EVERY NIGHT'S
A SATURDAY
NIGHT

EVERY NIGHT'S A SATURDAY NIGHT

THE ROCK 'N' ROLL LIFE OF LEGENDARY SAX MAN

BOBBY KEYS

By Bobby Keys with Bill Ditenhafer

COUNTERPOINT

BERKELEY

Library of Congress Cataloging-in-Publication Data is available.

ISBN: 978-1-58243-783-5

Cover design by Sharon McGill
Interior design by meganjonesdesign.com
Photo Editor: Loni Efron

COUNTERPOINT
1919 Fifth Street
Berkeley, CA 94710
www.counterpointpress.com

Distributed by Publishers Group West

10 9 8 7 6 5 4 3 2 1

For Mom, who bought me my first horn, for Skip Eckenrod, for getting the ball rolling, and for each and every musician I've ever shared a studio, stage, or twelve bars of music with. And last but not least, for my wife, Holly, for her support and recollections, my son, Jesse, and my dog, J.J., leader of the pack.

Every night's a Saturday night,

And every day's a Sunday—

I know I've been wrong before,

But I'm gonna try it one more time.

—TRADITIONAL TEXAS SAYING

CONTENTS

BOBBY KEYS
IS A MASTER OF BLOWING
HOT AIR THRU A BRASS TUBE
BY MANIPULATING A SERIES OF
VALVES. THIS MUST BE TRUE
BECAUSE I HAVE PLAYED
ALONG SIDE OF HIM FOR OVER
40 YEARS. HE HAS ALSO TOLD ME
THAT A RICO REED HAS SOMETHING
TO DO WITH IT.
  IN OTHER WORDS HE IS THE HOTTEST
SAX (NOT TO BE CONFUSED WITH SEX)
PLAYER ON THE PLANET.
  MY MOST TREASURED FRIEND, THIS
BELOVED MAESTRO IS GOING TO
TAKE YOU ON A ROCK & ROLL JOURNEY
THAT WILL LEAVE THE READER
GASPING. WE HAVE BEEN THRU THICK &
THIN TOGETHER, AND I'VE ALWAYS
FOUND HIS LOVE OF MUSIC & PEOPLE
TO BE AN ANTIDOTE FOR THE BLUES.
  Bobs: I LOVE YOU.

- '11

1

MUSIC. IT'S BEEN my driving force. And it's been that way since the first time I heard it, even before rock 'n' roll came around, although that's when I really started to listen. I was born on December 18, 1943, and by the time I was twelve years old, Fats Domino was on the scene, Little Richard was on the scene, Chuck Berry had "Maybellene," and a guy named Alan Freed had given this new type of music its name. Call it divine intervention, fate, whatever, but rock 'n' roll and I came of age together.

As a matter of fact, it *was* fate, because where I grew up had a whole lot to do with the way my life turned out, too. I was born at Lubbock Army Airfield, which was in the town of Hurlwood, Texas. The base shut down in 1997, and I guess that was the town's only reason for existing, so when it went, the town went. The base itself was a few miles west of Lubbock proper. Sometime before I came around, my father, Bill Keys, had decided to join the U.S.

Army Air Corps, so my mother, Lucy, being an Army Air Corps wife, went through her pregnancy care at Lubbock Army Airfield while living with my grandparents—my father's parents, Harrison and Lou Ann Keys—in Slaton, Texas, about fifteen miles southeast of Lubbock on U.S. 84, at 610 South Ninth Street.

My mother was quite young, just sixteen or so, when I was born, and with my father off with the Army Air Corps, my parents probably hadn't spent a whole lot of time together, so when the war was over in 1945 they went to get settled on their own. My father had gotten a job with the Santa Fe Railroad in Belen, New Mexico, so they moved there. I guess my grandmother had become sort of attached to me while she was looking after me during the war years, so when my parents said they wanted to have some time together—and, plus, my mother was pregnant with my brother Gary by this time—my grandmother said, "Well, just leave young Robert here." I was around three years old.

So I grew up in Slaton. My parents came to Texas to visit every once in a while, and we'd go to New Mexico to visit them. From Slaton to Belen it was about an eight- to nine-hour drive. We had a big ol' massive '48 or '49 Mercury, and it had a good radio in it, and we'd listen to the hits of the day. I remember the feeling of being panicky when we'd go to Belen—I didn't want to be left there. All of a sudden I had a younger brother who I didn't know that much about, but I knew it was better off when there was just one kid around. With my grandparents I was completely happy, I was my grandmother's pride and joy. In Belen, there was competition.

When I was five, my mother gave birth to twins, Debbie and Daryl, and that pretty much cemented me in Slaton, which was just fine with me. That's where my friends were. It wasn't exactly a typical family arrangement, but as far as childhoods go, mine was pretty idyllic. Although my grandparents were blue-collar working class, I didn't really want for anything. I had a bicycle—it was a used bicycle, but my grandfather had painted it to look new. I think my grandfather probably made maybe $500 a month as an assistant foreman for the Santa Fe Railroad, which had a big presence in town. I used to love to go down there when I was a kid. Those train yards were the biggest thing about Slaton.

The little town I was raised in was probably pretty typical of the South at the time, or at least of West Texas. It was divided into four different social groups: There were your white Anglo-Saxon Protestants, which is the group my grandparents were in and so therefore I was, too; then there were the Catholics—well, they drank all the time, according to the Protestants; then there was the Mexican population, they lived in their own specific part of town; and finally there was the black population, and they lived in *their* own specific part of town. So it was extremely divided. And what it was acceptable to do and what social lines you could cross—what the social structure was—was always present, always a factor. There were just certain things you didn't *do*. Like, there was some ordinance that essentially said that black people could not be in the white section of town after the sun went down unless they were going to or from a specific job, usually a custodial job at the hospital or something like that. It was extremely divided.

But I'd ask questions. I remember my first experience with racial divisions was when I signed up to play Little League baseball. Little League baseball, because it was a national thing, had no "whites only" version. I remember I was on the Indians, and we were sponsored by the Brotherhood of Railway Trainmen. The first time I had any contact with black kids my age was at that time. It was the summer of 1952, when I was eight years old. I remember going to the baseball tryouts and there were these two guys, Charlie Curtis and a kid whose nickname was Snow Cone ('cause he liked to eat so many snow cones), and they were really good players. So after practice, after we'd gotten the teams chosen and I was on the team with these two guys, we walked back together from the baseball field—my house was sort of midway between where they lived and where the baseball field was.

My grandfather had a little garden in the backyard where we grew corn and radishes and rhubarb and watermelons, so I asked the guys if they wanted to come over to have some watermelon straight from the vine, and they said sure. When we got to our backyard, I went through the back door and said, "Hey, Grandma, I'm home from baseball practice and I got a couple friends of mine with me I invited over for some watermelon." I remember my grandmother saying something like, "Oh, well, that's nice, that's sweet," and then she comes out through the back porch and sees they're two black kids, and all of a sudden, man, the whole situation changed:

"Hey, well, Robert, where'd you meet these fellas?"

"They're on my baseball team."

"Well, OK, but you can't bring 'em into the house."

"Well, why not?"

"Well, because."

"Well, *how come* because?"

"Well, *because.*"

Never got a reason. It just *ain't done.* Don't ask questions and just do what I say. Well, I *did* have questions, but of course these guys said, "It's OK, it's OK," and my grandmother cut some slices of watermelon and we had 'em in the backyard. But that moment really brought into focus the social divisions of the world I lived in. I mean, in a lot of ways I had an ideal childhood, but sometimes it's the other things you remember. Anyway, that incident made a very big impression on me.

Meanwhile, my interest in music was growing. I remember listening to my grandmother's radio a lot—she loved Eddy Arnold and the "Grand Ole Opry"—but the music that really started to grab me was rhythm and blues. And that was not what was played on my grandmother's radio. That was down in The Flats.

The Flats was a poor neighborhood down by the switching yards and the Paymaster Cottonseed Oil Co. in the black part of town. This was Texas in the early '50s, real *In the Heat of the Night* stuff. The only white people you ever saw down there were the people who came to buy bootleg beer or whiskey. But Slaton's a small town, and I could hear this music through my window coming from this place a few blocks away called the Black and Tan Café. I was maybe ten years old. So I'd sneak out my window and go through the alleys and the back roads and sit outside this place and listen to the music. I had no idea who I was listening to at the time, but I found out later it was folks like Howlin' Wolf and Muddy Waters and some of those other guys who'd do these circuits of small towns throughout the South. Legends now. But back then, I'd just sit out there in the parking lot and listen to the music.

I remember the smell of that place—it was like whiskey and sweat. I thought it was really cool.

Turns out there was a lot to see in that parking lot, too. Slaton was a dry city, no alcohol sold, so the only booze available was bootleg beer or whiskey, and there was a bootlegger right next to the Black and Tan. Every once in a while I'd see a big ol' Buick or a big ol' Oldsmobile pull up there to the window, flash its lights, and, by golly, hell, that's ol' Joe T.! Why, he's the drugstore owner and a deacon in the church! I'd see some of the so-called respected city fathers and captains of industry of Slaton down there associating with this element that was completely taboo. Not only that, they were buying alcohol. And I thought, Man, somethin' ain't right. The whole thing just seemed to have a compelling effect on me. I was always being told, "Don't ask, don't do it, it's wrong," and "If you do it you're gonna die and go to hell!"—whatever "it" was—and then I'd see the same people who told me not to do it doing it themselves. It was just a feeling, a very strong feeling, and I still get it, and I still can't really put it into words.

Of course, I was always drawn to the forbidden fruit, too, and I never tried to claim otherwise. Tell me don't go someplace, that's pretty much the first place I'm gonna go. And The Flats, well, that was about as forbidden as it got in Slaton for a white boy. I found out how to hot-wire my grandfather's car around that time, too. All you had to do was short-circuit two posts on the ignition and you were in business. I don't remember who taught me that skill. I'd wait for my grandparents to go to sleep, and then quietly push the car out of the garage. My granddad had bought this old Dodge or Chrysler or DeSoto or whatever, and it had what was called a vacuum shift, which was an automatic transmission, but it also had a clutch you had to use for the first gears. I didn't know how to drive the damn thing. I just guessed.

And so I did that until I got caught. But not before I'd gotten a taste of what was out there, and that planted the seed. It complicated my life somewhat because I was doing things I wasn't supposed to do, sneaking out of windows and hot-wiring cars, going to hotbeds of sin and degradation. But I was hooked.

Still, whatever adrenaline rush I had been getting from hot-wiring my granddad's car and sneaking over to the wrong side of the tracks was no match for what came next—and it just floated through my bedroom window. I was ten years old, it was 1954, and one random day—I guess it was a Saturday—I was just lying in bed at my grandparents' house in Slaton when suddenly I heard this music. Of course, I'd heard this type of music on the radio before, but this wasn't on the radio, man, this was somewhere outside my house! So I jumped up and went outside and there he was: Buddy Holly. Buddy and his guys were playing on the back of a cotton trailer with the sides taken off, just a flatbed wagon. He was playing for the grand opening of a gas station just half a block away from where my grandparents lived. Of course, I didn't know who Buddy Holly was at the time. I was just drawn to that sound—it was the first time I'd ever heard anyone play an electric guitar live.

I remember the bass player—this was before the Crickets, so it would've been Don Guess, I guess—had a stand-up bass with different colored strings, and I remember he had his fingers taped with Band-Aids because he was just *slappin'* the bass, man. The whole thing was just like . . . I don't know, it was like a *mountain* had fallen on me. And right then and there I knew I wanted to have something to do with that music. There was just this *power*, just something about it, and I thought, Well, by golly, they're doing it right here in Slaton, so, you know, *it must be available!* And that just kinda lit a fuse that started burning then, and it's still burning now.

It's clear to me now, in retrospect, that I didn't choose rock 'n' roll so much as it chose me. It said, "Here I am," and I said, *"I'm comin'!"* When I first heard Buddy Holly playing the electric guitar and heard that bass fiddle thumpin' up there and the drums and cymbals, I mean, I knew right then. I was like a kid following the Pied Piper, man. I wanna go where that music is. Who's making that music and how do they do that?

By pure coincidence, just a few weeks later I'd get a chance to find out. I went along with my grandmother over to my Aunt Leora's, who had just started a tea room up in Lubbock where on the weekends she'd host these bridge parties for the various ladies' clubs in town. I, of course, and for good reason, was exiled out to the backyard. Well, almost as soon as I got out there I remember hearing this music coming from across the street. I hopped the fence and went over to go check it out. I recognized him right away—there weren't that many people around who played guitar and sang. As it turns out, my Aunt Leora's house was across the street from Buddy Holly's parents' house.

My grandmother continued to help my Aunt Leora start up her tea room business, so for the next month or so we went up there every weekend. And though Buddy and the guys weren't there all the time, I did manage to weasel my way in and listen before our trips to Lubbock slowed down. But it cost me.

Buddy and his band were in high school at the time, maybe six or seven years older than me, which was a big difference at that age. So when I showed up and tried to hang around, I kinda didn't know what to say and got some hard looks. The only way I could think of to keep from getting physically removed from the area was to volunteer to go down to the Hi-D-Ho Drive-In and get french fries, burgers, Cokes, and the like for everyone. Of course, I didn't have the money to do it, but I was determined, and it didn't take long for me to find a way. My grandmother, I knew, collected S&H Green Stamps and put 'em into books, and there was an S&H stamp-redemption center not far from my aunt's house, so I sorta light-fingered a couple books of Green Stamps during the week and then, when we got to Lubbock, I took 'em down to the redemption center and turned 'em in for cash money. After loading up at the Hi-D-Ho, I went back to the garage and said, "Hey, here you go, burgers and Cokes—*now* can I stay?" I had to pay my way, but I was in.

And then, right in step with me becoming a teenager, rock 'n' roll seemed to be *everywhere.* I can't recall the day or the month when it happened, but there was a time when all of a sudden rock 'n' roll gave a whole generation an *identity.* It was just such a heavy cultural shock. First off, it was *our* music—it was teenage America's music, something that separated us from the parents and the grandparents and the aunts and uncles. We had our own colors, pink and black; our own hairstyles, ducktails and pompadours. Blue suede shoes, leather jackets, all of it. Car styles, the way you talked, the language you used. Of course, a lot of that was derived from the movies, like James Dean in *Rebel Without a Cause.* And the music was great: Bill Haley and His Comets, Chuck Berry, Jerry Lee Lewis, Elvis Presley. It just stirred something inside me.

I remember *Blackboard Jungle* was the first time I heard rock 'n' roll music played full blast in a movie theater, the Lindsey Theater, 1019 Main Street, Lubbock, Texas. I was twelve years old, and, I mean, that was just *it*—like, OK, there's something here, people are making movies about it and they've got these records and everything. It's hard to put into words what an impact that had on my tiny little teenage mind. I just remember that it felt really good.

From then on, I'd stay up to listen to rock 'n' roll on the radio late at night because Lubbock radio stations weren't playing it that much during normal hours. The only time I could listen to it was after hours, when there was access to these fifty-thousand-watt clear-channel stations from places like Del Rio, Texas, and Shreveport, Louisiana. At the time, the powers that be considered it dangerous, a corruptor of the youth, sorta the devil's music, or so it was said. People were burning rock 'n' roll records in the city squares back then: *Don't let your children near it, it'll rot your teeth, it'll stunt your growth!* All sorts of things were attributed to rock 'n' roll.

And it was so discouraged by all the parents. I mean, they had these *meetings.* I remember you'd see these paper fliers stapled to the telephone poles and at various locations around town that'd say things like: RACE MUSIC—BEWARE, BEWARE, BEWARE! or DON'T LET YOUR CHILDREN LISTEN TO RACE MUSIC, which is what they called black music back when they had songs like "Work with Me, Annie" and "Annie

Had a Baby" and all that other stuff. Popular blues and R&B were starting to cross over to a white teenage audience, and the parents didn't like it. You have to understand, this was a very big church part of the country. *Really* big. Baptist, Methodist, Presbyterian, and Church of Christ—Church of Christ was *real* big. And they were all really down on this new rock 'n' roll. Which only *enhanced* my desire.

I refused to listen to Frank Sinatra, Tommy Dorsey, any of that big band stuff. I thought that was just *death*. It's Elvis, it's Gene Vincent, it's Eddie Cochran, Little Richard, Fats Domino, guys like that! I purposely sought out primarily—aside from Elvis and Gene Vincent—Little Richard and Chuck Berry, black R&B acts. I loved Fats Domino, I loved Fats Domino's *band*. Most of 'em were guys from New Orleans. I didn't know what made 'em sound different, but I could really tell the difference between Fats Domino's band and Little Richard's band. Little Richard's band was *keepaknockinbutyoucan't-come-in!* and Fats Domino was *I—found—my—three-ill* . . . It was a lot easier and it *swung* more.

It was just so compelling to listen to that music. And just the fact that someone right there in Lubbock could create that sound, that fascinated me. So that's what really lit my fuse. It was a combination of all the taboo stuff, the movies and the culture—just the growing reality of it all—and then also, of course, seeing how the chicks reacted. That was a *big* selling point right there.

I remember when I first went to see Elvis at the Fair Park Coliseum in Lubbock—I was probably thirteen years old—and just the sight of seeing that music being played live and feeling this feeling that was just so, so *different* from anything prior to that. Plus, seeing how these girls just *lost it*, man. I mean, *"Waaaahhhhhh!"* Wow. That was really cool. These were girls who I went to school with, who I'd known all my life. Went to Sunday school with 'em, went to MYF—Methodist Youth Fellowship—and all that jazz. But all of a sudden, boy, when Elvis came out these girls *just lost it.* And I gotta admit, it evoked a feeling that had a hell of an impact on me. I didn't know what I was gonna do or how I was gonna do it, but I knew that I *had* to be a part of this somehow.

I'D WANTED TO play guitar but I didn't *have* a guitar. I didn't have anything. I had a harmonica, but I couldn't seem to get much out of that. And my grandparents, they weren't gonna spring for an instrument for me just 'cause I stood in front of the mirror and pretended I was Elvis or whoever. So the first instrument I ever had was provided by Slaton High School my freshman year.

In Texas, in a small town, man, if you didn't participate in athletics of some kind or other, you just didn't have much social status. And I liked baseball, I liked basketball, I liked football, but I was really skinny and light and wasn't much of a football player at all. I did play a little baseball. I got hurt playing it, though, so I couldn't even go out for the football team. No big loss, except the only way to go to the football games and be involved in the program was to join the band. And the only instrument they had left, the absolute last instrument available, was an old baritone saxophone, which I had no idea how to even put my *lips* on. But I figured we had a large band, so one guy who didn't know what he was doing wasn't gonna really throw the band off. I didn't even have to try out, all I needed to do was be able to put it together.

Before that moment I'd never thought twice about the saxophone, never mind wanted to learn how to play one. I wanted to be
a guitar player but I didn't have a guitar. I wanted to sing rock 'n'
roll but I didn't have a voice. So, by virtue of the band giving me an
old saxophone, and then listening more closely to what was on the
radio—there was a lot of R&B stuff at the time that featured saxophones, as in actual solos—I mean this was *really* a good period
for saxophones—I thought, Well, by golly, I've *got* a saxophone,
maybe this is my ticket in. But the baritone saxophone wasn't the
way to go: It was too big, and besides that, it belonged to the school.
It didn't belong to me. So I started campaigning heavily with my
mother in New Mexico and anyone else who'd listen to me for a
new saxophone because I wanted one so bad. I campaigned long
and hard enough to get my mother to buy me a used alto saxophone from a music store in Lubbock, a Conn Connstellation made
in Elkhart, Indiana, probably $175. (I thought I had a better chance
with my mother if I asked her for an alto because it was smaller,
thinking it'd be less expensive—I didn't know a tenor sax from an
alto sax from a bass fiddle on a record.) Getting that horn was one
of the biggest moments of my life—now I had something to actually join in with.

'Course I didn't know how to play the thing worth a damn. But
for some reason I was lucky: I could blow one, and just learning
the basic mechanics of it, like where your fingers go on the keys
and what keys to push down to reproduce the basics like C, D,
E, and so on, came pretty quickly to me. Plus, I had a good ear. I
didn't know what I was doing, but I could play some things that
sounded OK. So that *double*-reinforced my desire to be more and

more involved in this rock 'n' roll music. Aside from the chicks, it was fun, the clothes were cool, and I just might be able to play it.

So I practiced. And I practiced. And eventually, a guy named Doc Babb got wind that there was a budding saxophone player in Slaton and he sought me out. Truett Babb was a true character. He was about five-foot-ten and built like a frog, all kinda fat at the bottom and slender up top. He had black hair slicked back, smoked a cigar, had a cookie-duster mustache, and wore black horn-rimmed glasses. When I met him he was Slaton's FFA teacher—Future Farmers of America—and a Norman Petty wannabe. Norman Petty was the guy who, as manager and producer, helped Buddy Holly and the Crickets hit it big, which they very much had by 1957. Doc was interested in putting his own little band together.

Doc lived about five minutes away from me by bicycle, fifteen by walking. Through his involvement with the FFA—and, I guess, his own interest in getting in on the ground floor of the rock 'n' roll business—he often had a guy named Sonny Curtis at his house. Sonny, when I met him, was going to Meadow High School in Meadow, Texas, about twenty miles away, but more importantly he was the official state FFA entertainer. He played guitar and sang and wrote songs. He'd even been out on the road already. He used to play with Buddy, but he got out of that band because he didn't have much confidence Buddy was ever gonna amount to anything. A pretty big mistake, looking back, but then Sonny went on to write a bunch of hits throughout a long career, everything from "I Fought the Law" and "More Than I Can Say" to the theme to *The Mary Tyler Moore Show*, among a whole lot of others. I don't know how he got hooked up with the FFA gig, but once he did, he was sorta taken under Doc's wing. His last year of high school, Sonny pretty much lived at Doc's house so Doc could take him around to all the FFA events, where he'd provide the entertainment.

Anyway, I remember prevailing upon Sonny to show me notes on his guitar and where the corresponding notes were on the saxophone. The first song he taught me, the first song I ever learned note for note, was "San Antonio Rose." I knew how to play the scales, your major scales, but things like sharps and flats—I didn't know *anything* about music. But I started to figure out how to play what you'd call chromatically. And it seemed like if I heard something once, I could reproduce it. I would hunt and find it. All I needed was to get a start and the rest of it sorta fell into place. I mean, it wasn't an *overnight* thing, it took a while to do, and it took a lot of patience on the part of some of the people who I'd play with, but I was starting to get the hang of it.

Or at least I thought I was. Anyway, news had gotten around that there was a kid who owned his own saxophone and who could sorta find his way around a few songs. One of the few people who was interested in this piece of news was a guy named Stinson Behlen. Stinson was a plumber in town, but he also played the accordion and led a little band that would play Catholic wedding dances and socials at St. Joseph's Hall and things of that nature, and he wanted me to join, which I did for a while. Through that band I learned a bunch of songs that were standards at the time, things like "Cherry Pink and Apple Blossom White," "Sentimental Journey," and "Harbor Lights," as well as some polkas and a thing called a schottische, which is a German dance that's got a certain rhythm to it. It's a silly little dance but it was big with the

Germans, who liked to drink beer and whoop and holler and do it as their wedding dance. My first public appearance ever was with Stinson and the boys, and it's a gig I will never forget—but for all the wrong reasons.

Slaton, once a year, had this sort of city holiday. Western Day, they called it. And they had a parade, had the fire truck and the police car—this was a small town, remember—and then they'd have a little concert in the town square in a little gazebo. I was scheduled to play one song with Stinson and his band. Well, since this was gonna be my first appearance in public, I went and bought some white pants and a red knit golf shirt with a penguin on it, Penguin by Munsingwear. This was gonna be my big moment. My classmates were *real* skeptical of me having anything to do with the direction that I had chosen for myself, so this was where I was gonna prove 'em wrong. So I got my girlfriend, my classmates, and my friends out there, and I'm getting ready to go up there, and, boy, I had learned this song "Cherry Pink and Apple Blossom White." I knew it backward, forward, and sideways.

The thing I *didn't* know was that you can't let your reed dry out. A saxophone's made of brass, but the reed is a small, thin piece of wood which fits into the mouthpiece. It's what produces the sound, through its vibrations. Now, wood—not just cane wood, which is what most reeds are made from, but any type of wood— when it's sliced real thin, will kinda pucker and curl up around the edges if it gets wet, which in the case of a saxophone reed makes it impossible to play. The reed has to fit snugly, and for that to happen you're supposed to wet your reed beyond the warping point. Put it in your mouth and suck on it like a lollipop. You have to saturate the cane fibers with saliva. You have to moisten it, and when it's thoroughly moist, it'll hold its proper form.

Well, I knew that. That's one of the first things you learn about any horn that uses a reed. So the morning of the show, when I was getting ready to head out, I'd gotten my reed all lathered up and set up in my saxophone and packed it all away. I didn't take my horn out of its case until it was time to get up on this gazebo and play, and the minute I wet my reed—*re*-wet it 'cause it had completely dried out by then—it warped. It looked like a potato chip. That first note I hit was *the worst note ever heard by anyone, ever.* My saxophone wouldn't play, it just emitted this series of squeaks and honks. It was so humiliating. In one fell swoop I'd lost *any* support that I'd tried to gain with folks. It was really horrible—everybody was sayin', "What *happened*?" and I'd say, "Well, I didn't *know* . . . " Never, ever, *ever* forget to wet your reed before you get up onstage, buddy.

After that, I went underground. I didn't display my saxophonic prowess outside the living room or to anyone besides the fellas I eventually started playin' with over at Doc's house, which was a band called the Sla-tons. The Sla-tons from Slaton. Real creative name. That was Randy Sanders, Gary Ward, Leo Hensler, and myself. And ol' Doc Babb, who by this point had become the principal of Slaton High School, let us rehearse over at his house.

Music, despite my inauspicious debut, had taken over my whole focus, my whole life. I'd given up on being a New York Yankee or a Baltimore Colt, I wasn't gonna be the next Bob Cousy, and anyway, this music thing was a whole lotta fun. It wasn't endorsed by my grandfather or my grandmother, but that didn't matter. I mean, I didn't give 'em much of a choice—I didn't always tell 'em where I was going or what I was doing. I'd just make up a whole bunch of stories. I don't recall what they were, but I remember I had to lie my way outta the house to do it. Not so much because of what I was doing, but because of where I was doing it.

The first gigs Doc got us were in the spring of '58 at a place called the Cotton Club, which was on the outskirts of Lubbock. All the clubs were on the outskirts of town because they weren't allowed inside the city limits—the Christian community just wouldn't stand for that. He'd arranged for us to play a few Sunday afternoons in a row. I don't think we made any money or anything, but it didn't matter. We went up there and played, and this time I wet my reed and it worked, and it was on a real stage, not in a gazebo, with people out there—not very many people, but a few people. I remember thinking, OK, this is it, no matter what else, this is what I'm gonna do with my life. From that moment on, it just never occurred to me *not* to be playing rock 'n' roll.

It was at one of those Sunday afternoon gigs at the Cotton Club where I was first introduced to one of the major nonmusical aspects of rock 'n' roll, although I didn't realize it at the time. Sometimes those gigs went long or we'd just stay afterward to listen to the next guys or whatever, and one Sunday night after we played we were up late and this steel guitar player, an old guy with the house band, heard me worrying about getting up for school the next morning. Trying to be helpful, I guess, he said, "Well, here, take two of these and one of these." He'd given me two bennies—Benzedrine pills, which are amphetamines—and what he called a Red Bird, which was Nembutal or somethin', some kinda barbiturate. Anyway, I was told they'd help me get up and go to school the next morning. So I took 'em.

Well, when I got home at around one in the morning, I was *wide* awake, my heart was bangin' outta my chest, and I remember thinking, Oh my God, I've done it now. I've taken dope. I have *done* it now! The next day I couldn't go to school 'cause I was still too jacked, and so I finally worked up the nerve to go and see the family doctor because I really thought I was gonna die. Dr. Payne was his name, believe it or not. So I went in there and he asked, "Robert, what are you doin' here?" and I said, "I gotta be honest with you, doctor, I played last night and I was real sleepy and this guitar player *got a bottle out of the back of his amplifier and he said there were two bennies and a Red Bird and if I took 'em I'd be OK*! Am I gonna be OK?! Am I ever gonna be all right again?!" And he looked at me and said, "Don't ever do that again." I asked, "Well, what can I do?!" and he said, "Go home and go to bed. Go to sleep. You'll wake up in the morning and it'll be gone. But, Robert, don't ever do that again." Well, of course I did. But not for a while.

Once I was in with Doc Babb, I had the opportunity to actually meet guys like Sonny and Buddy and the Crickets' drummer J.I. Allison and bass player Joe B. Mauldin. Sonny hadn't had his hits yet, but of course J.I. and Buddy and Joe B. had been to New York. They'd played the Brooklyn Paramount, the Brooklyn Fox, and they also played the Apollo. They were one of the first white groups to have played the Apollo, mostly because the guy who booked 'em there didn't know they were white.

At some point on tour they'd met this fella named King Curtis, who was a saxophone player. He'd played on all the early Coasters stuff, "Yakety Yak" and "Charlie Brown," just an endless list. He was my saxophone *hero*. Well, in October of 1958 I got a call one day from J.I. because he knew I had a car, a '51 Chevrolet—I was a sophomore in high school, but you could get your driver's license as early as age thirteen in Texas in those days—and they'd come back from New York and they'd gone to Norman Petty's studio in Clovis, New Mexico, where they'd recorded this stuff, about a hundred miles west of Lubbock. Anyway, they'd hired King Curtis to come to Clovis to play on a couple of Buddy's tracks, but there was no passenger service into Clovis, you flew into Amarillo. Well, I forsook my high school basketball game—didn't tell anyone I wasn't gonna show up—and went and picked up King Curtis and drove him to Clovis, drilling him for tips and insights and advice the whole way. When word got around that I wasn't deathly ill and that I had in fact gone to pick up a black cat at the airport, well, that sorta ground my social life in Slaton to a halt. But it didn't matter. Basketball? *Pffff.* Saxophone, music, chicks, rock 'n' roll? *Yeah.* I didn't care what anyone in Slaton thought.

By that time, I'd phased the marching band out and was focused solely on R&B and rock 'n' roll, both trying to play it and, failing that, trying to just soak up whatever I could from the people who *could* play it, which meant spending more and more time at Doc Babb's house. I always knew when everybody was there because there'd be all these new cars in the driveway. I especially remember this one white Jaguar XK150 that belonged to Joe B.—when I'd see that, I knew there was a celebrity about. Joe B. and J.I. were already big successes with Buddy, they were on an actual album cover, and I was just so big on anything to do with rock 'n' roll, especially people who'd recorded music and gotten out of Lubbock. Which was not easy to do.

Anyway, they'd congregate down at Doc's house, and I'd get to listen to the latest thing that they'd done at Norman Petty's studio in Clovis. They used to bring the acetates back, those big ol' twelve-inch things. They were like platters. After you'd record a song, they'd make an acetate of it, a "dub" is what they called it.

And we'd go to this radio station to hang out, too. There was a guy named Doc Stewart at KLLL who had a radio show. Waylon Jennings had a radio show there, too, as did Don Bowman, the country singer and comedian. We'd go to the top of the Great Plains Life Building, which was where K-triple-L was located— "The tallest point in West Texas," they'd say, and it was, I suppose, although it was only twenty stories high or so—and Doc Stewart would play music late into the night. We could get in there late at night because I was with a genuine, honest-to-goodness rock 'n' roll guy when I was with Joe B. That opened up a lotta doors in Lubbock—what doors there were, that is.

The Sla-tons, meanwhile, only lasted for a few months, but just by virtue of owning a saxophone I started to get other gigs playing around Lubbock. One of the bands I played with was called Jim Solley and the Lu-bocs—I'd gone from the Sla-tons in Slaton to the Lu-bocs in Lubbock—which had a regular gig playing Arthur Murray Dance Club events. We'd get this list of songs we had to play, a waltz, a cha-cha, a merengue. I didn't even know what a merengue was. That's when I actually started getting paid for playing. I don't recall what it was, probably no more than five or ten bucks, but, you know, gas was twenty cents a gallon back then.

Buddy Holly died in a plane crash on February 3, 1959. I was fifteen, a sophomore in high school. After that, J.I. and Joe B. spent a lot more time in Lubbock, and I spent a lot more time with them. It was around that time that they opened a studio in town. Buddy might've had something to do with that, too, before he died, I don't know. I know he wanted to develop local talent, guys from around West Texas like Waylon and others, 'cause, hell, Orbison came from Wink, Texas, and there were a lot of other folks who had come out of that neck of the woods. It seemed like there were so many people in Lubbock who were so talented. 'Course, there were a whole bunch who combed their hair better than they played the guitar, but that's true of anyplace, I guess. For myself, I was getting a little better, and by this time I was playing in a band called the Ravens with a neighbor of J.I.'s, Ernie Hall, also a drummer, so J.I. let us go into their studio and make a record. That was probably my first recording.

I started staying in Lubbock pretty much full time not too long after that, sleeping on people's couches and living with various other musicians like Joe B. from the Crickets and Bobo Yates, who was the drummer in another band I was playing with, Tommy Hancock and the Roadside Playboys. My grandmother had passed away in 1960 when I was sixteen, and after that, I'd just kinda left Slaton behind. Although Lubbock was only fifteen miles away, it was a whole *world* away. There wasn't a lot of directions to go in Slaton except *out*. The town was supported primarily by agriculture and the Santa Fe Railroad, and neither of those fields were ones I cared to get into—didn't wanna chop cotton, didn't have a farm, didn't wanna *get* a farm. And I was developing musically. I didn't get fired, people didn't tell me to shut up and go away, so I just kept playin'.

The rest of high school just kinda cruised on by, it seems, mostly because I was hardly ever there for it. I started my senior year, I got my class ring, but I hadn't shown up for most of my junior year, and if it hadn't been for Doc Babb being the principal, I wouldn't have made it into my senior class. I just didn't like school. I'd go to Lubbock, go up to Bobo Yates's house to play music or listen to music or just . . . anything. I'd do anything instead of going to school.

I lived with Joe B. at his parents' house my senior year pretty much because that's where I preferred to be. Plus, he provided me with a job, at least for a while. The couple of jobs I'd had in Slaton didn't work out all that well. One of 'em was just for two weeks when I was younger, and that was just to get my first BB gun. I swept out the Hoffman hardware store. My first job, and it was to *arm* myself.

JOE B. MAULDIN: *We didn't do anything for a year or so after Buddy died. We weren't gonna work as the Crickets, so that band was on hiatus, I guess you'd say. That's when Bobby and I played together a bit. We even lived together for a while. That's also when we'd break bricks for my girlfriend's father. They were on this old two-story house, and we'd get up there and push and push and push until part of the brick wall would fall and land in the yard and partially break up, then Bobby and I'd go down and finish breakin' it up one brick at a time so the bricks could be used again.*

Joe B.'s girlfriend's father had a company that would go out and buy houses that were being torn down, brick houses, and Joe B. and I would sit out in the sun with our little hammers knocking the mortar off of bricks so that his girlfriend's father could resell 'em. That was a *horrible* job. That had *nothing* to do with music at *all*, man, bangin' on bricks with a hammer. I'd have never done it had I not been getting into show business by virtue of the fact that I was breaking bricks with a guy who'd been on *The Ed Sullivan Show*, by golly. When I was living with Joe B., I'd notice that he had these pants and shoes that he'd gotten in New York, things you couldn't get in Lubbock, and I remember asking him all these questions about the music and what it was like while we'd drink beer, and he'd tell me. I remember distinctly this certificate he'd gotten from Pan Am for flying over the equator or the International Date Line or something hanging on his bedroom wall—I'd just stare at it in amazement. I was just looking off into the future.

JOE B. MAULDIN: *We'd go home after workin' all day, gettin' dirty and stinky and sweaty, and we'd go to Bobby's grandfather's house and shower and clean up, and then we'd go drink some beer or drive around. I had a 45-rpm record player mounted on the floorboard of that Jaguar, and I had a speaker in the grille. I could put a record on and switch it to the grille. So we'd go down to the tennis courts and get out and rock 'n' roll dance. I liked a record called "Isabella." The intro to it was killer. I could cue that up, and when one of the waitresses at the drive-in restaurant would come walkin' out with a tray of dishes,*

I'd turn that on the grille and you'd hear, "Ah, you tender spring chicken, girl! What's yo' name?" Bobby and I'd do stuff like that all the time.

Bobby seemed to know every song on the radio. And if anybody wanted to hear somethin', Bobby knew how to play it. I asked him if he was a [music] reader and he said, "I don't read enough to hurt my pickin' any." That was the first time I'd heard that phrase. But it always amazed me. I never saw Keys read any music at all.

We'd drive around Buffalo Lake or wherever. Back then, you did a lot of drivin' around lookin' for chicks. I was on the hunt, man. Especially in that Jaguar. But more importantly, we were starting to play music together in a band called the Hollyhawks.

JOE B. MAULDIN: *Before I'd ever met him, I'd heard Bobby playing somewhere, and I was just amazed that a fifteen-year-old kid could blow the saxophone like he invented it. I was highly impressed with his ability to play the saxophone. And I was equally impressed later on when we ended up playin' together in the Hollyhawks. We played Tucson, Phoenix, and Albuquerque. When we put the Hollyhawks together, I thought we were puttin' together a band for posterity.*

I did, too. That was the biggest deal for me. Finally, I'm in a band that's goin' out of town, playin' gigs, and Joe B.'s in the band. We'd play stuff like "40 Miles of Bad Road" or some Duane Eddy song that was popular at the time, and I think we played "Tequila."

We played a couple Crickets songs, a couple Elvis songs. Shoot, I thought I'd made it. It was a big deal for me at the time to get outta Lubbock. And Arizona was pretty far outta Lubbock. 'Course, then I couldn't wait to get *back* to Lubbock so I could brag to all my friends that I'd been to Arizona.

We all went in one car, all five of us. I don't remember whose car it was. And we had a trailer, a little one-wheel trailer that kept falling apart. The wheel kept coming off the damn thing. I don't know where we got it. But it didn't matter, man, we were out of town, we were on our way. That was just such a lovely feeling, seeing Lubbock in your rearview mirror and nothing but the horizon in front of you. It was the first thing in my life that made any real impact on me, the first thing that I'd come across that I really, truly wanted to do—play music in a rock 'n' roll band and just get outta town. New people, new places. It was everything I thought it would be. And no matter what it took, I knew I was gonna find a way to keep doing it.

But the Hollyhawks didn't last. A couple of things happened right around the same time that split the band up for good: Joel Searsy, who played guitar and sang, committed suicide—he'd been having problems with his girlfriend and he turned the engine of his car on inside his garage. Unfortunately, unbeknownst to me at the time, Joel was only the first in a long line of rock 'n' roll casualties I'd be acquainted with. The other thing was much more positive: I was offered the chance to go out on tour with Buddy Knox.

Buddy Knox had a few hit records—"Party Doll" was his big one—and he was getting ready to go out on the road to do a concert and dance tour of the Midwest and Canada. He and J.I. were

friends—Knox was from Happy, Texas, just north of Lubbock—
and he needed a saxophone player for the tour and asked J.I. if he
knew of one. At that stage I was living on people's sofas and just
wherever I could, so when J.I. asked me if I wanted to go out on
the road with Buddy Knox, I said, "Yeah, *hell* yeah. You betcha."
There was only one catch: I was still too young to sign a contract
and I had to join the union. So J.I. drove me back to Slaton to talk
to my grandfather. Luckily, my grandfather, by that point, was fed
up with anything to do with me, so he said, "You got somebody
who wants to take over, bring 'em on." Fortunately, it was J.I. who
signed for me. I've been grateful to him ever since.

> J.I. ALLISON: *I remember talking to Bobby's granddad,*
> *because Buddy Knox—in those days, rock 'n' roll was*
> *considered a terrible thing to do. The preachers called it*
> *sinful music and all the older people said Elvis Presley*
> *had a weird look in his eye, he must be on dope—but*
> *Buddy Knox said he needed a sax player in his band. He*
> *was doin' a lot of touring, he had a hit record, "Party Doll."*
> *I knew him from even before the Crickets. Real good guy.*
> *Anyway, I recommended Bobby to him, and so Bobby and*
> *I went and asked his granddad. I remember his granddad*
> *askin' me, "Is Buddy Knox a good guy or is he on dope or*
> *a drunk?" I said, "No, no, Buddy Knox is fine."*
>
> *In fact, of anybody you could go out on the road with,*
> *he was probably the most wholesome. He played football*
> *at West Texas State. Graduated, did ROTC, and became a*
> *lieutenant in the army. He was a tank commander.*

So that was it, man, the starting gate was open. My grandfather signed me over to a drummer for me to be allowed to do it. I never did graduate from high school. In the fall of 1961, I took my first airplane ride ever from Lubbock to Amarillo, Texas, and was picked up there by a guy named Donny Lanier, who was the guitar player in the Rhythm Orchids, Knox's band. He drove me into downtown Amarillo to this house where the local musicians' union representative lived—he worked out of his house—a guy named Tiny Fogel. He had lots of cats and the longest fingernails of anybody I'd ever seen in my entire life. And *ugly*. I was just taking it all in because here I am entering the world of rock 'n' roll, show business. It was just unbelievable.

So I joined the union. I had to sign a paper and give Tiny $25 to pay my dues. And the next morning we took off for Sioux Falls, South Dakota, and met up with Buddy Knox and the other guys, who were from that area. We had a couple days of rehearsal, and then it was on up into Canada. And it was rock 'n' roll for pay.

2

THAT FIRST KNOX tour was sixteen weeks long, all across Canada and then across the Midwest. There was a week or so off in between. It went from Prince Edward Island, near Nova Scotia, to Vancouver Island, British Columbia, with every little jerk town in between, and there are a *lotta* jerk towns in Canada. That was Buddy's bread and butter: the U.S. Midwest and central Canada.

I was nervous, scared to death—until I got onstage. Because onstage I knew what I was doing. Besides that, Buddy Knox had no saxophone on any of his records, which meant I only did the first part of the show. Back then, especially in these Midwestern ballrooms, they'd hire an artist and it would be billed "Buddy Knox Show and Dance." Well, the band would come out, which was guitar, bass, drums, and me, and play for the dance section just doing honky-tonk stuff or whatever, and then they'd bring on the star of the show, Buddy Knox—"*Here he is, Mr. 'Party Doll' himself!"*—and, since there was no saxophone on that stuff, I'd kinda fade off to the side of the stage.

Of course, being the youngest guy in the band, I got the privilege of carrying the amplifiers and the two microphone stands and a Bogan PA amplifier and two big ol' black Voice of the Theatre wooden box speakers and setting 'em up. Plus our lighting system, which was two spotlights with four different colored gels on a disk that would go around and around. I got to unload it and then I got to load it back up into our trailer—no bus, just a couple of cars and a trailer. But, you know, it was *show business.* It was my ticket outta town, and even though I went to a very cold place, *I didn't care.* I was playing music, and this fella's had records that've been on the "Hit Parade," so, shoot, I was shittin' in tall cotton and fartin' in silk sheets.

Being on the road with Knox and going to larger cities, I hit a spurt there where I started to get pretty comfortable on the saxophone. I could actually think of things I wanted to play and I could play 'em, instead of just blindly blowing notes and tapping my foot. I don't recall exactly what it was or if there was a parting of the clouds and the sun shone in and all of a sudden I was enlightened, but it was something like that, albeit without the flair. One day I just seemed to be able to play more than I could the day before. I don't know how it came about or why—I suppose just from practicing and playing and getting used to the instrument. I'd also like to think there was some talent involved in there somewhere. Whatever it was, I was getting better.

Going on tour was teaching me other things, too. I remember learning how to break open a Benzedrex nose inhaler and cut the cotton filament out of it—the cotton that had the medicine in it—and chop it up and put it into a piece of bread so you could swallow it. That shit would keep you *awake*. But it made you belch really horrible-tasting gas outta you, too, unfortunately, and it made you kinda edgy, a little belligerent. 'Course, the other guys in the car were just like you, which made for a volatile situation. But, you know, I hardly ever thought about stuff like that back then. The only thing I thought about was playing the next gig.

I ended up doing two tours with Buddy Knox and the Rhythm Orchids, two sixteen-week tours. On long tours like that there was usually a break around the middle, and when our week off came up on that first tour, Stuart Perry and I decided to take a little trip down south so we could drink as much beer as we could as cheaply as we could, and maybe visit a whorehouse or two. Stu was my best buddy on the road with the Knox band, he was my drinking partner, and he was the drummer for the Rhythm Orchids. He was also from Gibbon, Minnesota, and had never been south of the border so, after I'd spent the first half of the tour telling him all about my teenage high school adventures in Juarez, Mexico, and how you could go over there and buy anything for a dollar, he was all for it. So we got drunk and lit out from Gibbon in a red Corvair, a very little car, and headed out for Juarez and all the pleasures of the flesh that could be achieved. Back then we were into boozin' and girls.

Gibbon, Minnesota, to Juarez, Mexico, is a long drive. I don't really know how long because we were drunk when we left and pretty much stayed drunk till we got there. When we did, we left his car on the American side of the border and walked across, and our goal was we were gonna, by God, get drunk, go to a whorehouse, and buy a sackful of bennies to bring back. Bennies, or

Benzedrine, by that point came in pill form and were used as stimulants—we were doing a lot of driving in those days and that was part of the equipment needed for long drives—but they were prescription-only in the U.S. Back then, though, you could go to any *farmacia* and buy fistloads, bucketloads of all these uppers.

Once we got across the border, we went into the first bar that we saw and started drinkin', and pretty much maintained that pace throughout our visit. And even though it's cheap, cheap, cheap, finally, at some point, you do run outta money. And we ran outta money. I don't know what on—booze and pills and shit, I guess— but we ran out. We were at a bar and feeling very, very drunk and very, very broke, and I don't recall how it happened exactly, but I got pissed off at the bartender for some reason and I threw a bottle at him. I remember it bounced off his forehead, didn't break, and hit the mirror behind the bar, smashing it. So this guy pulls out his whistle and starts blowing his whistle and all of a sudden a bunch of guys, *policía*, just descended on us, man, and just wadded us up like old newspaper and toted us down to the fuckin' slam. And this is in Juarez, Mexico. This is not a nice jail.

So we get in there and now I see that we have a problem. We're broke and have no way out. I don't remember exactly how it came about, but somehow I got a call in to my mother: "Momma, momma, your baby boy's in jail in Juarez, Mexico, and I've got a friend with me and we're broke and we need to get *outta* here, please!" Well, my mom came through. I don't know exactly what that entailed, and it took a couple more hours before the wheels of Mexican justice spat us out, but we got out.

I didn't think of it much at the time, but the fact that we weren't killed, the fact that we were able to return to Minnesota and return to playing music seems pretty lucky to me today. It was one of those things that I used to get into blindly, *willfully* blindly. I'd just make a decision—whether it was wrong (and most of 'em were) or right—and just go for it, and the hell with whatever consequences may ensue, I'll deal with that when the time comes. It was an attitude that worked for me for a long, long time, just relying on being lucky. And having a momma who could get you outta the hoosegow. Thank you, Mom.

Mexican jails are not fun. They weren't then, and I'm sure they aren't now. But what might've been even less fun was dealing with the fallout from our little escapade across the border. I'd been telling my mom up to that time—because my mom was the only person from the family who I really had any kind of contact with after my grandmother died—that her son was actually doing good, that he was coming up in the world, that he was making a good living and making an impact in the music world, only to have to call her up from a jail in Juarez. And then, of course, Stu had to call *his* parents and get them to wire us some money for gas so we could drive back from Juarez to Minnesota. Thank God we left the car on the other side of the border. I remember that car had no air conditioning, and it was hot, and I had, I think, the worst hangover I've ever had in my life all the way from Mexico to Gibbon, Minnesota. We tried to spin the story the best way we could, but it still boiled down to having to call your momma up to get you outta jail and send you money so you could get home.

I didn't just rely on luck back then—sometimes it came and found me. At one point during the 1961 Knox tour we were in New York City and I got the opportunity to play on a session with Dion, who'd been a part of Buddy's ill-fated Winter Dance Party tour. To be honest, I don't quite remember how I weaseled my way into that session—just bein' in the right place at the right time, I'm sure—but however it happened, I ended up recording the sax part, solo and everything, for "The Wanderer."

Now, here's the kicker: Unbeknownst to me until very recently, during my take of "The Wanderer" I was slightly out of tune, so they had somebody come in after me and copy what I'd done, but in tune. Well, I always thought that it was me because the solo on the record was exactly what I'd remembered playing. The licks were exactly the same. And it sounded really good. But it wasn't me playing. After forty-five goddamn years, I found out it was somebody else playin' my solo. Somebody else played it more in tune, I guess. And no one thought to tell me I'd hit the cutting room floor.

Another, more successful instance of being in the right place at the right time came in the spring of 1962 when, back on tour with Buddy, we had to make a detour out to L.A. Buddy was signed with Liberty Records, and for some reason they needed to see him. By chance, an old acquaintance from Lubbock, Glen D. Hardin, who'd moved to L.A. to become a songwriter and arranger, heard that I was in town. He was doing a session and the guy who was booked to play the session couldn't make the gig, so Glen D. called me. Well, I wasn't gonna turn down a recording session in an L.A. studio, so I said sure, even though I had no idea who it was for.

I had an old baritone sax, which as it turns out was the reason I got the gig—I guess it was easier or cheaper or both to use a guy who already had a baritone sax. Anyway, I went down there and was immediately confronted with sheet music, which I couldn't read except to see that I had the very first notes. The song started with the baritone sax. It was all written out, but it looked like a Chinese puzzle to me. So Glen D. played it for me on piano and I picked it up from there and played it, and then throughout the session, whenever I saw the formation of notes on the sheet music that matched what Glen D. had played for me, I knew that that's when I was supposed to play. The rest of it was just playing the root notes of the chord changes.

Once I got the music down I started picking up on a strange vibe about the session but I couldn't quite figure out what it was. There was a big control room in the front but this was an over-dub, so I was in the studio and there were no musicians in there with me. At some point during the playbacks, though, there was a sudden perceptive change in the air. I'd seen these people come into the control room booth, but they were on the other side of a glass plate, and I couldn't really see that well because it wasn't very well-lit. But I had a minute before I was expected to play so I squinted a little bit and there he was: Elvis fucking Presley. The song was "Return to Sender."

I think I was told right after that, "Oh, didn't you know this was for Elvis?" *Fuck* no, nobody told me anything! I mean, shit! Of course, suddenly I was very, very nervous, but it didn't take that many takes and we got it. It wasn't the first take, unfortunately. Or the second, or the third. It took a few times, but I got it down. The whole time Glen D. was saying, "It's OK, man. Take it easy. It's all right." Stuff like that to calm me down. Elvis didn't really say much.

But I met him. It was quick, but I met him. I remember he said something like, "I'd like to thank you, son. Oh, you're from Texas, you knew Buddy?" I didn't exactly get to sit down and say, "What kind of hair oil do you use?" or "Where'd you get them blue suede shoes?" Actually, he wasn't wearing blue suede shoes. I looked.

No, I didn't say much, man. I was a teenager, eighteen years old. I didn't say anything. This was the king! The *undisputed* king of rock 'n' roll, and I just played on one of his records, and if I don't die of a heart attack before I get outta here it'll be really cool. I mean, that was the coolest thing I did for a long time, in *my* mind, anyway. It's *still* one of the coolest things I've ever done.

WITH KNOX, THERE were breaks from touring that were not always planned or to do with his record company. Knox had his Cadillac, and he and Donny Lanier, the guitar player—they were college buddies—rode in the Cadillac while the Rhythm Orchids, of which I was first chair saxophone player slash sound system and lighting roadie, followed in a different car that pulled the equipment trailer. But Knox also had a wife, and his wife wanted him to come home. Buddy was a good guy, but he had this young, pretty girl in Macon, Georgia, who I guess was the demanding type, and one day he just kinda left, and left me with a U-Haul trailer and a sound system and some pissed-off musicians who didn't get paid.

I don't recall which city we were ditched in that first time he left us, but I do remember, after we sold the sound system and the microphones, Stu and I went to Kansas City and got a gig in a place called Club Michael's. Stu knew a bass player there who was looking for some musicians. And while it wasn't the same as being on the road, it was a whole new chapter because these other guys, they were actually better than some of the guys in Knox's band. And we played primarily black music, too—gone were the Elvis covers and all that other stuff. Now we were playing James Brown–type music, which I really, really enjoyed. For one thing, they have even more horns than they do in rock 'n' roll music, so that was fine with me. And we played all the time—this ol' boy who ran the place had us working all the shifts that he could possibly squeeze out of us. I learned a lot during that period.

But there was a catch. Club Michael's was a strip joint part of the time, and part of the time it was like a supper club, people'd come in to eat. It was also, according to rumor, owned by this Kansas City mob guy who didn't particularly care for music, or at least not our type of music. So the rule was, whenever the owner comes through the door, you stop playing. Not another note. You get off the stage, no questions asked. You didn't want to piss him off because apparently he might beat you up or shoot you. I don't know if that was really true or not, but that was the word goin' around.

And that didn't set sit well. I mean, who wants to play in a club whose owner doesn't want to hear you make a sound? So after a while, as much as I loved playing all that R&B, I started looking for a way out. It was during that time that I met a guy who was a pool hustler. Back then, I thought I was a shit-hot pool player, which I *wasn't* when it came down to really playing, but this guy, Steve Bankston, truly was. So when I'd had enough of being at the mercy of the musical whims of this mafioso guy at Club Michael's,

I took up driving Steve Bankston around. I was a pool hustler's driver, caddy, and all-around aide-de-camp.

Turned out Bankston needed a driver mostly because he was a drunk. But he gave me fifty bucks a day, which was more than I was making playing at Club Michael's, so it seemed like a worthwhile proposition at the time. We'd go to these places, these little towns like Sioux City, Iowa, or Dubuque, find the VFW halls and little pool halls and do a small-town hustling thing. He'd go in and play some nine-ball or play some fourteen-rack call and lose—win some, lose some, win some, lose some, but always lose a little bit more than he won so he could leave there saying, "All right, you gotta gimme a chance to win some of my money back." And then he'd come back the next day and just clean everybody's plow. Where I came into the equation became apparent very quickly—as soon as things got ugly, which they almost always did, we'd have to make a quick exit outta the VFW hall and into his Buick and hit the road hard, with folks running out the door after us with guns and shit, cursing and threatening us.

So I did that for a while. And people actually took shots at us—not a whole lot, but it did happen. (I will never set foot in the town of Mankato, Minnesota, again for as long as I live.) It was probably only a couple, three weeks. It wasn't a *long* period of time, it was just one of those times when I didn't have a saxophone gig. I was finding out that being a professional musician didn't always mean you'd be playing music. Not every night ended on a stage. Sometimes you had to take a job driving the getaway car for an alcoholic pool hustler just to make ends meet. So I tried to look at it as an adventure. And it *was* an adventure, but in the end it wasn't furthering my saxophonic career any. Plus, I didn't like getting shot at.

I did manage to finagle one pretty significant gig during this break from Knox: my first major rock 'n' roll show in New York. King Curtis got me the gig. It was with the house band for an Alan Freed rock 'n' roll show at the Brooklyn Paramount Theatre. They had two concerts a day and a double feature, one of which, I remember very clearly, was "I Was a Teenage Werewolf" with Michael Landon.

The band onstage for this particular show was a couple of trumpets, trombone, and two saxes—a baritone sax and myself. We were sitting behind these little orchestra setups, stands that were kind of like podiums where you put your music. And then they had one microphone set up at the front of the stage for solos. If you had a solo, you got up from your little spot behind the stand and went up to the microphone to play your solo. And I had a solo during Little Eva's "The Loco-Motion."

Before the show, all the guys from the other acts were backstage in the dressing room—Little Anthony and the Imperials, Major Lance, Round Robin, guys like that. And Ernie Wright, from the Imperials, he was back there with the guys smokin' pot. I'd never smoked pot before, but when I walked in and saw what they were doin'—and *smelled* what they were doin'—I figured out what they were up to. So Ernie Wright turned around and looked at me and said, "Hey, Texas, you want some of this?"

Well, I'd never tried marijuana before, but I was in New York and I didn't want to appear to be the clodhopper from the panhandle, so I said, "Sure, yeah, I do this all the time!" So he passed me the joint and I took a big drag on it and exhaled immediately. I didn't know how to do it. Ernie said, "No, no, Texas, lemme show you how to do this. Try it my way." So he tore off the back page of the program—there were a bunch of the show's programs laying around—and rolled it up into a giant straw. Then he held it up to one end of the joint, gave me the other end, and told me to suck in as much as I possibly could, like I was gettin' ready to play a sixty-four-bar solo without takin' a breath. So I did. I wolfed it back, man, sucked it on down, and held it till my eyes started buggin' out. Then he suggested that I do it again, so I did it again. I did it about three times.

All of a sudden, or what seemed like all of a sudden, I heard the cue for Little Eva to come up onstage, so I had to hustle my ass onto the stage. I barely made it behind my little stand. Meanwhile, I noticed going up the stairs to the stage that everything around me was different, just looked slightly *different* than anything I'd seen before in my life. Anyway, I skidded out onto the stage just in time and I was playin' away and eventually it got time for my solo. I was really having to concentrate on my movements by this time, and, man, the lights were brighter than they'd *ever* been and more colorful than I'd *ever* seen 'em. And so I walked up to where I thought the microphone should've been, but I couldn't see anything but the lights, so I walked right on past it into the area where the footlights were, where I fell forward off of the damn stage into the damn orchestra pit—*Crash! Bang! Wallop! Bam!*—and ended up in a kind of ball down on the orchestra pit floor with a broken saxophone and a *wrecked* ego, wondering what the hell happened—'cause I had *no idea.*

Anyway, an usher picked me up and carried me back and people were asking if I was all right and what had happened, and I just said I got blinded by the light. But there were a few of 'em who knew *exactly* what happened, and they enjoyed it thoroughly. I did, too, once I got over it. And it certainly didn't deter me from havin' another puff. Of course, Ernie and the boys were always only too happy to oblige, hoping to get a repeat performance.

I was back out on the road with Knox and the Rhythm Orchids not too long after that on another sixteen-week tour. This time we made it as far as South Dakota before Knox's wife called him back home in the middle of the night. We had to get this guy from Tulsa to drive up in a pickup truck and pick us up. There were three of us, so there were four of us riding from Sioux Falls, South Dakota, back to Tulsa, Oklahoma, and it was cold as a son-of-a-bitch in that pickup truck. It was wintertime. I remember that. The other guys were gonna go home, but I stayed there in Tulsa. That's how I got swept up in the Great Okie Musicians' Migration to Los Angeles, California, a year or so later. It's also where I nearly got inducted into the army.

I got hooked up with a guy named Jimmy Markham, a singer and harmonica player. Jimmy and I established a friendship that carried on from Tulsa through Los Angeles and all the way up to today. When I first met him, though, he didn't have a sax player and I was ready to go, so I started playing gigs with him. I don't know if they were actually *looking* for a saxophone player or not, but I was a saxophone player and I was there. And because I had a miniscule, teeny-weeny bit of a resume from being out on the road with a guy who had a couple of hit records, it gave me a little bit of credibility. We were playing a lot at a place called the Fondalight Club, and Charlie Daniels was actually playing there at the time, too. This was back when his band was called Charlie Daniels and the Jaguars. It's also when I met guys like Leon Russell and Johnny (J.J.) Cale for the first time. Tulsa had an impressive number of good musicians back then.

I supplemented my living expenses at that stage by living with a barmaid from the Fondalight. I don't think we ever made $100 apiece. I think it was more in the neighborhood of $25 to $40. It wasn't a lot of money, but it didn't matter. When we weren't at the Fondalight, Markham would book us at a couple of NCO clubs at army bases around Tulsa or wherever else he could. But it was work. It was great. Nobody bitched or complained, except maybe about the condition of some of these clubs, which were a little less than extravagant.

Anyway, I decided one afternoon to give my grandfather a call because I hadn't talked to him in ages, so I called him up and said, "Hi, Grandpa, this is Robert."

He asked, "Well, you know what you've gone and done?"

"No, Grandpa, I don't."

"You've got the FBI lookin' for ya."

"What do you mean?"

"You're a draft dodger."

"No, I'm not!"

"Well, you got a letter here sent to the house that says so . . . "

It was a notice saying I had to show up to take a physical and be classified. Which, of course, I didn't show up for because I didn't *know* about it because I didn't get the *letter*. So when I didn't show up for that, they sent me another letter saying, essentially, "OK, you are being *inducted*. You just come right on down and we're gonna give you a nice, pretty, autographed uniform and a gun and a helmet and you're in." And of course I didn't show up for *that*. So they sent another nasty letter saying they categorized me as a draft dodger. That I was a wanted man, basically, is what my grandfather conveyed to me. I asked my grandfather why he never sent me any of those letters but, of course, he never knew where to send 'em.

Back then, you had to sign up for the selective service. So I called up the guy back in Slaton, Don Crow, who owned the Chevrolet dealership there, who was also the selective service contact, and I said, "Don, this is Robert Keys. I've talked to my grandfather and he tells me that I'm in trouble with the government. I'm not trying to evade the draft or anything, but what can I do to get this straightened out?" He said, "Well, the only thing you can do is join the army before they find you."

Oh, God. All right. This was before Vietnam, but it was getting close. We were involved in Laos, I think. So I went down to volunteer in Tulsa because I thought it was either that or Leavenworth. I remember I had to get there at five o'clock in the morning, get on a bus, and the bus went somewhere outside of Oklahoma City where the induction center was.

So I went through the written exams, the physical, and everything else, and at this point I was really trying to get into the army because I thought the only other option was *jail*. After all of the testing was done, I was sitting in a waiting room with a bunch of other guys who'd gone through the process. Every once in a while the recruiting sergeant would come out and say, "OK, Jones, Smith, Brown," whoever, and then take the guy into this one room. By the time he said, "Mr. Keys, come with me," I knew what was supposed to be happening and I realized it wasn't—he was taking me into a *different* room! To me, that meant only one thing: They found out I'd been evading and I was going *directly* to jail and that's all there was to it. I don't recall ever having been as panicked in my life up to that point.

"Robert, sit down, I've got some bad news for you," I remember the sergeant saying said to me, and I thought, Oh *no,* I'm goin' in for *life!* Then he said, "Robert, I'm sorry, but due to your medical history of ulcers, we're not going to be able to accept you—we don't have a special diet, everybody eats the same thing." I'd had ulcers when I was a kid, and I'd written it down—I wrote *everything* down, I was 100 percent truthful because I was actually *trying* to get into the army—and now it turned out that my honest efforts had gotten me denied. I said, "Really? I can't join?" and he said, "No, sir. I'm sorry, Robert. I'm sorry to dash your hopes like this, but you're not qualified."

Well, all right! I thanked the sergeant for letting me down gently and then went immediately out to a phone booth and called Don Crow and said, "Look, I tried to get in, now they won't *take* me. What do I do now?" He said, "Well, have your recruiting sergeant there send the papers showing that you tried to join but were deemed unacceptable, and we'll see what happens from there." So that's what I did. And I never heard from 'em again.

Aside from my brush with the army, Tulsa was fun, but after a while I was itching to get back out on the road. It's hard to explain.

I wasn't driven by the lure of easy money because the money *wasn't* easy. There weren't any riches except for the few folks who made records and sold records and made a name for themselves that way. I just seemed to have this drive to make music and to keep experiencing things, to be someplace different almost every day. Pretty soon I got my chance.

Buddy Knox's booker was a guy named Jimmy Thomas—he booked all our gigs throughout the Midwest. Myron Lee Wachendorf, from Sioux Falls, South Dakota, meanwhile, had a band that Jimmy managed, and Buddy and the Rhythm Orchids would sometimes play gigs with Myron Lee because he had a following up there, a regular gig at a place called Shorty's. Myron Lee would open up and we'd go on and close it out. Shortly after this period, Myron Lee and his band hooked up with Bobby Vee to play Dick Clark's Caravan of Stars tour. The Caravan of Stars tour brought together six or seven of the top rock 'n' roll acts of the day, put 'em all together on a bus, and drove 'em around the country, and Bobby Vee had a bunch of hits at the time, "Rubber Ball" and "Take Good Care of My Baby" and some others. I don't know what exactly happened, but the guy who played saxophone for Myron Lee, a guy named Fred Scott, couldn't make the gig or got fired or quit, and all of a sudden I had an offer from Myron Lee to go out and do this Dick Clark tour with Bobby Vee. So once again I was an afterthought—or maybe once again I was in the right place at the right time.

Being in Bobby Vee's band, we also had to back up the other acts on the show that didn't carry bands on the tour. The headliner got his band and then there were six or seven supporting acts. And the supporting acts, I thought, were cooler than Bobby: Little Anthony and the Imperials, Major Lance, the Shangri-La's, the Detergents, Billy Stewart, Round Robin, Freddie Cannon, they were all really good. Aside from the debacle in New York City on the Alan Freed show, these were my first really big gigs—they weren't actually that big, but they were bigger than the dance halls and the places where I played with Buddy Knox.

Ever since my grandmother had died, I didn't keep in touch with my family all that much. I'd call my mother occasionally, but my father couldn't have cared less. My family was really the guys I was playing with on the road. My buddy Stu Perry, for instance, who also lucked into the Caravan of Stars gig, was with me. I'd left Texas. There was no reason to go back. I didn't *wanna* go back, I wanted to keep doing what I was doing. Which I did. I had a Samsonite suitcase with my clothes in it, a suit bag with a black mohair suit, a couple shirts and a tie, and my saxophone. And that was it. Very economical traveling. But it was all I needed.

Touring back then was much different than it is today. We were on a regular bus, for one thing. Not one of these tricked-out tour buses they have now that have bathrooms and beds and television sets and stereos, but a *regular bus*. And while they were miserable, I thought they were great, too, because here in one place were all these acts that've got these hit records out . . . *and I'm with 'em*. It was pretty cool. There was a lotta gambling going on in the back of the bus, a lotta shootin' dice. There were occasional disputes, and a couple times knives were drawn. There was always a bottle being passed around on the bus—wasn't supposed to be, but what else were we gonna do? We'd be driving for hours and every seat'd be taken. It's not like there was anyplace to go sprawl out. And this was before Walkmans, before anything like that. This was when there were transistor radios, that's about it. So on the bus you'd either sit there and look out the window or you'd talk with the other guys in the band or the guys in the other groups. I mostly listened. I didn't do a whole lotta talking because I was still young, very young. I was just soaking it all up.

That tour was great. We played a lot—we did matinees, we'd do two shows a day. We didn't have any days off that I can remember. Dick Clark himself would be on certain legs, the ones in the bigger markets like Philadelphia. He even rode on the bus a couple of times, or at least once that I remember for sure because I remember everyone saying, "Hey, Dick Clark's up there, you can't smoke, you can't gamble, put those dice away!" Dick was a very clean-cut boy, just the way he was portrayed. I remember we always had plenty of Dr. Pepper. They were one of the sponsors of the tour. We had loads and loads of Dr. Pepper, but beer was not allowed on the bus. 'Course, that was what was *said*, and while it's true there wasn't a lot of beer on the bus, there was plenty of whiskey and plenty of wine.

This was a whole new experience for me: a whole bus full of rock 'n' roll musicians. Sometimes I'd find myself thinking, Man, not long ago I was listening to these people on the radio and now I'm sitting here watching 'em shoot dice and drink wine and we're all having a good time rollin' down the highway. Pretty soon, though, I got the feeling that there was something of a caste system, although it wasn't spoken out loud. There were the guys in the backup band, like me, and then there were the stars. I mean, I knew there was a reason for the division—these were the guys and girls who people paid money to come and see. They didn't pay a dime to come and see the guy from Slaton, Texas, playing saxophone. And although most of 'em were nice, there were a couple of guys who were snooty. Usually they were the least talented of the acts.

At this point in my life, I played all the time. I used to shine my saxophone every day. My saxophone guy was still King Curtis, even though the music I was playing didn't call for any King Curtis–style solo playing. In fact, I didn't have any solos *period*. I'd play lines. King Curtis used a lot of tonguing and a lot of phrasing that was more like a country fiddle-playing-type approach. It was very precise, very difficult to do. He didn't play any jazz notes at all, just straight-ahead rock 'n' roll. Hardly any blues notes—sevenths, fifths. He had such a distinctive style, really up-tempo. It was fun music. To me it was, anyway. Years later he'd end up getting stabbed in his doorway. Some asshole wanted some free money. I played on his last album, I was on a track called "Ridin' Thumb."

I was starting to feel good about my playing on the Caravan of Stars tour. It wasn't hard at all. I felt relaxed. I felt good. And I felt *particularly* good when I had a little buzz going. It was during that time when I really developed a fondness for pot, reunited as I was with Ernie Wright and Clarence Collins from the Imperials. This was before the hippie movement, way before peace and love, way before the Vietnam War. These were New York fellas who used to just go down to the candy store and get a $5 brown bag of ganja.

This time around it was Clarence Collins who offered me a toke, saying something like, "This is African black ganja. You better watch out, Texas boy, 'cause it'll kick your ass!" I didn't know if it really came from Africa, but that's what he called it, so, hell, that's what it was. Ernie Wright, Sammy Strain, and Clarence Collins, they were the Imperials. Sammy also sang in a spiritual group, so I don't think he smoked pot. Maybe he did, I don't know. But I know for sure I smoked a lot of pot with Ernie and Clarence.

I hung out with them a lot. I think I was tolerated by them because I was sort of a novelty—this young, white Texas boy who had a taste for ganja. All I know is I loved hanging out with them. They were the coolest act on the stage. They all dressed alike and had three different tuxedo options: One was wine-colored, another was dark blue, and then they had the real special white tuxedos. They were really smooth. They were like the Temptations, but before the Temptations.

Stu Perry was my other pot-smoking partner on the Dick Clark tour. He was the only guy I let know about my new pastime. I remember one time we'd gotten a couple of joints from a friend in Tulsa before heading to New York with Bobby Vee to do a Dick Clark gig. I put the joints in a vial for some pills or something, and I'd also put some poppers in there—amyl nitrate, which came in a little capsule encased in cotton and mesh. Poppers were officially for people having heart attacks—you broke the mesh and inhaled, and it gave you quite a rush. It was a vapor. You'd break it and smell it. Like smelling salts. It was a liquid in glass surrounded by cotton and mesh, and you'd smell it and go, "Whoo-hoo!" But I didn't know that it had a detrimental effect on pot. So I'd put three or four joints in this prescription bottle with this used amyl nitrate and somehow or other it effected the pot. I remember getting to

New York and heading up to our room thinking, We're gonna get high in New York City and hang out of the window and watch all the taxis! But the shit didn't work. It tasted bad and put us in a bad mood.

We finally did score, though. We were at the Hotel President— either the President or the Roosevelt, I don't remember which— and we were sitting up in the room getting stoned and looking out the window, down at our bus and Myron Lee's station wagon and trailer with all of our shit in it parked down below. As we were doing this, Stu sees somebody start to run off with his drums. We were on the twentieth or thirtieth floor of this hotel and somebody was stealing his drums outta the back of the trailer. So we were up there screaming, "Hey you! Hey you!" And we were stoned. So we went downstairs and told the other guys that somebody was stealing our shit, and someone said, "Get a cop!" and we said, "No! Don't get any policemen, we're high!" The other guys in the band were trying to tell us it was OK, but Stu said, "No, no, no! I'd rather get more drums! I can't let my parents know I'm high!"—like as soon as the cops saw us they'd have known we were high, as if there was a neon sign above us that said STONED! STONED! STONED! So the drums were stolen, and Stu had to buy a new set.

One of the first places we went on that tour was to Hershey, Pennsylvania. I remember smoking a joint and getting off that bus and, I mean, the whole *town* smelled like chocolate! The air was just *permeated* with chocolate. Talk about the munchies. I wanted to just jump in a vat of chocolate and eat my way across. It's funny, but back then it was considered a real sin to smoke pot, although I never had that opinion. I never felt like I was sinnin'. To me it really didn't seem like there was a damn thing wrong with it. It sure did make fried chicken taste better than it had ever tasted before. I still to this day religiously smoke.

I used to smoke cigarettes, too. I had a bad cigarette habit until I realized I couldn't finish playing a solo on one breath that I used to be able play on one breath. I found out it was affecting my playing, my breathing, and I shut it down. I didn't need any patches or anything because I knew if I blew the gig with the saxophone, I was fucked. I had no plan B. Outside of crime. I just remember finding myself having to take a gulp of air when I didn't use to have to take a gulp of air, and that really impressed me. Man, if you got no lungs, you got no gig, and if you got no gig, you are up shit creek without the proverbial paddle. Because I didn't have any other skills. Other than being a tightrope walker. A drunk tightrope walker.

Those were some good days, though, on that Caravan of Stars tour. I remember looking around at the people riding on the bus and thinking, Entertainers, when they're not onstage entertaining, they look different. On the bus they just looked like ordinary people. Sometimes when I looked at 'em I'd think, OK, now, that's Freddie Cannon—but he doesn't look like the Freddie Cannon that you see in pictures in *Hit Parade* magazine. It was a trip. Other times I'd think, Two years ago I was sitting in Slaton, Texas, doing nothing, wondering how I was gonna get my girlfriend back, and now I'm on a bus going down the road with guys who have hit records in the Top 10 and Top 20, and I'm playing in front of all these people. It was like a rock 'n' roll dream come true. And then I met the Rolling Stones.

3

N JUNE OF 1964 I was at the Teenage World's Fair in San Antonio,
Texas. The headliners were Bobby Vee, who I was playing
with, the Rolling Stones, and George Jones. George Jones had
"White Lightning" out at the time. This was the Stones' first tour of
America. All of the acts were staying on the same floor at the San
Antonio Ramada Inn. I was staying in a room next door to Brian
Jones and Keith Richards. The Rolling Stones' current record was
"Not Fade Away," which opened a natural avenue of introduction
between Keith, Brian, and me. Brian's the first one I met because
he was a saxophone player. He played alto sax, and not very well.
But he was also a guitar player and a really good harmonica player.
Anyway, because of my knowing Buddy Holly and being from
Lubbock, that opened the door for a friendship.

The Stones were fascinated with the idea that in the States
everybody changed clothes before they went onstage, so before

they went on, they all switched clothes with each other. In the Bobby Vee band, we were all wearing these black mohair suits. At that point, I'd had mine cleaned so many times by one-hour Martinizing cleaners that the fabric was paper-thin at the crease, so when I went to put the pants on and my toenail caught the fabric, it just ripped right down the crease line. I tried to duct-tape 'em together but that didn't work, and I knew I couldn't wear 'em like that, and the only other thing I had to wear was the pair of old Bermuda shorts I'd worn to the gig. It was summertime, it was hot, and so that's what I wore: Bermuda shorts and cowboy boots. If you ask Keith or Charlie Watts or Mick Jagger, that's what they'll say they remember about meeting me for the first time.

Anyway, after the show we spent the rest of the time talking, Keith and I, and Brian. They asked me about Buddy Holly and Roy Orbison, who was from around Lubbock. It was just one night, and the next day everybody went their separate ways. And I didn't run into 'em again until Philadelphia, at the Spectrum. I played there with Bobby Vee—and this time the Rolling Stones were headlining.

That first meeting made a big impact on me, though. Within the first minute that I actually sat down and talked with Keith, I knew this was a special guy. I had no idea how much further down the road, or if ever, our paths would cross again, but somehow I knew it. I remember when I saw him, when I was looking at him, that I saw a lot of characteristics in Keith that I'd noticed in Buddy Holly. I've always told Keith, "Man, if you had known Buddy, you would have scared the shit out of yourself," because even though they didn't look alike physically, they had a lot of the same qualities. They were both highly motivated people. I mean, Holly *knew* he was gonna make it—here he was, a stained-toothed, four-eyed, glasses-wearin' guy, but he had no fear. And that's what I saw right away in Keith Richards. It was one of those moments, like a chill-down-the-spine moment. He just had that same look in his eye.

Aside from making some new friends in the Stones, I didn't like the British Invasion much. But I could see why the time was ripe for a change. Rock 'n' roll was undergoing a major shift by the mid-'60s. Elvis had started to change; his music was more the music he did in his movies—*Kissin' Cousins* and *Paradise, Hawaiian Style*. There were a ton of 'em. And then it got diluted with all those boy-next-door types while guys like Jerry Lee Lewis and Little Richard and some of the other founding fathers were sort of fading from the foreground. It was pretty vanilla until the Beatles came along. That was in February 1964, the same year I met the Stones for the first time.

The Beatles changed a *whole* lotta stuff, and not particularly for my good because there were no saxophones in their songs. They led the whole British Invasion, and the only band with a saxophone in that bunch was the Dave Clark Five, and they weren't my cup of tea, to tell you the truth. I liked the Beatles, but they didn't have horns. And they weren't the blues. Fortunately, I knew where I could find some fellas who were into the blues as much as I was: Tulsa. So when Dick Clark's Caravan of Stars tour ended, that's where I went, but by then the Great Okie Musicians' Migration out to L.A. was already well underway.

There was a huge amount of talent in Tulsa in the mid-'60s, I guess too much for one Midwestern town, so people just naturally started heading out West. There was a lot more opportunity in L.A.—Leon Russell lived out there by that point and there were a few other Okies who had gone there and made some money at it, so a lot more followed. And I was among those who followed. This was in 1965. I rode from Tulsa to California with Tommy Tripplehorn, a guitar player. (His daughter's the actress Jeanne Tripplehorn.) Tommy was going out there to be in Gary Lewis's band. I was going out there to reunite with Jimmy Markham.

California opened up a whole new chapter for me. I didn't think about it at the time—I'm a musician, I didn't think about much except where my next gig was gonna be—but if I hadn't moved to L.A. in 1965, I wouldn't be here today. The Buddy Knox and Bobby Vee tours opened me up to what's out there in the rest of the country, but it was California and the people I met and played with there that opened me up to the rest of the world.

Actually, if I'm gonna be totally honest, all the good things that happened to me go right back to Lubbock, as much as I detested being in that town. The opportunity to play with people like Joe B.—just getting a taste of it—spurred me on. And I would never have gotten the gig with Buddy Knox had I not known J.I., and the thing with Knox ultimately led to other things, the Caravan of Stars and Tulsa, which led to Leon Russell and Delaney & Bonnie, which in turn led to other things. When I first met the Stones, my main pass into being accepted by those Brits was the fact that I knew the Crickets and I'd known Buddy because the record they had out at the time was "Not Fade Away." That set up a relationship that's still going to this day. I guess I have Lubbock, Texas, to thank for that.

But that's not how I thought at the time. Back then, I was just happy to be somewhere else, and L.A. in the '60s couldn't have been a better place. Well, most of L.A. The Watts Riots were in August of 1965, and Markham and I were living together during that time. This was right when I first moved out there. We were staying in the basement of this big old house on a hill above Griffith Park, four or five of us. The people we knew who lived there were these two brothers, the Quick brothers. Maybe they just rented the place, I don't know, but back then if one guy had a house, everybody just kinda crashed. This was one of those places. It was a very grand old home. I remember you could see downtown L.A. from up on top of this hill. It was up by the Griffith Observatory, and the places we were trying to play—the only clubs that hired bands that played blues and R&B music—were being *set on fire*. So that was kind of a bummer. I mean, they were torching the place. It was serious shit. This did not bode well for our incomes. They were burnin' our gigs, man!

Fortunately or unfortunately, I don't know which way you'd put it, but the blues weren't a real big item in California at that time. Surf music was the big item. Real big. Never real big with me because it never had any brass in it. It just never appealed to me. Aside from the lack of the blues, I found out that session work wouldn't be easy to come by, either. Out there, all the horn guys read really well. Plus, they had established themselves, these guys, as the session guys. So when a producer needed some horns, they got the call. It was really hard for me to break into something like that because I couldn't read music. So at that time the only playing I did was with Markham and a few other bands that were around, like Gram Parson's International Submarine Band. The other guys who played with Markham at the time were Jesse Ed Davis and J.J. Cale—both Okies—and Gary Gilmore. By then, pretty much everyone was living in Leon Russell's place out in Studio City, 7709 Skyhill Drive.

Leon was the only guy who had a steady gig. The goal back then for most of us was just to survive. We were havin' fun. I mean, we weren't striving for any record deal or anything like that. Leon was working with Snuff Garrett, who'd been a DJ back in Lubbock and had been friends with Buddy Holly and who was now a producer in L.A. Leon was doing a lot of sessions and arranging at the time for Snuff. He was also working with Jack Good on the *Shindig!* TV show. He did some arranging and got paid for that.

As musicians, we all thought we were pretty good, but everybody knew Leon was superior. He was a phenomenal pianist and stylist. He brought a lot of gospel in with blues and boogie-woogie. He could play Jerry Lee Lewis licks—in fact, I think he played with Jerry Lee Lewis for a little while. Leon was what all the other Okies and Texans were aspiring to be: He had a black Cadillac, he had his own house in the hills, he had a studio in his house, and he had chicks up there day and night.

One album I remember doing there was a thing called *A Trip Down the Sunset Strip*, which was coproduced by Snuff and J.J. Cale, who'd put together a band they called the Leathercoated Minds specifically for that purpose. It was not one of your big sellers or one of your more memorable albums. We did it during the let's-see-how-much-LSD-we-can-take-and-see-if-we-sound-like-the-Beatles stage, when everybody was convinced that all the Beatles' songs had triple and quadruple meanings if you only knew how to listen and what to listen for. Of course, you had to be in a receptive state of mind, which meant several hundred micrograms of LSD. Then, hell, you could hear all *kinds* of messages.

That was a talent pool that was pretty deep, though. Jesse Ed Davis went on to work with Taj Mahal and on various Beatles' solo projects, Johnny Cale became J.J. Cale—these were some great players. But before we went on to do other things, we played with Markham. And we had some good gigs, man. It was the blues: We were doing covers of Jimmy Reed and Howlin' Wolf and Lightnin' Hopkins. One of the best gigs I remember was down at Peacock Alley, which was right across the street from the old Ambassador Hotel in Los Angeles, where Bobby Kennedy was shot. It was run by this guy, George DeCarl, whose claim to fame was that he could play the trumpet quieter than anybody else. We played there semi-regularly, Markham and me and Johnny Cale and Jesse Ed Davis and Gary Gilmore, who also later played in Taj Mahal's band, and on drums we had Levon Helm . . . Yeah, it was a good gig. Markham played harmonica and sang.

Mostly, though, we were playing blues clubs. You put Markham in front of a bunch of black people and he turns black *immediately*. That type of music—blues, R&B—it centered what I was doing back then. I wasn't a schooled musician. I didn't read, I didn't depend on arrangements or a section to play with. So, being the only horn player, I started playing rhythm. It was kind of a wide-open field because nobody'd ever really done it that way. I mean, there were songs that had saxophone solos in 'em, but unfortunately the songs of Buddy Knox never had a single saxophone solo in 'em, so all I did was rhythm stuff. With Markham, it was pretty much all harmonicas and shuffles, which was right up my alley— that was my meat and potatoes, man, I loved that stuff.

We got *no* money for doing what we did, hardly. We made, I don't know, maybe twenty bucks a gig or something like that. But it was right when it seemed like there was this nucleus of musicians from Oklahoma, with a few additions here and there, and everybody just got together over at Leon's house. Just a nest of Okies down there. It was serious fun.

And then, with the advent of flower power, that brought about a resurgence of a lot of blues guys' popularity. All of a sudden places like the Troubadour and a few other clubs started bringing in people like Howlin' Wolf and Muddy Waters and Jimmy Reed. And I know from talking to Chuck Berry and some other players from that period of time that flower power did more to revitalize the blues than anything. The English particularly, with Clapton and the Stones and the Yardbirds—after they became popular, when they were interviewed, people would ask them where their sources of inspiration came from, and it went right back to Lightnin' Hopkins, Muddy, and that bunch. So even though I didn't care for the British Invasion when it began because of the lack of saxophones in the game, they did help to bring about a resurgence of American blues music.

There was a *lot* of stuff going on out in L.A. in the '60s. There were people unhappy about the war, which I happened to be one of 'em, although I didn't demonstrate actively. But I certainly didn't agree with the policies of the government. Things were changing. There were all these Renaissance fairs and love-ins, and all-afternoon and all-day events started taking place out at places like Topanga Canyon at somebody's ranch, or at a park sometimes, although the police didn't like assemblages in large numbers without a permit. Out in Topanga Canyon, there were places like the Topanga Corral, where Taj Mahal used to go and play, lots of people played there. I'd play out there with Markham. Gram Parsons played out there in the International Submarine Band. And I played with them, too.

Back then, musicians just seemed to find each other. There was a lot of hanging out together, especially at these Sunday afternoon get-togethers. Everybody'd bring a guitar or harmonica or something to bang on, a tambourine. And there'd just be circles of people playin' blues and stuff. I didn't walk around with my saxophone because it was too heavy, but it was nice just to go out and roll up a big fat joint, man, and walk through the hills and see all these flower children.

I never considered myself a flower child, particularly. I didn't even get into tie-dye that much. To be honest, even if I'd wanted to be one, I wasn't really the flower child type. But I liked the vibe. I had love beads, but I didn't wear flowers, particularly, except, you know, if someone gave 'em to me. When you were at one of these Renaissance things, somebody'd always come up to you and offer you flowers and, well, you *gotta* take the flowers. You'd be a *jerk* not to take 'em.

It was kind of like when rock 'n' roll first started, when teenagers had their own badges of distinction like pink and black wardrobes and their own language and stuff—this was kind of like a resurgence of that. All of a sudden there was long hair—it just scared the hell out of the establishment when kids started letting their hair grow shaggy. And there was a lot of dissatisfaction with the government about their policies in Vietnam and a whole bunch of stuff. It was really a division of culture. We were the counter-culture, the youth, and then there was the establishment with their billy clubs and bullhorns. So to get around all that, there were lots of people playing music and, let's say, *experimenting*.

But even more than flowers, music was everywhere. It seemed like you could play all the time back then if you wanted to. You could always find somebody to jam with. With Markham and Levon, we played lots of weekends and lots of Sunday afternoons. And those were always fun because we'd go and we'd just listen to Howlin' Wolf and Muddy and all the guys and then be able to go out and play that kind of music. We weren't really playing rock 'n' roll, we were playing blues boogie tempered with a little Chuck Berry here and there. We'd play Snoopy's Opera House in North Hollywood, we'd play a couple places down in the Valley, and then a lot of those gatherings.

We played one gig—it was a Markham gig—that was an early-morning thing, so the day before, we went down to the Supply Sergeant, which was a place where you could buy cheap clothes. It was an army surplus store but they had fashions, cheap fashions. You could get your bell-bottom jeans there for ten bucks a pair; you could get an outfit for twenty-five bucks. Which is what we'd do: go buy white pants and these flowery shirts to wear out in the desert.

Arnold Rosenthal got us the gig. He went under the name of Georgie Dee as a bass player, but actually he was with a group that already had a bass player, a classic one-hit wonder group called the T-Bones. Maybe he was their manager. Their song was "No Matter What Shape (Your Stomach's In)." It was a takeoff on the Alka-Seltzer commercial. Short-lived.

James Drury, the Virginian from the TV show *The Virginian*, was also there with his lasso. That was his deal: He'd do lasso tricks at his personal appearances. And there was a girl group, a '60s version of the McGuire Sisters, on the show. And us. Which was an odd bill. Especially first thing in the morning. It was one of those things where you had to stop and think, Now, is this why I got into playing the saxophone, to be out here in the middle of the desert at nine o'clock in the morning with polka-dot queens over here and this fella James Drury over there?

Actually, James Drury was cool, except he was all hungover, too. He wasn't shaven, and his corset—he was all trussed up—was bothering him so he was bitchin' about that. But I remember we got paid. That was the only reason we'd do things like that. During that time, man, it was just a matter of survival.

But even when I didn't get paid a lot, I didn't mind because every time I played with somebody, one thing would lead to another and there'd be a new opportunity. L.A. was really good in those days because there were a lot of clubs and there was a lot of live music. It was during that time that I met Delaney Bramlett. I played a lot with Markham at Snoopy's Opera House, and Delaney's band at the time played there, too. There were so many good musicians, so when a band finished playing there was always another band playing down the road. That's when it was really fun for me, and it seemed like it was really fun for everyone around me, too. There was a lot of music goin' on, a lotta pot, a lotta LSD. And lots of women.

I was living off and on at that period of time with Levon—we were both staying at this place called the Villa Carlotta in Hollywood at the corner of Franklin and Argyle. He had left the Band—before they were called the Band, they were Ronnie Hawkins's band, and they'd been playing with Bob Dylan—because he wanted to go to school or something like that. Anyway, it was a very formative time. We used to take LSD every damn day together. He had the smallest Harley-Davidson motorcycle ever manufactured—not quite what you'd see clowns ride around on at the circus but suspiciously similar—and we used to get on that thing just *blazin'* and go down Sunset Boulevard nearly to the ocean to this place that was called the Self-Realization Center, which was established by some yogi or somebody. Someone who had all the answers. We'd go there looking for peace within and all that shit, but we'd just end up laughing. We weren't trying to be rude, it just all seemed so funny to us.

Actually, I learned a lot from Levon. He turned me on to Little Walter, a harmonica player, and that was crucial. He's the one who suggested that, instead of playing like a saxophone player in a big band, maybe I should play like a harmonica player. And I took him at his word. A good piece of advice he gave me there. Thank you, Levon.

From that point on, I started taking a lot of my solos and a lot of my phrasing and approaches to playing the saxophone from blues harmonica players. I'd taken my rock 'n' roll influence from King Curtis, but actually all I was doing, really, was mimicking King Curtis. Which wasn't a *bad* thing, but not particularly original.

I'd developed some licks: double-tonguing, triple-tonguing, and just some sorta standard King Curtis–type licks. And then Levon turned me on to harmonica players like Little Walter. If you want to think of what I do as having a style, it was fashioned from King Curtis and from Little Walter and harmonica solos, and kind of fusing all that together. I don't play a lot of notes. You don't see me running a lot of scales and stuff like that. It's pretty much straight- ahead rock 'n' roll.

And then, just when I was starting to hit my stride in L.A., I almost threw it all away.

I was playing at a place called Carol's Cottontail Club in the Valley with Jimmy Markham, and this guy came up to me on a break and asked, "Hey, man, you got some good weed?" Back then *everybody* was smoking pot, *everybody* had joints, but anyway, this guy came up to me, so I said, "Yeah, man, I got good weed." He said something like his connection had gone defunct, whatever. So we split a joint and right away he was complimenting the band, and especially my saxophone playing, so it didn't take him long to sink the hook in my lip. Then he came down to the gig a couple more times—we had a regular gig there for a while—and the second time he asked me if I could I help him out.

Well, it just so happened I knew this guy in Laurel Canyon who sold pot for $125 a kilo, so I said, "Yeah, I can do that." "First off," he said, "get me a lid and let me see what it's like." And I did, and he said, "OK, can you get me some more?" and I said, "Yeah, how much you want?" and he said, "How much can you get me?" I said, "Well, I don't know, I can probably get you a kilo." He said, "Well, all right—you go get it and let me check it out, and then if my man wants it, I might be able to get fifty kilos, one hundred kilos, whatever, and of course you'll make four or five hundred bucks." And I thought, Wow, that's *easy*. Easy money. In retrospect, I don't think he ever did actually smoke with me. I should've known. There could've been a tell there.

Anyway, I got the pot for him and he called me. He wanted to do a bigger deal. He wanted me to introduce him to this guy Howard who lived up in Laurel Canyon. And he kinda started pushing me about it. Finally, he showed up at my apartment door with this other guy—it was his partner, which I didn't know at the time—and I said, "Look, man, I do *not* want to be involved," and he said, "Well, I'm sorry, you're *already* involved," and he whipped out his badge. At the time, I was living with this chick who was dancing down at the Body Shop—I had to supplement my income, and she was a regular earner.

So they put me in jail. I guess they picked me out when they saw me smoking in the parking lot—"Here's a dumb one, let's see what he can turn up." So when I told them I wasn't gonna do that, they put the cuffs on me and we went downtown and it started a whole 'nother branch of experience for me. A very depressing time. I had to call Mommy. I was in deep. So I called my mother and she got me Harry Weiss and Peter Knecht, the two top defense lawyers in California at the time.

I thought I was going away for ten years, or five years at least, but when I went to my lawyers' office and told them what happened, they said, "*Pfff*. This is nothing, this is entrapment." Which it was—they came to me, they asked me to do it. I did not approach them. And so I got off. But there was this whole procedure after I got busted—I'd meet with my lawyers and they'd take me before a judge and they—my lawyers—kept putting my case off to a different date, trying to maneuver it in front of a friendly judge.

It seemed like I showed up to about a dozen appearances with my lawyers, during which time I'd gotten so used to them taking care of everything—because they *told* me they were taking care of everything—that when, finally, something happened, I wasn't even aware of it. They went through some kinda motion or other and I was just sitting there not really paying attention to what was going on because I didn't understand it, it was legalese. At the end, when the cops and my attorneys and the judge were through, some guy said, "OK, see the bailiff and he'll give you instructions about what to do." And so I got the instructions, folded 'em into my pocket, and didn't bother to read 'em until the night before I was supposed to go back to court. I pulled 'em out to check the details, to make sure I got the date right, the time right, and the address right, and I happened to notice on there that it said, "Upon receipt of this, proceed directly across the street to department such-and-such to be interviewed by a probation officer." Which I obviously neglected to do.

So I called the probation officer up and said, "Hi, this is Robert Keys, and I'm case number blah-blah-blah, and I see here where I was supposed to see you." And he says, "Mr. Keys, take a toothbrush with you tomorrow 'cause you're goin' to jail." I said, "What! Why? Why am I goin' to jail?" He said, "Because you didn't come over here to be interviewed and I can't give any sort of recommendation to the court because I don't know anything about you. You chose not to come and see me." I said, "I didn't *choose* not to come, I just didn't turn the paper over!"

Sure enough, off I went to the L.A. County Jail, to an area called the Glass House. Which was a *charming* place, really. It was a regular melting pot, a cast of characters that you wouldn't find many other places. The Glass House was where people were held for ongoing trials. They hadn't yet been sentenced, they'd just been charged. It wasn't prison, everybody was just going through the system. No one had been proven guilty yet.

I got in as good as I could with the guy who was our cell block leader, captain, whatever. His name was Mendoza and he played chess. Got in with him, hell—I was in a *cell* with him. I played a lot of chess in jail. He was a good chess player. Don't quite know what he was in there for. There was one guy in the cell next to us who was in there for murdering his wife and her lover—they only found parts of her. Not even all the parts. I was in really good company there.

So I had to stay there until my next court appearance and until my probation officer could come over and interview me. When they first nabbed me and I knew I was going to jail, my attorneys said, "It's all right, all you have to do is let this judge interview you, fill out the papers, and you'll be out." Well, I kept waiting and waiting and waiting. As it turns out, the judge waited until the next court appearance, which was a month later. A month I spent in the slam. I went in at first thinking it'd be a day or two and I'd be out, but then it turned into three or four days, five days, a week, and I wasn't getting out.

So I'd call my attorney—you only get one phone call a day— and he wasn't much help. He'd say, "Well, you can't *force* the judge to do anything." So, finally, I guess about the third week—and by this point I'd just about given up; I thought, Hell, I'm going to prison for five, ten years—my attorney said, "Maybe you should write a letter to the judge telling him you're sorry." I remember thinking, You're supposed to be the hottest attorney in L.A. and *this* is what you come up with? I need to write a *letter?* But I did. I don't know what I said, but I know it was pitiful. Meanwhile, I'd spent the whole damn month in there until that next court date, and then I got out. They essentially just sent me home for bein' stupid. And it really was just stupid. After that, I had to be on probation for a year, and I had to go see a probation officer once a month, twice a month in the beginning.

Anyway, it's all there in the court records. They exist. Believe me, the Japanese are *well* aware of them. They sent me home. The first time I went to Japan with the Stones, I got all the way there—and I'd come in, for some reason, from some other place, so I'd come in on my own—and they took me into a little room and said, "Uh-uh. Nope." And they sent me back. They put me on a plane. When I talked to an attorney with the Stones about it, they said the Japanese have really cracked down on issuing visas to people with drug arrest histories. And I thought, Well, hell, man, look at the *band.* There are two guys at least who I *know* ran into similar problems.

But anyway, they sent me back and I had to write this letter— well, actually, the lawyers composed the body of it—that was essentially to the emperor or whoever, promising that I will not have anything to do with leading the youth of Japan astray, that I will not bring in any pornography, drugs, or alcohol, and I flew back and they let me in. I missed a couple of rehearsals, but I didn't miss the gig. But from that point on, anytime we go to Japan, it's me and Keith and Mick, we get pulled out every time. It's to the point now—we've been back to Japan three times—that when we land, they say, "Mr. Jagger, Mr. Richards, and Mr. Keys, remain on board." Everybody else goes, they take us to the room, and now it's gotten to be where our road manager will go in there with Mick and Keith and they take some eight-by-ten glossies, they sign some piece of paper and then get their picture taken with all of the customs authorities, hand out autographed pictures, and then we go on our way.

SNOOPY'S OPERA HOUSE doesn't exist anymore, but it was a great melting pot at the time, and a great training ground. Plus, playing there with Markham eventually led to my Delaney & Bonnie stint. We spent the formative part of that band playing at Snoopy's, too, in late 1968, early 1969. J.J. Cale, who'd been playing with Markham as well, was actually our first guitar player in the Delaney & Bonnie band. And then he decided that he'd rather concentrate on his own material and his own career, which turned out to be a pretty damn good move, though I didn't see it that way at the time.

Johnny Cale played a beautiful guitar, and he loved the music because it was a really good band, but he kept maintaining that, although he appreciated what everybody was doing, he wanted to do his own thing. I thought he was *nuts*. I remember I called him up and said, "Johnny, you're *crazy*, man, this is a golden fucking opportunity!" But he stuck to his guns. A couple years later I remember calling him up when Eric Clapton recorded "After Midnight," which J.J.'d written. I was in the studio in London when it was recorded, and I called Cale up and held the phone up to the playback speaker and said, "Listen to this, you son of a bitch!" I was happy for him. He'd been right.

The first incarnation of Delaney & Bonnie and Friends, aside from founding members Delaney Bramlett and his wife, the singer Bonnie Bramlett, included a guy named Jimmy Karstein playing the drums. He lived over in that area of the Valley with that whole nest of Okie friends of mine—Markham lived over there, the guitar player Bill Boatman, the drummer Chuck Blackwell—a bunch of players from Tulsa. When we first started with Delaney & Bonnie, we'd play a gig and go back over to Karstein's house and still be buzzed over the gig because we were the only band around that was playing original music with a very Southern, very Stax Records–like sound. There wasn't anybody else doing that in L.A. And with the vocal power of Delaney and Bonnie and also Rita Coolidge, who was singing with us at the time, we had *damn* strong vocals. And we were doing original stuff.

It was a helluva band. People in the industry *loved* us. I'd wake up in the morning just itching to go to the gig that evening. *Really* looking forward to it. And then, after it was over, we'd all hang out and talk about the gig.

Delaney Bramlett was one of the most influential, smart, truly great musicians of that period, and a wonderful songwriter. He wrote some beautiful stuff. He'd worked with Leon in the Shindogs, the house band for *Shindig!* They mostly did covers. It was a nighttime rock 'n' roll show. They'd have the Temptations on, the Supremes. Delaney was born in Mississippi. He was a real talented guy: He was a great singer, he was a good-lookin' guy, he wrote good songs, and he was real personable. He had a real good and easy way about him. In the beginning, anyway.

Delaney was the guiding factor in damn near every aspect of Delaney & Bonnie's music. He was like me in the sense that he just played by ear, he wasn't formally schooled. Didn't write down music notation. But he had a great ear and a great feel. And during that time in the late '60s, boy, he and Bonnie—it was like listening to Otis and Aretha. It had the same impact. They were such a strong musical couple. It made playing in that band really fun.

It was at this point, during the formative stages of Delaney & Bonnie and Friends, when I first hooked up with a musical partner who'd be by my side for years to come: Jim Price.

We'd tried a couple of other trumpet players before Jim, but they didn't work out. One guy who was pretty good wanted to play flügelhorn, but the flügelhorn just didn't have enough bite in its sound for what we needed. I mean, the flügelhorn's a beautiful instrument when it's played by someone who knows how to play it, but it's not a rock 'n' roll instrument. Not live. And when you have two horns, you need something that has a little edge, and Jim had a real bright sound. He's a real strong player.

Jim Price went to school at North Texas State College in Denton, Texas, for music. He played piano and trumpet and trombone. He didn't play guitar or anything like that, but he did play piano and keyboards and he read and wrote music. He also had, I think, perfect pitch. And I didn't. Even though I could hear it once and play it, doesn't mean I was gonna play it in tune. Jim always used to get on me about being either a little sharp or a little flat, and I couldn't argue with him because I knew the son of a bitch could tell—I mean, you could play a note and he could tell you what it was, so I didn't have any room for argument. Finally I'd just say, "Jim, it's our damn *sound*, man! It's the oscillation between your pitch and my pitch that gives it that edge!" And that seemed to satisfy him. Of course, I'd just made that shit up. But then I got to thinking, Well, hell, man, maybe there's a greater truth there. Because if we were exactly the same I don't know what it would've sounded like. There was never any chance of that, though, 'cause I never played perfectly in tune.

Delaney played the biggest part in coming up with the horn parts in the beginning of the endeavor, and we would voice them to suit the needs of each song because he didn't know how to voice them. But he'd hear the parts in his head. And then I'd just have to memorize it. And because of the way the recording process worked, you could be playing a part and, if you screwed up and hit a wrong note, you could stop there and punch it back in and go on from that point forward. Which I was very happy for—we did a lot of punching in because Delaney also wanted to have everything just exactly right. At times I thought he was taking it too far, but I appreciate now that it was a good idea. We'd go back sometimes and punch in just one single note to get it right.

We did a lot of that same formula later with the Stones. We'd pick up something that Keith had played and follow that. Songs like "Bitch"—the horn line on that is the same thing the guitar's playing. The notation is a little bit different, but the rhythm and the feel is exactly the same as the guitar. Jim and I used that same approach on a lotta stuff that we did. If you listen to some of the horn lines on George Harrison's album *All Things Must Pass*, you can hear that some of the things we're doing are exactly like what somebody else is doing. We're just taking that element and using it ourselves.

I was playing the tenor saxophone exclusively at the time, so what we started doing, because there was just the two of us which meant we couldn't do your traditional horn-section-type parts, and two-part harmony is not very effective—and I've got to credit Delaney with this—is we concentrated on playing unison parts in octaves, and finding something that was in the song that wasn't necessarily a traditional horn part. We didn't play traditional horn stuff so much. We took our horn parts out of the song, and Delaney would help with that.

Traditionally, three horns was the minimum, but bands like Chicago had four or five horns: a trumpet or two trumpets, two saxes, and trombone. And Al Kooper's band, Blood, Sweat & Tears, they had four or five horns. A two-horn section had never been done before. When we first started playing, we did a lot of Stax-influenced blues stuff, and those Stax records all had horns in 'em, the Memphis Horns. It first started out with just me playing with Delaney, and then when Bonnie came in it was still just me. But I wanted to get a trumpet player. Back then, the economics of the time didn't allow you to get a big horn section. You couldn't pay everybody. So Jim and I decided that we could make it sound like more than two horns if we augmented it with, for instance, the keyboard player playing the same lines, like in thirds. And then it evolved from that into Jim and I playing in unison and picking out a part from the guitar or keyboard and augmenting that. And it just produced a different sound. It gave us an opportunity to do stuff that we probably couldn't have done to the same effect if we'd done it with a horn section. We had to look at it from a different perspective, take a different approach.

The tenor sax has always been looked at as producing the closest sound to the human voice, and a trumpet's more like a violin. But with the right voicing you can make two horns sound like more than two horns, just by the strength of two people playing the same thing. Plus, Jim was a strong player, and I played pretty strong. So we were loud.

The first Elektra Records album, *Accept No Substitute*, was released in the fall of 1969. Actually, Delaney & Bonnie had done a record earlier that year with Stax, but it had been done mostly with studio guys in Memphis, not our full-time lineup. It hadn't done so well. Anyway, we had a big meeting with Group 3 Management—which was Alan Pariser, who was our manager, Barry Feinstein, and Tom Wilkes—and our attorney, Owen Sloane. When the deal was signed, Group 3 Management got a chunk of money—back then, record labels would give groups a lot of advance money to buy clothes, buy instruments, rent studio time, all that stuff. So they got the money, put it all in the bank, and set it up so that Delaney & Bonnie and Friends would be a family-type affair—everyone had the right to look at the books at any time, all the money's going into one fund. Of course, it was to be seen over by Delaney and Alan Pariser. From that, we were allocated a certain amount of money each week to live on, which was cool because none of us had had any steady income up to that time anyway, so it was a bit of a relief. And we were going into the studio to make the record.

Actually, before we even got into the studio, we'd gotten some serious attention. Al Pariser, it turned out, was friends with George Harrison and Ringo Starr and Co., so he brought George out to the club that we were playing at in L.A. at the time. But he didn't let us know he was bringing him. Next thing we know, George Harrison's out at this club, which was a pretty big deal because the Beatles were still the Beatles. After the set, he said something like, "Oh, you guys were wonderful, you guys were great, I love the Southern gospel thing, love the horns." He just loved everything. And I loved him 'cause he was a Beatle.

The Beatles ruled the whole music scene back then. Their records, from beginning to end—especially toward the end with *Rubber Soul, Revolver, Sgt. Pepper, Magical Mystery Tour*—I mean, the Beatles were a *must*. You just weren't socially relevant unless you had a Beatles album. But as a horn player, although I really liked 'em, I cursed 'em, too. Because anything that cuts into the brass man's portion of the pie, musically speaking, had to be considered a threat—and, I mean, the Beatles just ate the whole damn pie and left nothin' but crumbs.

Still, it was a pretty big deal to have a real live Beatle at your gig, and liking it. He even wanted to sign us to Apple Records. Our manager was all eaten up with Beatlemania, so of course he wanted us to be one of the first acts signed to their label. And it would've been a prestigious thing. As it turned out, it might've been what we needed to do because, unfortunately, the album we released on Elektra didn't sell beans, man. At least compared to what it was thought it was gonna do. To this day, I cannot figure it out. We didn't sell any damn records! Not as many as I thought we would, anyway. As the old saying goes, they're all hits till they're released.

But I didn't know any of that at the time. All I knew was it was a good period. It was always productive. Delaney was prepared when we went into the studio. There wasn't any boozin' or drugs or anything. I mean, we might've smoked a joint every now and then, but it was pretty focused. The sessions would be six or seven hours, but there'd be a break in between. It was fun, so nobody was really watching the clock anyway.

We did most of the creating of the music over in Alan Pariser's living room. He had an A-frame house up in the hills, one of those houses you see in Hollywood that's up on stilts and you think, Oh, man, when the next earthquake hits that one's gonna come tumbling down. And he had a tape recorder, a pretty nice little ReVox two-track and nice microphones, so we'd record up there. We got a lot of the stuff worked out before we went into the studio.

In terms of arranging the songs, that was Delaney's bailiwick. I made suggestions a few times, but actually Delaney was doing a good job with everything—I couldn't see anything he was doing I could suggest he do differently. Nothing he'd listen to, anyway. Hell, as I saw it, he was doing everything just right. The music was good, it was fresh songs, and he wrote the songs. Plus, Leon Russell was in the band at the time, and Leon had some ideas about arrangements and things. Delaney would acquiesce to Leon musically. He was the kingpin of our Okie/Texas/Southern bunch of good ol' boys out there. Leon had the big, long, black Cadillac and the rest of us didn't. I don't know what makes Leon Russell tick, I have no idea, but I know that he plays the piano better than just about anyone I've ever heard. He was a child prodigy, as I understand it, which is a story I believe because he's *so* good.

By the time I was playing with Delaney & Bonnie, I'd also stepped up to another level. I had more confidence in what I was playing, I knew more what I was playing, and also, too, we were playing in a kind of heightened state of awareness because it was such a good band. You couldn't really slough off because you wouldn't be in the band, you'd be out. Plus, as a two-piece horn section, Jim and I had to try new things. It made us get creative. And I'll give Delaney credit here, too: He heard some of the horn parts more as voice parts, gospel church voice parts, so we'd voice the horns in a gospel voicing where the lines were more like vocal lines than horn lines. That's not true on every line, but in general, the horns were used in a different way in that band.

Back then, a studio would have three or four recording studios in it and they'd all be going at the same time, so you'd be in studio A and Janis Joplin and her band'd be in studio B and Stills and Nash would be in studio C, etc. That's how I met Jim Morrison. The Doors were recording *The Soft Parade*, I think it was. In fact, the guy who was engineering and producing our album had engineered their album, and I guess there was a kind of a rivalry between label mates—you know, the Doors were the big act for Elektra at the time, and Delaney & Bonnie were the new big-buzz act coming in. We'd come in and taken over their engineer and sorta taken a little bit of the limelight off of them, which I guess they found upsetting. There wasn't a lot of love. So when Jim and I happened to pass each other in the hallway one day it was kind of a tense moment. I'd seen them before at a gig, I forget where it was, and they were terrible, I thought. Maybe they just had a bad day, I don't know. Anyway, when we passed each other in the hall we almost immediately got into an argument. I forget what it was about, but it nearly came to blows.

Well, we got to be friends. Actually, his wife and my wife got to be friends, they hung out a lot, so Jim and I got to talking and I found out he wasn't out of his skull like everybody seemed to be at the time, or a lot of people anyway, especially singers, who seemed to be particularly obnoxious. Hanging out with Jim generally involved drinkin' tequila and gettin' drunk and listenin' to music. Mostly he'd play me music that *he* liked, and then we'd drink and get drunk and I'd play some music I'd brought. It wasn't a close relationship—we were friends, but we were also kinda like stablemates. What we had in common was we both liked to get *ripped*. I really liked to get ripped back then and he did, too. And I could stay with him, whereas a lot of people couldn't. We were never what you'd call soul mates, though. But he had a presence. He definitely did.

During the pop festival era, I met everybody. *Everybody* met everybody. But due to a lot of people's state of mind at the time, it's hard to remember who those people were. Of course, some people are hard to forget. Janis Joplin fits into that category. And like Jim Morrison, I met Janis under circumstances that were not what you'd call ideal.

Bonnie did an excellent version of "Piece of My Heart" before Janis did. And Albert Grossman, Janis's manager—that's Albert Grossman's Rolls-Royce that's on the front of the *Delaney & Bonnie On Tour with Eric Clapton* album, and those are Bob Dylan's feet stickin' out of the window 'cause Albert also managed Bob Dylan— saw us do "Piece of My Heart" on a show that Janis was headlining and told Janis, and naturally she got very upset about it because that was one of her tour de force numbers and Bonnie just blew her away. Of course, we had a better band than Janis did—I thought so, anyway. We had horns. I ain't takin' nothin' away from Janis, I thought she was great. They were just different styles. But so there was always this thing about who did a better job. Anyway, despite all that, since Janis was from Texas, and I was from Texas we got along great—listened to music together, drank that syrupy shit she used to like to drink, Southern Comfort, and got completely ripped from that.

Some real, lifelong-lasting friendships came out of that period, too, though, primarily Jim Keltner and me. He came in and replaced Jimmy Karstein. I didn't like him for doing that for a while because, hell, I'd known Karstein a lot longer than I'd known Keltner. In fact, I didn't really know Keltner at all. Leon Russell wanted to bring Keltner into the scene for recording because Keltner had done a lot of work in the studio, and Karstein hadn't done that much. That may have been the thought process behind that. 'Course, Keltner was from Tulsa, too. They were all Okies out there—I swear to God, I couldn't throw a stick without hittin' an Okie, or a couple of 'em. There was sort of a modern-day exodus from Tulsa out to the promised land: California.

JIM KELTNER: *My first remembrance of Bobby is playing with Delaney & Bonnie at Snoopy's in L.A. I had just been called by them. I think they just wanted to see how it felt to play with me. I took Jimmy Karstein's place with Delaney & Bonnie. He was the drummer right before that and they let him go and took me. The irony there was, with Gary Lewis and the Playboys in 1965, approximately four years prior to that, Jimmy Karstein had taken my place. They let me go and they took Jimmy. Anyway, I remember playing that night and I remember feeling real good about it. It was real fun. It was a great band and the music was fantastic. And I also remember that Bobby, at some point, had lit a cigarette—I think he was onstage when this happened— he lit a cigarette and somehow put the match back in his pocket while it was still burning. Something like that. And so there was a big commotion, and he'd burned a hole in his shirt.*

That was the first night that I met Bobby. The thing that's funny about that story to me is you would've thought that this would've introduced a klutz into your life, but it was far removed from that. Very quickly, I found him to be a very erudite guy. Cunning, you'd almost say. He always had a plan. He always knew what he was gonna do, and you pretty much would have to get involved with it if you were his friend. I can say, with a smile on my face, that I got in some trouble being with Bobby at different times, but for the most part he was always just great.

As a player, I realized right away he was different. You see, I was coming from the jazz world, so I'd been playing with tenor sax players who were John Coltrane disciples, and it was a far cry from that, playing with Bobby. Bobby played with so much soul, so much conviction, and no apologies—he was a rock 'n' roll sax player, and that's it. And you had to love that. And so, musically, I went from the ridiculous to the sublime with Bobby in my life. I've always treasured Bobby for what he is, which is a real original. And then when he got teamed up with Jim Price, they were a formidable team there for a while. They were like San Fernando Valley's answer to the Memphis Horns.

WHILE KELTNER WAS coming in, Leon was on his way out. He always had something else goin' on. Once the record was done, we were booked on *The Tonight Show*, which Leon played with us, and also on some of the first gigs we played, but then it was just Bobby Whitlock on keys. Bobby sang really well and he played a really good B3 organ. So the official lineup at that point was Delaney Bramlett, Bonnie Bramlett, Bobby Whitlock, Carl Radle on bass, Jerry McGee on lead guitar, Jim Keltner on drums, Rita Coolidge singing backup, and Jim Price and myself on horns. That was the lineup that went on tour opening for Blind Faith in the summer of 1969.

Opening for Blind Faith was great because before that, we'd played a couple of gigs as part of a multi-band lineup—not ever headlining, but in the lineup—at the Fillmore East and Fillmore West, and some pop festivals, Atlanta I remember, and one outside of Milwaukee or Chicago. So Blind Faith was the first national tour that we'd ever played on as a band. Blind Faith was a great band: Steve Winwood, Eric Clapton, Ric Grech on bass, and Ginger Baker on drums. Ginger and I got to be good friends, although later, not on that tour—on that tour he disappeared after every gig. It was rumored that he was going back and forth between London and wherever we were for "medical purposes," I suppose is one way of putting it.

Wherever we played, man, the people dug it. They weren't quite sure who we were, but they always dug it. I remember having the feeling of being on a team that's going for the championship with that band: You know you got a good team, and when you're getting ready to go out and play, you know you're gonna go out and kick everybody else's ass. And that was a good feeling. In the beginning, especially, it was really cool because people'd come up to us and say, "Who *are* you, man? Where can we get a record?" I remember thinking, Shit, all we need is for people to hear us and everybody's gonna run out and flood the record stores with money and buy our product. It felt like a magical record company fairy tale.

The band had a hell of a lot of energy onstage and it generated a lot of energy in the audience. And we were filling a niche that nobody else was into—this was before the Allman Brothers, before Southern rock, as such. It was a precursor of sorts.

On tour, we had a representative from the record company with us, and of course Delaney and Bonnie were doing a lot of press interviews, which left time for us, the blue-collar workers of the band, to do what we wanted to do. At that time, what we did mostly was get out and walk around and just take in the new cities we were going to and the new culture that was springing up and being a part of it. It felt good to see hundreds and then thousands of people getting into it, really digging the music. It just felt so good waking up in the morning and you couldn't wait to get to the gig because you loved the music, you loved the band, and people loved you, and pot was plentiful. Wine was cheap. Everything was working, man. We were all young, all in our twenties, and we were playing original music that was the buzz, the new hottest thing, so, you know, what could go wrong?

During the tour opening for Blind Faith, Eric Clapton and Delaney got very tight in the dressing rooms and at the hotels where they started hanging out and doing some songwriting, and that precipitated us doing a tour of Europe with Eric playing with us. Eric really liked the band. After that U.S. tour he'd split with Blind Faith, so he got his manager, Robert Stigwood, to book a tour, but they booked it as an Eric Clapton tour. Instead of being billed "Eric Clapton with Delaney & Bonnie," it was something like "Eric Clapton's New Band," and so when we played in Europe, the kids who had bought tickets, they were expecting Eric Clapton material exclusively. When we did our material, while I think they liked it, it wasn't quite what they were looking for—you know, they wanted to see Eric Clapton burn the place down with his guitar, and it didn't happen. So we got kinda mixed reviews there.

In England, though, it went well. We had George Harrison playing with us on that tour, too. The band was killin'. And the kids got into it. We recorded some of the gigs live, and they were really good and everybody got real enthusiastic. We got a Beatle with us, we got Eric Clapton with us. So I thought, Well, this is *definitely* it—the first album didn't sell, but, I mean, now we got

Eric Clapton, hell, we have a damn *Beatle*. That became Delaney & Bonnie and Friends' *On Tour with Eric Clapton* album.

In the States we'd supported Blind Faith, but in Europe and England it was just us, along with Eric and George. The most fun on that tour was on the bus. Everybody was together, everybody rode on the same bus. And another singer, Lesley Duncan, who wrote "Love Song," which Elton John did with her as a duet, was on that tour, too. But the bus rides across Scandinavia and Germany, that's when Delaney and George and Eric would break out the guitars and Bonnie and everybody'd be singin'. It wasn't a tour bus as such, it was a big European coach—it didn't have a kitchen or berths or anything like that, it was all seats, but it was nice. George started "My Sweet Lord" on one of those bus rides. They were singin' "Hare Krishna, Krishna Krishna," just playin' that chord progression. That's where it all started. Rita Coolidge and Bonnie and Delaney and George and Eric. Quite a busload of people.

Rowdiness went hand in hand with rock 'n' roll, but generally any rowdiness was generated by people just having a good time and good fun and then add in alcohol. There was some drinking going on on that bus, but no cocaine and very little pot. George didn't do any of that shit. Eric didn't either, really, at that time. It didn't appear that he had any problems with excessive use at that time, anyway. I mean, we took some acid at his house, but on the road it was pretty together as far as stayin' sober. It wasn't hard. I mean, there were a couple times. *I* was probably the biggest instigator of unruly behavior.

The one place we did do some drinkin' was at the hotels. We'd get sloshed at the bar. But mostly on beer and wine, not tequila and Jack Daniel's. Of course, when we'd go into different countries we'd drink the alcohol of the realm—Jägermeister in Germany, etc. But on that bus, we'd pretty much just stick together, travel, enjoy the experience. It was all about music. The only bad part was that the promoter had put it in such a light that people were expecting one thing and got another. But I know when the band got up and played, we kicked ass.

George picked up on what Jim and I were doing in terms of horn arrangements when he played with us on that tour. And from listening to the albums and during the course of conversations, too, but it was onstage, I think, where it really clicked for him. George played rhythm guitar real nice. When Jim and I went to his house to do some recording for *All Things Must Pass*, he would get his guitar out in the kitchen and he'd play the song that we'd be playing on, and he played great. But on stage during that European tour, I never really could hear him. 'Cause, hell, we had three guitar players, Delaney and Eric and George, and they *all* turned their guitars up. Dave Mason played guitar with that band for a while, too. He was also managed by the same people we were.

Unfortunately, one of the things that started coming up at that period of time was that Delaney and Bonnie's personal life was not going well. They'd get in fights and yelling matches and shit before we'd go onstage, and that was disconcerting. Didn't really set the tone for a good gig. They were where the energy came from, or anyway where it started. That was the first sort of chink in the armor. That and the fact that Delaney was starting to put more distance between himself and the band. The physical proof was in the billing: It started to be just "Delaney & Bonnie," and we were just the band. It wasn't even "and Friends" anymore. The

"Friends" moniker seems to have been only a name for the first album. And while Delaney got romanced by the Big Time—Eric and George and the record companies—we were just kinda pushed aside, which pissed everybody in the band off 'cause we weren't exactly day-old bread. We were a pretty damn good band.

Of course it didn't help that our record deal wasn't proving to be quite what was promised. We were told everybody was gonna share in the rewards and it didn't quite work that way. Back in L.A., it was described to us that everybody was gonna get a piece of the pie and it's all for one and one for all, we're just gonna centralize the money here, and anytime anybody wants to know the books and where we stand you can feel free to call up and you'll have access. You know: "Nothin' to hide here, we're all on the same team goin' to the same place." And the first time that was put to the test, it was like, "Well, no, uh-uh, we've been told by the management that without their permission we can't open up the books." I don't remember exactly what precipitated that—probably me callin' up to see if I could get an advance or something—but that was another one of the first sorta flies in the buttermilk that came along.

In retrospect, I believe Delaney got led by other influences, and a lot of it had to do with our manager, Alan Pariser, who seemed to go the way of a lot of other managers—he concentrated on Delaney. He looked at Delaney as being the golden boy, as where everything comes from. The musicians are good, they play good, and they look good and all that, but if we have to lose them, no big deal. As long as we got Delaney. And Bonnie, of course. And that's essentially what happened. Delaney really had his ears filled with people telling him that he was the king and that all things came from him and the rest of us were just dressing, and he started to believe it. I don't know how much convincing it took, but that's when the wheels started comin' off the train.

Of course, Delaney *did* lead that band. He was in charge, he was very much in charge. And he wrote the material. I didn't begrudge him—obviously there wouldn't have been a band without him. But what got my goat was, why say you're gonna do something and then just blatantly not do it? He should've just said, "I'm in charge, and we're all gonna get a percentage, but I'm gonna get more of a percentage because I write more and I do more. I write it and I sing it." That would've been *fine*. No problem. But by setting it all up as one happy family in the beginning, where everyone has access to the books at any time, no problem, and the first time you put that to the test you get the door slammed in your face, you say, "What the fuck is this?" One irritating point was our management was always saying, "Well, leave everything to us and we'll decide what's best for you." Well, that might work when you're nine or ten years old, but it doesn't sit well with adults.

As soon as the European tour ended and we were back in the States, things went sour fast, and it culminated in a gig in San Diego in which Delaney threw something at Keltner and Keltner threw his sticks at Delaney and we rode back to L.A. in just an awful silence. It was right after that gig that the Mad Dogs & Englishmen thing came up with Leon and Joe Cocker, which was very fortunate. One day we were Friends and the next day we were Mad Dogs and Englishmen. Not *literally* the next day, of course, but awful close. I don't think there was ever an official breakup, like Delaney saying we were fired. I think *we* fired *Delaney*. That's the way I remember it. There'd been bitchin' prior to that because things weren't playing out like they'd been portrayed, but it was at that San Diego gig where that band officially broke apart. No more Friends for Delaney & Bonnie.

After that, I reconnected with Delaney only one time, years later. I did a session for him. It was like he still thought I worked for him. Well, he hired me, so I guess technically I did, but it was . . . well, it wasn't a pleasant experience. I remember going in there and hoping it would be. I knew we hadn't left on good terms, but this had to have been ten or fifteen years after the fact. I mean, he was OK and I was OK, but it was real strained. And then when it came time to get paid, I never got paid. It was one of those, "Listen, I gotta turn this stuff in. I'll get the money from the record company and then I'll pay ya." But I never got paid. I don't remember exactly what the record was.

So, no, I never really got anything resolved with Delaney. For one thing, he never thought he was wrong. He was as hardheaded as anyone I'd ever known. And of course I knew that *I* wasn't wrong. I guess I'm kinda hardheaded myself. Even so, it doesn't lessen the whole experience. I'm really proud of that music and that band. That was a *damn* good band, man. It was one of the few times I was in a band that'd get together after a gig to listen to a recording of the gig and talk about the gig, and then wake up the next morning ready to play another gig again. More importantly, without that band I wouldn't have gone in the direction I went in. I met a hell of a lot of people through Delaney & Bonnie and Friends. That band was a springboard for a lot of people to do other things. I know it was for me.

5

N 1970, I was twenty-six years old playing onstage with people everybody listened to, people I really respected. That was good stuff. Then all of a sudden it was over, and before I had a chance to really think about it being over, there was another gig with primarily the same people I'd been playing with plus about thirty or forty other people, including the dogs and kids and Space Choir. It was the Mad Dogs & Englishmen tour.

Mad Dogs & Englishmen was a Joe Cocker album, but it was more than that, it was an *event*. It was like a circus, a traveling rock 'n' roll gypsy carnival. Joe, of course, was already an established guy before the Mad Dogs & Englishmen tour came along. He'd done Woodstock. Joe's one of those really gentle souls. He's so talented, and he's got so much good in him. What I remember about Joe is all good, positive stuff. Joe always kept things inside of him. He never screamed or got pumped up. The only time he got pumped up was when he was onstage singing. He saved it for the stage.

Leon Russell and Denny Cordell put it together. Denny Cordell was Joe Cocker's record producer. Joe had had a falling out with the Grease Band, his original backing band, and he had a tour to do that his manager had signed him up for, which he couldn't renege on or he was gonna get sued and lose everything he had. So when the Grease Band went one way and he went another, Joe found himself in the position of having to do this tour with no backing band. This occurred simultaneously with the departure of Keltner, Jim Price, Carl Radle, and me from the Delaney & Bonnie band. So Leon, who'd been working with Denny Cordell, thought he'd put us all together.

JOE COCKER: *The Grease Band was Alan Spenner on bass, Bruce Roland on drums, Henry McCullough on lead guitar, and Chris Stainton, that's when he went over to the keyboards. He always played bass with me before that. This was from '67 to the end of '69. At one point, we wanted to get Jimmy Page into the Grease Band—we'd done "A Little Help from My Friends," and he was on it— but he said, "Nah, I'm workin' with these new guys. I want to do something a bit heavier." And Denny was affronted. He said, "Well, what could be heavier?" 'Cause at the time we were supposed to be the bee's knees. When next we heard him, though, the volume level had gone up a bit.*

By the end of '69, I'd done Woodstock, and the Grease Band and I weren't getting along well. Chris Stainton and

I stuck it out for the most part, but Woodstock was the last show. Mad Dogs was next. I stayed at Leon's house in L.A., 7709 Skyhill Drive. People were very naked. I got the clap there. God.

Onstage Joe did externally what a lot of people internalize—although I thought he was just off his nut. The first time I saw him was at the Atlanta Pop Festival in 1969, and I was convinced that the man had some sorta medical issue. I remember thinking to myself, God bless that poor boy—look at him, he's up there and he's struggling through all these physical problems, his tongue's comin' out, his eyes are rolling back, and he's gettin' sorta spastic. I mean, the guy's singing his ass off, but what kind of a tortured life must he lead? I really thought that. I was sure the boy was whacked-out on some sort of psychedelic or had some sorta serious medical problem. But then when I met him, there were no spastic motions or anything. Couldn't understand a word he said—he's from Northern England—but he was obviously coordinated. The press used to make some mention of that in the early days, that it was like watching an electrical appliance that had short-circuited, but he sings so good that those comments just fell by the wayside.

JOE COCKER: *Leon surprised me with his arrangements of some of those songs. I mean, one day he came up with "The Letter"—he just said, "Hey, Joe, what do you think about this?" It clicked instantly. It fit right in with the way we were rearranging songs. Like "A Little Help." People have told me that the version of "A Little Help" that I do is, in their minds, the definitive version of the song, and I think that's 'cause it wasn't just a cover, we did a whole reinvention of it. Even [Paul] McCartney was nice enough to say that—that he thought it was the best version around.*

And then Leon and Bobby and Jim Price: I mean, it didn't even strike me when they came on board as a horn section how good they were. Nowadays when I work with brass you have to give 'em some time to put their act together, but it seemed like Bobby and Jim, at that time, it was just instant arrangements. It was fascinating stuff.

The horn parts were not very demanding. We weren't playing Buddy Rich charts or anything. It was more a matter of doing your job and being able to exist in this type of environment. Which I found no problem existing in this type of environment. I *flourished. I thrived.*

Denny Cordell took the name Mad Dogs & Englishmen from a Noël Coward song—"Only mad dogs and Englishmen go out in the noonday sun" is one of the lines. Anyway, it seemed to fit. It was really fun being up onstage with that much power behind you: Jim Gordon and Jim Keltner bangin' away back there, Carl Radle on bass.

JOE COCKER: *I don't remember anyone doing that before us, using the two-drummer format. Keltner would really hit the snare hard while Gordon would do the faster stuff. It really set up this incredible rhythm. It was like a train coming.*

It was basically the Delaney & Bonnie band, but without Bobby Whitlock. Or Delaney, or Bonnie. And with some added accessories. It was a great band. Not everybody had their own Space Choir on the road. Those singers really added so much. It was like being in church sometimes. Ninety percent of them were such good singers—there were some folks in there who were just along for the ride, which was fine, that was the spirit of the thing—but Rita Coolidge and Claudia Lennear, I mean, those were classy singers. Danny Moore, Matthew Moore, Pamela Polland. That wasn't karaoke. And when you get that many voices together it really did sound like a space choir. Plus there was this great juxtaposition between Joe's voice and the choir.

In concert, man, it was just raw, live stuff. No flash pots, no big screen, none of that shit. Just raw rock 'n' roll. I loved that period of time. That kind of freedom was such a big part of that period of time. You were given an opportunity to create on the spot. You weren't locked in to any one specific thing.

It was a really great feeling going onstage. It was primarily done just for the love of music. And getting to go out with so many friends, just heading out en masse. As I recall, there wasn't any strict regimentation of the set. It was more like, "We'll do this, this, and this." There was a flexibility. Everybody knew what was goin' on. Except for endings. And sometimes beginnings.

JOE COCKER: *It's evolved into a thing where I do all the stops now, and the breaks, but back then it was just Leon going, "One, two . . . " Everybody thought he was doing some sort of trip on me—which he did, I mean, mentally, but everybody found their way to the end eventually.*

All those endings were great, except ol' Leon would just carry 'em on out and on out, and I don't know that anyone who's not a horn player can have any idea of how thin the air gets when you're hittin' those real high notes. Because you gotta put a lotta extra effort into those. So by the time that it actually got to the end of the song, I was able to see molecules with my naked eye—you know how when you run out of oxygen you see the little squiggly things in the air? I'd think, "Goddamn, I've reached another level of awareness!" I never passed out, but there were plenty of times I thought I'd reached another plateau.

One of the reasons this would happen was because Leon was the focal point for cues for the ending and to count us off in the beginning, and there were times when Leon was not in sight. We'd be on the opposite side of the stage from him. So, yeah, there were some multiple endings, but I don't think anyone really noticed or minded. It was kinda like, OK, we missed it, we'll do it again, and then the next eight bars'd roll around and we'd give it another try. Onstage, there was a lotta license to stretch out. I mean, "Delta Lady" ends about three or four times.

Backstage and in between shows the atmosphere was equally relaxed. This one woman who was part of the entourage did everybody's daily star chart: "Now, Bobby, stay away from the color purple today," things like that. "Don't walk under any trees." This was back in the day of love beads and all that stuff. Everything was so easy, so gentle. A lotta gettin' high. Man, the stage, after these concerts, was *covered* with joints. It was just this attitude of, "Hey, yeah, share the love, share the love."

But not everything was shared. I remember Dee Anthony, who was Joe Cocker's manager, showed up backstage one day with two Sony TC-120s. This was back when Sony first came out with personal cassette players. Came in a case with two speakers, I mean *everybody* wanted one. The first stereophonic portable cassette system. *Really* cool. Dee Anthony had gotten Leon and Joe each one, and then he said, "If anybody else wants one of these, just raise your hand," so, hell, everybody raised their hands. Well, he took all the orders, and shortly after that we all got our brand new Sony TC-120s. And then the next week I noticed I got no paycheck. They'd deducted the damn cost of the cassette player. They didn't mention that part when they asked us if we wanted one.

That particular incident wasn't captured on film, but a lot of that tour was because not only were they recording the shows so they could make a live album, they were also filming everything so they could make a movie of it: *Mad Dogs & Englishmen.* The first scene in the movie's got me reciting one of my very favorite Texasisms: "Every night's a Saturday night, and every day's a Sunday." I'd like to say that line was mine, but I don't think so. I remember the original quote was "Every night's a Saturday night, and every day's a Sunday—I know I've been wrong before, but I'm gonna try it *one more time.*"

What's funny is I don't remember the cameramen really being around all that much. I remember a few times in the hotels the guys would come into the rooms and we'd be in there smokin' away. This was back when we'd think, Man, we're cool and we don't mind if the whole world knows we're smokin' pot, but then we'd think, after the guys were gone, Shit, man, you think that's gonna get into the wrong hands?

But just because we were being filmed and recorded for posterity doesn't mean we were living lives of luxury. For one thing, we had no roadies. Well, no, we had *a* roadie. He was Joe's primary assistant. He was the guy who'd go down and make sure the hall was ready for rehearsal or ready for sound check or whatever. But otherwise, we had no real staff at all. There were some local stagehands, but that's about all I remember for help.

And that plane. We had a Lockheed Constellation to fly us from gig to gig, the latest model of which was made in 1958, and this was 1970. It had four propellers, triple tail fins, and was shaped like a submarine. It was old. The normal flight time between L.A. and New York on a jet is about four hours. On this plane it took us something like eight or nine hours because we had to stop to refuel and then take off again. But it didn't matter. We had things to entertain us. Guitars.

JOE COCKER: *That airplane, the Constellation. That was a farce. I remember the pilot, one day, I saw that he'd got this little flask of whiskey. I thought, OK, I better drink somethin', too. It all seemed to fit. Everyone was part of the team. I remember flying one night and saying, "Doesn't it seem like we're leaning at the back?" 'Cause everyone was at the back, like it was the designated smoking section, the drug center. It seemed like the plane was flying tipped back that way.*

BY MAY OF 1970, the Mad Dogs tour was winding down, and some of us were starting to hear rumors that Eric Clapton was looking for a new band. There were phone calls made between Clapton and Carl Radle and Jim Gordon, and Jim Price and I were always included in the plans that were being made. Eric had disbanded Blind Faith, that was over with, and he was gonna do his own thing, form a new band, and Jim and I were of the impression that we were a part of that band. Robert Stigwood, who was the manager of Eric Clapton at the time, told us, "Oh, yeah, man, you guys are comin' in—what we're gonna do first is record the album and get the basic tracks down, and we're still in the process of writing and picking material, so we're gonna do that, and then we're gonna bring you guys on in and you're gonna put the cherry on the sundae."

So, OK. I kept waiting for that cherry. Finally, after calling back and forth between England and L.A., which is where we all came home to after the Mad Dogs tour ended, we got the word that our tickets were gonna be waiting for us at LAX, and Jim and I were to go out there and take our suitcases and our instruments and get on the plane and go put the cherry on the sundae. Well, unbeknownst to us, somewhere between the time that we'd taken off from Los Angeles and the time we'd arrived at London/Heathrow, they'd decided that the sundae didn't *need* any damn cherries.

We were expecting to be met at the airport by Eric Clapton's representatives; instead, we got off the plane, we got through customs, and we saw this fella, Mal Evans, who we recognized as being George Harrison's associate. He'd been with George when George'd done his gigs with Delaney & Bonnie. He was George's right-hand man. So, OK, at least we had a ride. So we got in the car, and at this point, Jim and I were still of the impression that we were part of Eric's new band. Mal didn't really say much of anything. All we knew was that Robin Turner, the guy who was supposed to be there to pick us up, wasn't there, but Mal *was* there. Mal said he didn't really know what was going on, but that George and Eric had spoken, and we were on our way to George's house. Well, hell, that was fine with me! I could put up with that.

George had just bought this estate, Friar Park, and it was enormous. Really huge place built by this mad monk—or friar, I guess—named Sir Crisp, I think it was. Jim and I were still in the dark about what was going on and then Mal, as if he was drivin' the point home, led us down into this subterranean network of caves and underground passageways. Suddenly Mal's sorta taken on the persona of a hunchback, sayin', "Right, follow me," in this real exaggerated voice. As we're following him, I'm looking back at Jim, thinking, These English are weird, but this is really weird.

What we didn't know was that this was just some sort of elaborate joke that George had cooked up to break the mood. After we'd been wandering down in the catacombs for a while, George jumped out from behind a wall and scared the hell out of us. Anyway, so we had a laugh, and went upstairs and joined his wife, Patty, and that's where we got the news about why we're at George's house and not at Eric's house.

George said Eric had called and, knowing that George was still working on his album and that he wanted to use Jim and me on it anyway. Since things still seemed to be up in the air with Eric and how we were to be involved, he kinda passed us on to George for the time being. In fact, Jim and I were beginning to think that we weren't as involved in Eric's new project as we thought we were gonna be, but, what the hell, here we were at a Beatle's house and we're gonna play on a Beatle's record, so, shit, how bad can it be?

It wasn't bad at all. We got up the next morning, got into George's car, the biggest, most super-duper Mercedes sedan they made at the time, and drove to Apple Studios on Abbey Road. George's house was about an hour's drive from London, so on the way into town, George explained to us what he wanted us to do in the studio, which was primarily just to listen to what he had so far and see what we thought. And to see what Phil Spector thought because he was coproducing it.

The night before, George had played for us some of the tracks he wanted us to play on—including "What Is Life?"—so when we got to the studio it was just a matter of he and Jim getting together on the whens and whats, as in when we came in and what we played. Jim was a lot better at voicing the horn parts—he had an actual education, a diploma. That was his gig, and he did a damn good job of it.

At one of those first sessions there was a full orchestra that George had hired—the London Philharmonic Orchestra, as a matter of fact, or most of it. Anyway, we'd done these horn parts and George and Phil were happy with 'em, and this string section was there and we're getting ready to do another take when everybody just stops. London has a very strong union, I guess, for string players, and it had come time for the union tea break. The British are very, very fussy about their tea.

Meanwhile, Phil Spector's out there buzzin' around the place— he had a lotta energy, he was always in motion. We were getting ready to do another take when the concert master tapped his bow on his music stand and everybody just got up and walked out. Phil said, "Wait! Where're you going? Where're you going? *Come back here!*" All thirty or forty people were exiting and he couldn't do anything about it. Here's this little guy spinnin' around in the middle of the studio tryin' to grab hold of exiting string players, and nobody's paying any attention to him. So he jumped up onto the piano and slammed the lid down and started ranting and raving—"You idiots! You can't do this!"

I'd met Phil on the Dick Clark tour because he was involved with the Ronettes, and when we played someplace back east he came to the gig. So we'd met. He wasn't a warm, fuzzy guy. The other time I worked with him was with John Lennon a few years later, in 1973, for his *Rock 'n' Roll* album.

Anyway, Jim and I were just kinda sittin' there watching this whole surreal scene go down, and I overheard this one guy turn to another guy and he said something like, "Can't someone shut that noisy Yank up?" Well, Phil heard this, and that just set him off to another level, at which point the guys in the string section decided they weren't gonna put up with this, so they left. For good. They walked right out of the studio.

George was there the whole time but he was leaving it up to Phil, and things just got to escalating and going so fast—it doesn't take long for Phil to piss people off. He can do it in a real hurry. And that's what happened. Everybody split. And then it was just me and Jim and George and Phil. And all this extra studio time.

At this stage, we still hadn't heard anything from the Clapton camp as to where Jim and I stood with regard to Eric's new band, but we did hear that the band had got itself a name. Apparently, shortly before Jim and I had arrived in England, they'd done a surprise gig with this guy Tony Ashton, who was part of the band Ashton, Gardner and Dyke. They'd been the opening act on the Delaney & Bonnie European tour that Eric did with us. Anyway, the way I understand it, Tony Ashton introduced the band onstage, and it was Tony who dubbed them, pretty much on the spot, Derek and the Dominos.

As it turns out, Jim and I were never destined to be Dominos. Eric never told us directly we weren't gonna be a part of the band, it just kinda became apparent as time went on that we weren't gonna be involved. Jim and I were kinda left hanging. It was a disappointment 'cause I was looking forward to working with Eric again. I'd been on his first solo album, produced by Delaney Bramlett. I played on "After Midnight," which the horns were taken off of, and I played on "Let It Rain."

I'd met Eric on that first Delaney & Bonnie tour, and later we stayed at his house before the European tour. He was real affable and friendly. A real nice guy. Very talented. Not loud. All music. He was a silent runner. He was involved in all kinds of things I never knew anything about. Women, for one thing. I never saw him with anyone—or not a *lot* of women, at any rate—but he was. Then, of course, he ended up with George's wife Patty. The English are strange about switchin' wives. They really are. And then the guys go on and remain friends. I don't know if the wives stay friends or not.

A few years later, I kind of wrote Eric off when I heard what happened when he fired the Dominos—he rehired a band and told my friend Carl Radle he was gonna be in the new band and then, when Carl got fired, too, he didn't even bother to call him up personally. Had his manager call him up. And this was after years of playing together. Carl deserved more than that.

Well, I held that grudge against Eric for a long time. I mean, I don't really hold a grudge against him anymore, but it's always a fly in the buttermilk every time I think about it. 'Course, I can understand—he had his drug problems at the time, he didn't want to talk to *anybody*. Or see anybody. So I think maybe that was a big part of it. Because Carl was involved with the same thing Eric was, and maybe Eric was tryin' to get away from anyone who was involved. But he should've had the balls to call him. Anyway, Carl ended up overdosing and dying. And that always left a real bad taste in my mouth 'cause I know he'd been trying to get in touch with Eric real hard right before he died, and Eric wouldn't take his calls.

Anyway. That has nothin' to do with Eric's skills as a musician or an artist. He was a hell of a musician. Still is. And back in 1970, Derek and the Dominos were shaping up to be a hell of a band. Just not with Jim and me.

So, OK. Big disappointment not being in a band, but we're living in a Beatle's house, recording with a Beatle—newly former Beatle at that time—so life wasn't so bad. I've never really talked to Eric about exactly what happened because ultimately it didn't really matter. We didn't have the gig. Instead, we did George's first solo album and lived out at his place for a month or so. Several weeks anyway, probably a month. More than a week and less than a year.

During that time, we'd go into the EMI studios there on Abbey Road every day and record. And sometimes George'd be in there and I wouldn't have anything to do, so I'd get bored and go down to a pub or something. One night, George was in the studio wrapping things up and I'd gone down to a club, the Speakeasy, and I ran into Mick Jagger. He asked me what I was doin' there and I told him what I was in town for, doin' George's thing, and he asked, "Well, how long are you gonna be here?" I said, "I don't know, I'm probably gonna be goin' back pretty soon 'cause there's nothin' else to do," and that led to Mick saying, "Well, we're doin' this album at Olympic Studios, would you and Jim be interested in coming by?"

One thing led to another, and throughout the course of the conversation, Mick said, "You're welcome to stay at my place for a while if you wanna stick around, you know, and you can go to the studio with me." And I said, "Yeah, Mick, sounds great to me" because I really wasn't in the mood to leave England. So I went over to Mick's and stayed there for a while, and I'd go to the studio with him. I ended up playing on "I Got the Blues," and that worked out, so he'd say, "If you feel like stickin' around for a while, stick around," and so I stuck around and kept playing on first one track and then another. I guess Mick and their producer, Jimmy Miller, were looking to do something different on this album. This was gonna be the very first Stones album release on their new label, so they really wanted to make a statement. Jim had a girlfriend in England, so he was sticking around anyway.

At that time, I was the one who generated most of the work for Jim and myself. Just through my forceful personality. I'd say, "Look, you son of a bitch, if you want a hit record you hire people who play on hits." Or something to that effect. That's not Jim's character or makeup. He's very quiet. And I wasn't.

I loved staying at Jagger's place in Chelsea. Loved it, loved it, loved it. This was in London—SW1 is the postal zone. It was just me and him and a housekeeper. Mick and I got to be good friends. We'd play chess in the afternoon. He educated me in the finer vintages of wine and stuff. We didn't play much at Mick's house, but we listened to a lot of stuff. A lotta blues. He was very much into the blues and blues harmonica players, so I'd tell him all about the stuff that Levon Helm had turned me on to when I was livin' with Levon in California: Sonny Boy and Little Walter and all of those guys. Mick was really into that part of American blues music. He played a really good harmonica himself, surprisingly so. I never would've thought it at first—he was a vocalist and a dancer and a prancer—but the boy could play a really good harmonica. Plus, he'd always been a big fan of early rock 'n' roll, so I would regale him with stories from West Texas.

Mick was on his own at this point. He'd broken up with Marianne Faithfull, and Anita Pallenberg was with Keith. So basically I was living with—and going out on the town with—the most eligible bachelor in the Western Hemisphere. There was always a bunch of girls hangin' out. Mick had his Bentley parked out in front. It seemed like London was just one big party back then. Mick was very generous, too. He didn't make me pay for anything, he always picked up the tabs—and we were drinking champagne and very expensive wines.

This was back before everybody had migrated from London, so you'd go out and you'd see Ringo and you'd see John Lennon, everybody. Keith Moon, Pete Townshend, Eric Clapton, all out partying. And I was always with Mick. I was his wingman before the term existed. Which was an extremely good position to be in if you wanted to meet girls and drink good wine and eat fine foods and ride around in a brand new Bentley. The scene was great, especially if you were hangin' out with Mick Jagger. The world was definitely a shinier, brighter place to be.

At that time, the Stones were working on *Sticky Fingers*. They had just left Decca Records and this was gonna be their first release on their own label, Rolling Stones Records. They'd gone in one direction for a while and it had served them quite well, but now they were gonna do their own album and do their own music and they weren't gonna be dictated to by anybody else—not the label, not the producer, no one—as to what material they should use or what style they should take up. Once again, I was simply in the right place at the right time.

At some point while I was living with Mick and going into the studio, I got tapes of the Mad Dogs & Englishmen tour. This was before the album had been released. I don't remember how I'd gotten a hold of them. Denny Cordell, I guess—he lived just down the road from Mick. Anyway, I'd gotten these tapes, and Mick had this little garden house or shed right behind his flat in Chelsea that he'd turned into a wine cellar, and he had a little recorder out there, so we'd go out there in the afternoons and I'd play him these tapes, all the time campaigning: "Hey, man, you just can't do it without me! Listen to what I did, I'm Bobby Wonderful! I'm gonna change your life! You put some horns in the band and you'll *have* somethin'!" (That's still my rallying cry: "*More horns!*")

I wasn't aiming for a full-time gig, really. It didn't enter into my mind. But we were listening to a lot of Otis Redding at the time, and I could tell Mick was really taken with using the horns to bring another dimension to their music. And I was really touting it—"Hey, Mick, listen to how great these horns are! Listen to how Otis and the horns work together! Have you ever thought about doin' that?" So, yeah, I guess it was a weasel job. But I was weaseling because I *really* wanted to play the music. It wasn't because I wanted to be a Rolling Stone—I never had any fantasies about being a Rolling Stone. I knew they were already the Rolling Stones. I was just glad to play with 'em. And they paid me well, and I loved the music.

I had been in the studio with them once before, back in 1969. Played on "Live with Me." That was done in Los Angeles when I was in the studio with Delaney & Bonnie, and I ran into Mick in the hallway. We were recording the first Delaney & Bonnie album for Elektra Records while Jimmy Miller, who'd heard of our band, was in the studio down the hall with the Stones, finishing up the overdubs and mixing on *Let It Bleed.* Jimmy told Mick we were recording down the hall, so when I ran into Mick, he said, "Hey, if you can, get your horn and come on in. There's a track that might work well with a saxophone." So I took my horn and went into their studio. Which pissed Delaney off. They'd already asked Bonnie, I guess, although I didn't know this at the time, to sing the part that Merry Clayton ended up singing on "Gimme Shelter." Delaney wouldn't let Bonnie do it because . . . well, I don't know what his reason was. He was very possessive of her and her voice and whatever.

But when Mick asked me to come in, I went in—I don't have a voice, I have a saxophone—and I did the solo. A Rolling Stones record? Hell, yeah. Damn right. It only took a couple or three takes. It was Mick and Jimmy Miller and Glyn Johns. Keith wasn't there. Never got paid for it, either. I bring that up to 'em every time I remember it. And then I got a blast of shit from Delaney about doing it, too. You'd have thought I'd abandoned ship and let everyone else go down to Davy Jones's locker. "Oh, you're a big deal now, huh? You're gonna go off with the Rolling Stones now, I guess," and I said, "No, man, don't be silly." Little did I know.

So a year or so earlier I'd done my first solo for the Stones on "Live with Me," but the first *big* song I soloed on was "Brown Sugar," although before there was a horn solo on it there was a guitar solo. In fact, on the very first release of "Brown Sugar," there was no saxophone solo, only Mick Taylor playing guitar. It had originally been recorded at Muscle Shoals Sound Studios in Alabama, when the Stones were on tour in the U.S. in '69. Then, on December 18, 1970, Keith and I, who were born on the same day, had a birthday party at Olympic Studios in London and, through whatever process—Eric Clapton was there, a whole bunch of people were there—we ended up recording a version of "Brown Sugar" which I played the solo on. And it pricked up Mick's ears and Keith's ears. "Brown Sugar" had been considered pretty much a done deal, but when we played it at Olympic Studios on our birthday and I played the solo on it, I guess Jimmy Miller or Mick or somebody heard it and said, "Hey, man, let's do that again!" So I went in and I did the solo, and I remember it was one take. That's the way I remember it, anyway. Some other people might have a different take on that. No pun intended.

During that time I was doing a lot of sessions. After establishing myself in England a little bit, and knowing where the studios were and getting a sort of basic feel for how things worked, I got to know Pete Townshend and Ronnie Wood and Rod Stewart and Jimmy Page through Glyn Johns, who was producing the Rolling Stones but also some of these other guys, and so they would be recording and Glyn Johns would say, "Oh, I can get Bobby Keys for that." It was just word of mouth, networking, and the fact that I'd already been there with Delaney & Bonnie, too—we'd created somewhat of a stir with Clapton playing with us and George Harrison playing with us. So I had some A-list credentials in my hip pocket, which I didn't mind pulling out—"Hey, I'm Wonderful Bob! What do you mean, who am I? Who the fuck are *you*?" Ha.

As far as the Stones go, the song that I felt was really where I crossed over from being just an added musician, an overdub musician, to actually playing with the band was when we did "Can't You Hear Me Knocking." But it couldn't have been less planned. Originally, in the studio, the song wasn't designed to go into that long end part. That was just an added thing.

There was this percussionist, Rocky Dijon, a really good percussionist, who the Stones wanted on the record but he had a limited window of time, so they were doing it that night. And I was in the studio with him, I'd been jammin' with him, I had my horn out, but I got the vibe that there wasn't gonna be any horn on this, the song was already worked up and there wasn't really any part for horns on it. So, all right, fine. I'll just sit here and listen. So they play through the song, and the song, originally—this is how I remember it—was just the vocal part of the song. But when they finished that, Rocky and Mick Taylor just kept playin', the percussion just kept goin', and Mick just came in with that line that introduces the second half of that song, and my ears perked up because I knew this was just a jam—it sounded like a situation where anybody who wanted to can jump in, so I grabbed my horn and I started playin'. I came in something like eight bars after that section started, and I had no idea what I was gonna play. I just stuck my horn in my face and started to blow. I mean, I knew what note I was gonna start on, but that little trill thing, I didn't decide to do that until it just kinda happened, and I thought, Well, that sounds good. As it turns out, that became a real defining sound for me.

That was a first take, a onetime thing. When we got back in the mixing room I was feeling pretty good because I thought, Hey, man, I just got another solo. Then I heard Mick Jagger say something like, "I don't know if we're gonna use that. It was a fun jam, but . . . " The decision-makers at that time were Jimmy Miller, who was the producer—well, he had a hand in the decision-making—and then the final decision came down to Keith and Mick, whoever the last man standing was. I don't really know how it came about. I wasn't around when they were deciding what the final version should be. Anyway, they did end up using it, which worked out well for me.

Another song Jim and I worked on was something called "I Got the Blues," which we played primarily a Stax-format-type horn thing for. Mick was very much into Otis Redding and Wilson

Pickett and the Memphis Horns. And here he had his own Texas Horns. I remember telling him, "Hey, man, we're the *Longhorns!*"

I think the main thing at the point in time when Jim and I were playing together that stimulated the interest in horns was a lot of the soul stuff that was going on in the States. There was a big transition from go-go music—Johnny Rivers and Trini Lopez and shit—to soul brothers like, primarily, Sam and Dave, Wilson Pickett, and Otis Redding, who had horns all over the place. And that's where I think Mick wanted to go. In fact, I *know* he wanted to go in that direction.

6

CHARLIE WATTS ALWAYS loved horns. He loved the Memphis style, and that's what Jim Price and I brought—that Southern style. But we changed it up a little bit because we weren't a horn section in the traditional manner. We adapted what we played. And I guess Mick heard this when we played with Delaney & Bonnie. We'd take an element, generally a vocal line or a guitar line, and use that to put our two cents in. We could sound like the Memphis Horns if we wanted to—I was very much into R&B. And Jim, although he wasn't into Otis and Wilson and all that, he had the chops.

Not long after those sessions, Mick asked Jim and me if we wanted to do some gigs with the Stones, to which we said, of course, yes. There were some English dates first, so we did those and they worked out well. And then the band went across the Channel. I think probably the first couple of dates were strictly an audition to see how some of the material that they were doing with horns would translate onstage, and apparently it translated well—thank you, Jesus!

Well, most of it translated well. At that time the Stones were still a part of that rock 'n' roll hysterical frenzy—the minute you got out onstage it was pandemonium. We could've had monitors the size of the Tower of London and still not have been able to hear properly. Which probably wasn't the best scenario to try out a brand new song live, especially one that had become a completely different song than what they'd originally planned it to be, like "Can't You Hear Me Knocking." Also, too, this was a period of time when nobody thought that much about rehearsing— "Whaddya mean, 'rehearse'? We *wrote* the damn thing! We don't need to rehearse!"

Well, we got up onstage—I think we were in Liverpool when this happened—and sure enough Mick called "Can't You Hear Me Knocking," and it was pretty good all through the verses and choruses and vocals. When it got to the instrumental part it was still OK, except all of a sudden we realized we didn't have a percussionist, so it sounded a little weak. I went ahead anyway and steamed on in and gave it my big ol' twirling trill at the beginning even as I was trying to remember what the hell I had played in the studio, and thinking and playing at the same time do not work out well for me.

So the thing just kinda started to disintegrate, and it got, I don't know, not far—maybe a minute into that section—and I was already lookin' out of the corner of each of my eyes, lookin' for Mick Taylor to take over, or lookin' for *somebody*, Nicky Hopkins, who was on keyboards, to take a solo and just *get me outta this*, man, this is *horrible*. And of course it kept on goin' downhill until it just died out onstage. There was no ending, it just kinda fell apart. It literally just died. It's the only time I've ever been onstage with the Rolling Stones when the wheels just *completely* came off. So, for about thirty years after that, anytime any mention was made of that song—"Why don't we do 'Can't You Hear Me Knocking,' man?"—Mick would just immediately gag. "No! No, we're not gonna do *that* again!"

Other songs worked out much better, but even so, it took some getting used to playing with the Stones onstage. When we first started playing "Brown Sugar" on the road, I just played a different solo every night. Eventually Mick came to me and said, "Hey, Bobby, if you play something similar to what's on the record, people will love it," and he was right. I'd never thought about it before, but I realized that people would want to hear what they hear on the radio. And I thought about how I felt, too, like the one time I went to see the Coasters and the fella didn't play the saxophone solo the same way. 'Course, it wasn't King Curtis, but still, I remember thinking, Well, that's a gyp. So I kinda took that studio solo out on the road with me.

It's funny, but as many times as I've played the solo on "Brown Sugar"—which has been thousands and thousands of times, not only with the Stones but with other bands, too—I've never really grown tired of playing it. It's never become wooden to me. I could play a whole bunch of different stuff, but it wouldn't fit the song. It's a simple solo. There's no saxophonic virtuosity there. It just seems to fit.

And, too, this was before all the big, huge, mega sound systems where they have every single thing onstage covered with three, sometimes four microphones. You could play a completely different song and the audience wouldn't know it because from the time you'd hear the announcement, "Ladies and gentlemen, the Rolling—" and it wouldn't even finish. It was just "Ladies and gentlemen," and then a *blast.* We always played the song, but sometimes it would be difficult for us to hear each other on the stage. You'd have to look to see, Do we end now? Is it over? Is Charlie still hittin' the drums? People came from miles around, it was a hell of an event, but they didn't really come to hear the nuances of all the songs. You could hear the first couple of bars, or sometimes just the first note—like on "Satisfaction," that first note: *bah-bahh*—and then it was all over. Might as well play "Mary Had a Little Lamb."

But don't get me wrong: It was fun. Maybe too much fun sometimes. But while we most definitely had some wild times, not everything you might've heard is true. There are rumors out there that I got kicked out of the Stones because I wouldn't get out of a bathtub filled with champagne and a French model, for instance. That is absolutely untrue. Yes, I got caught in a hotel bathtub filled with champagne and a woman, but that wasn't my point of departure. That was years later. The champagne incident came about on that first European tour and was just rock 'n' roll overindulgence, pure and simple: "Well, Bobby filled up a tub with champagne and some broad he never even met before and blew his whole fuckin' tour profits in one night." Which was kind of dumb, but, you know, man, I'd do it again.

I never understood one word that girl said and I don't know if she understood anything that I said. But it didn't matter. We were stuck on one side of the Mont Blanc Tunnel for a night. Mick, Alan Dunne, and I got snowed in. We'd been taking a drive, we'd just gotten some board mixes from the album we were doing. Bianca might have been with us too, I don't recall—she and Mick started seeing each other around this time. This was back when Bianca and Mick really liked me.

Anyway, we stopped at this old chateau because we couldn't get through the Mont Blanc Tunnel, it was impassable. I remember I had my Sony TC-120 portable cassette player that I'd gotten on the Mad Dogs tour. Nothin' like a little music to set the mood. So I'm sitting at the bar and there's this beautiful, beautiful girl who I'm trying every trick in the book to win over, but there just aren't that many tricks when you can't speak the same language. You can't weasel your way in by touting your credentials and talking about how wonderful you are because she doesn't understand you. So the only way I could communicate was by doin' a lot of smilin' and bein' extra cute.

I think she may have been aware of who Mick was, and because I was with him, that might've helped, although I don't know. Anyway, through some series of eye rolls, gestures, and just tryin' to look like a little lost puppy—anything to gain some affection and attention—it finally seemed to start working. I mean, this was a *very* impressive-looking female.

Somehow I eventually got the point across that I wanted to play her some music that I was on. I don't remember how I did it, it was all done with hand signals and mirrors. She might've been the only woman I've never lied to when I first met her, come to think of it—I couldn't conceal my true intentions. Anyway, I bought a bottle of Dom Pérignon and I offered her a glass, and she accepted it. We drank that bottle and then I ordered another bottle 'cause there was really nothing else to do. Besides that, I thought it was all on Mick. Anyway, I never considered what I was spending 'cause, hey, man, this was something brand new—finally a chick who I can't bullshit, cajole, connive, talk into, promise things to because she doesn't understand a damn word I'm saying. So this presented an extra element to the usual challenge.

After a couple bottles of champagne, I somehow enticed her upstairs to listen to the music. We ordered another bottle of champagne to the room, and I'm sure we listened to the music, but at some point I was struck by this overwhelming romantic urge to bathe that night's memory in champagne. Literally. So with that thought, I called downstairs.

I didn't speak French worth a damn, though, and I didn't know how to count very high in French. I forget what my top number was, but as far as I could count in French, that's how many bottles of champagne I ordered. That poor waiter was runnin' up and down those stairs like crazy 'cause I could only order in increments of four or whatever, and for the bathtub that I wanted to fill up, I noticed, increments of four weren't really making a dent. It was a big ol' bathtub. So after about the second time up there, when the waiter gave me the bottles and turned to go I said, "Wait a minute!" and started pourin' it in to see if I'd need more. I didn't particularly pay much notice to the waiter at the time, but I can remember wondering afterward what this guy thought this

American was doin', taking perfectly good French champagne and throwin' it in the bathtub.

Well, finally I exhausted all the champagne they had and there were only a couple of inches in the bottom of the bathtub. By this time, I'm not sure, but I think the deal may have already been done, as far as me and my female companion were concerned. I don't remember. But I do know, one way or another, we got into that bathtub and splashed around. It may not have been full, but there was enough champagne to knock out my profit margin for the rest of the goddamn tour.

That's the thing about the rock 'n' roll lifestyle—when I was hangin' out with Keith and Mick, hell, I just lived the life that they did. Fuck it. But I'd forget, of course, that I was on a salary and those guys weren't. It just didn't seem relevant to me at the time. I thought, Well, if they can have it, hell, I can have it, too. Well, that was an error of calculation.

But, of course, it worked in my favor plenty of times, too. And not all of it had to do with rock 'n' roll excess. Like the time I brought my mom over to see me play with the Stones in Paris later on during that same European tour in '70. Lucy takes over France!

This was right in the middle of the tour, and we were playing the Palais des Sports in Paris for three days. One night I got the bright idea to call up my mother and invite her to come to Paris to see the gig. Of course, I never thought she'd come, but I thought I'd give it a shot: "Hey, Mama, it's your baby boy! I'm over here in Gay Paree gettin' ready to play with the Rolling Stones! How would you like to come to the concert?" And she said yes.

Of course, at the time I said, "Fantastic!" but in the meantime I'm thinkin', How the hell am I gonna do this? I said, "Well, I'll make the arrangements and I'll call you back." So I hung up the phone and I called Keith and said, "Hey, Keith, you ain't gonna believe this. I called my mother and asked her to come over here, *and she accepted.* And now I don't know how I'm gonna get her over here because I don't have the money for the plane ticket." He said, "Don't worry about it, man, if your mum wants to come, your mum will come."

So mom came. Jo Bergman, who was a Stones assistant at the time, made all the arrangements. First class all the way. A limo picked her up at the airport, brought her to the Hotel George V, where we were staying.

Now, when we'd made all these arrangements I was kinda stoned the whole time. I wasn't really considering all the aspects that my mother's visit might involve. I mean, I was asking my dear, sainted little mother to leave New Mexico, the so-called Land of Enchantment, to come on over to what was for all intents and purposes the Land of Oz. This was a whole different deal than the way life worked in Belen, New Mexico.

When it finally dawned on me that she was somewhere over the Atlantic and on her way, I made sure she had a room. But I also made sure that her room wasn't anywhere *near* my room because I had things goin' on there that I didn't necessarily want my momma to be involved with eyeball to eyeball. So I asked Jo to put her on some other floor and in some other wing.

In short order, everything was set. A car with an interpreter was scheduled to pick her up at the airport and bring her to the hotel, which it did, early that morning. Of course, I was asleep. Passed out. Done from the gig and the partying the night before. I remember realizing my mother was coming, but then I'd keep saying, "Aw, that's all right, I'll stretch it out for another hour or so, it'll be OK."

Anyway, when she showed up, I was out. Really out. *Deep* out. Gone. My wife at the time was shakin' me sayin', "Your momma's here, your momma's here!" and I'd just say, "Go away," not realizing where I was. Finally my wife said, "Your mother is *here*! Here in *Paris*!" Well, that got me. I said, "Oh. Yeah. OK. That's right. Where is she?" She said, "She's in her room."

So I started trying to gather my shit together real quick and it was just not workin' at all. I was thinking, Man, I can't see her. I love her and she's here, but—oh, God, what did I *do?*

Well, eventually I got it together and I went down, and, I mean, I looked like a *hay bale*. So I knocked on the door and here was my mother, all bright-eyed and chirpy—"Robert! Robert, my son!"— and I was standin' there lookin' like somethin' the cat wouldn't even *bother* to drag in. And she said, "Well, how are you?" I was thinkin', Well, *look* at me, but I said something like, "Well, I'm fine, Mom, how was your trip?" all that stuff. I distinctly remember, as we were going through all the niceties and stuff, I was thinking, I've got to get to bed, I think I'm dying. I mean, this was, like, seven thirty or eight in the morning. She'd flown to Paris overnight.

Finally, after saying hello, I made it back up to my room and got back to sleep, immediately forgetting she'd come. Suddenly the phone rang, and I heard, "Robert?" Nobody called me Robert except my mother, so I realized this must be my mother on the phone. "Robert, are you up?" "Well, of course I'm up, Mother! I've been waiting for your call!"

So I got up again and tried to get myself as presentable as I could and I went down to my mother's room and we went to go have breakfast. Meanwhile, the hotel was full of people from London—Rolling Stones fans, the whole London scene, all in velvet trousers and stacked-heel snakeskin boots and long hair with ribbons—and I was with my mother from the Land of Enchantment. I remember thinking, This is probably not the best idea I could've come up with. I mean, while I wasn't ashamed of what I was doing, I was very protective of my mother just being slammed into this mix all of a sudden with no warning. So I kept saying things like, "Well, Mom, these people don't look like Americans and don't act like Americans but they're fine, they're all fine." Of course, my mom was much hipper than I'd given her credit for being. She'd say to me, "Robert, don't worry, don't worry."

Well, we suffered through breakfast—or I did, anyway—and she finally said, "Robert, you look terrible. You'd better go back up and lie down." Oh, thank God! So I said, "I'll have Jo arrange a car and a driver to take you to the show." Which she did. So I told my mother there'd be a car waiting out in front of the hotel with a driver in a black suit. A limousine. I told her, "That's your car. The driver already knows you're gonna be there, and the driver already knows where you're going." So I was positive everything was taken care of. Mom was all set, the limo would get her at a certain time and take her to the show.

So off I went to the gig. Later, when I saw my mom, I said, "Hi, Mom, you made it. Everything OK?" and she said, "Yes, and I have to tell you, the man who you put me in the car with was just the *nicest* man. He's from Turkey." I said, "Turkey? Who was in the car with you, Mom? No one was supposed to be in the car with you." She said, "His name was Ertegun. Ahmet Ertegun. Do you know Ahmet?" I said, "*Ahmet Ertegun! He owns the record label!*"

Well, God bless Ahmet's heart. Ahmet Ertegun was the founder and president of Atlantic Records and probably one of the very most important people in the music industry. I had met Ahmet before. He was friends with King Curtis.

He never told my mother he was the guy in charge, the leader of the pack. She just came up to his car and said, "Oh, are you my driver? I'm Bobby's mother," and he said, "Oh, Mrs. Keys, yes, it'd be my pleasure," and she just got right in. She never did take the car that was sent for her.

This was all before the gig had even started. As it started, my mother was put on my side of the stage. Jim Price and I were on the right-hand side of the stage, me and Jim and Mick Taylor. So we were playin' along and here was my mom, safe on the side of the stage. And I was just playin' my little brains out when all of a sudden this pair of enthusiastic French girls started climbing up onto the stage. And they were takin' their *tops* off. There was no security around the stage back then, so they were right there in front of me and Jim, just shakin' what they got right in our faces. I remember thinkin', Oh God, my mother's right there! You can't be doing this! I mean, any other time at all I would've *loved* it, but not that night. So I was playin' along, but I was also furtively looking over my shoulder at my mother off to the side of the stage and she was just there smiling, taking it all in. I was thinking, Oh my God, this is an awful lot for my mother to be put through in the space of twelve hours.

When the show ended, she was taken back by security to the proper car and went back to her hotel room. We arrived back, I don't know, twenty-five, thirty minutes after her, and I went up to my room, off with the sweaty clothes, into the shower, got fresh clothes on, and called my mom's room. I thought maybe we'd go down to the bar and have a quick drink. Well, when she picked up the phone, I heard in the background that it was party central goin' on in her room! People hollerin' and yellin' and laughin' and stuff. I said, "Mom! Who's in your room?" And she said, "Oh, I've got some friends of yours here. Everybody loves you! That's why I invited them up to the room." I said, "Mom, what have you *done*?"

So I sprinted down to my mother's room and opened the door and there were just *clouds* of hash smoke rollin' out the door. I was thinking, Oh my God, my rock 'n' roll demons are followin' me around and now they're jumpin' on my mother. Then I recognized two of the guys in the room, Gene and Marty from Granny Takes a Trip, this haberdashery in London that makes clothes for all the rock stars. That was where I had all my velvet upholstery taken care of. Well, when they saw me, Gene and Marty started sayin', "Your mom's great, man!" And my mother said, "Well, Robert, you never told me you had so many nice friends!"

The entire ordeal was a whole lot more stressful for me than it was for my mom, apparently. The next day, she decided she was gonna skip going back to New Mexico and join the tour on through to its next date in Rome. Her being Catholic and Rome being Rome, she felt like she couldn't miss the opportunity. I couldn't blame her: That first Stones tour turned out to have been the biggest opportunity of my life. Who knows where I'd be today if I hadn't taken it.

I HAD COME into the Stones on Mick's arm, so to speak, but during those recording sessions and on tour through England and Europe, I got to reestablish the connection with Keith that we'd had from years before. And while Mick was really great and it was really fun living in London, at some point I started to feel a little bit like a toy, a prize, an acquisition—"Oh, here's my new loudmouth Texas friend; if you stick around, he'll get drunk and say somethin' funny. He's liable to puke at any time, just watch him!"

With Keith, though, it wasn't like that. I always looked at Keith as being a kindred spirit—if he weren't English he'd have to be Texan 'cause there were no other societies that would have him the way he was, but Texas would welcome him with open arms. Also, too, Mick didn't get high. He didn't really mind what I did, to his credit, but Keith and I just seemed to have more in common. More than getting high, although we did do that. I just always felt a very strong affinity with Keith—you know, the ol' December 18, 1943, double-Sagittarius half man, half horse and a license to shit in the streets, which is how Keith likes to describe our mutual birth date.

Anyway, Jagger was getting ready to go somewhere and I needed my own place because I was gonna be bringing my wife at the time and my kid over. At some point, someone at Apple Records told me there was this guy, Anthony Fawcett, who'd been retained by Yoko Ono for the past year or so to document every living, waking moment of John Lennon and Yoko's life, and John was fed up with it. So suddenly his house was vacant, and John said, "Come on out, move right on in," and he gave me the address.

It was a country cottage—a really, really *nice* country cottage—adjacent to their property. It was called Benacre, and it was on Horsegate Ride, Ascot, in the Royal County of Berkshire, about thirty or forty miles outside of London. From my house in Ascot to downtown London, it took about thirty-five or forty minutes.

I'd gotten to know John a little bit while I was staying at George's house. John would come over to George's when I was working on George's album, and George and I would go over to John's house. I'd actually met him a year or so earlier when we did the "Power to the People" sessions when I was with Delaney & Bonnie on our European tour with Eric and George. We did it at EMI Studios on Abbey Road. This was the first studio thing he'd done after he left the Beatles. But I didn't really see John socially, I didn't really hang out with John until I moved out to Ascot.

John's house was called Titness Park. He called it Tits 'n' Ass Park. It was a big, white, palatial estate. This was when I got to know John a little better. I had done *Sticky Fingers* with the Stones and I'd done *All Things Must Pass* with George, and in London, Jim Price and I had done everything from Harry Nilsson to Barbra Streisand. We were hot. I remember doing this thing with Jim Horn, another sax player and a good friend, where we'd pull into any damn studio, any of the bigger ones that I'd worked in, and I'd say to Jim, "Let's get our horns and see how many sessions we can weasel our way into today." So we'd walk into a place like Olympic Studios and somebody like Pete Townshend would be in there, and he'd say something like, "Hey, Bobby, listen to this shit, whaddya think of that?" and I'd say, "Needs horns." And it *worked.* "Not bad, but it's missing something: horns." "Oh, really? Do you have one with you?" "Yeah, and so does my pal Jim." Jim and I did a lot of sessions that year in London. Went to France occasionally to record, went to Ireland and recorded with Donovan for his album *Cosmic Wheels.*

This is when I started naming my saxophones. I'd get on planes back then and fly first class to wherever I was going, and inevitably someone would insist that I had to check the horn. The French in particular, for some reason. So I started buying a ticket for it. I told people who were gonna hire me that they had to buy a ticket for both me and my saxophone, and for them to do that, I had to have a name for my saxophone to put on the ticket. So I'd get on the plane going to, say, Paris, get to my seat in first class, and set the horn right there. Of course, I knew they'd question me—"Sorry, Mr. Keys, this is not allowed"—at which point I'd say, "Aha, but it *is.* Elmer has a ticket. Elmer will have the beef Bourguignon accompanied by the red wine." I always made them bring food and wine to my saxophone. If they were gonna make me pay, they were gonna feed my horn.

When you're doin' a lotta sessions, sometimes they all sorta blend together, but there were a few memorable ones during this period. I recorded with B.B. King in London, on his *In London* album, for instance. Jim and I did the overdubs. I think the main part of the recording was done elsewhere. That was such a wonderful experience. I remember Klaus Voormann was on the session, Eric Clapton, a whole bunch of guys. Gary Wright, Steve Marriott,

Jim Gordon. That was back when sessions were fun. I played a solo on a song called "Caldonia," the first song on the album, and then Jim and I put horns on a song called "Ain't Nobody Home," which was the last song on the album. We opened it and closed it. If I remember right, I did the solo on "Caldonia" in one take, and when I went in to listen to it, B.B. smiled and said, "That's just *fine*, son. That's just *fine*."

The thing I remember so much about B.B. King is that the guy is such a gentleman. There was no drinkin', there was none of that stuff. I don't think I even heard him say "damn" or "hell." Just really a gentleman. One of those people who made you feel thankful that you could play with him and, because of that, it made me wanna play really, really good for B.B. King. I can't speak for anyone else, but that's the way it made me feel. I sorta reached down that extra inch to make sure I was getting everything I could muster up 'cause this was *B.B. King*, man. Plus, you got your contemporaries playin' on the tracks, so you don't want to be left behind. But B.B., even among the Beatles, the Stones, the Faces, whatever—it was B.B.'s show. He was the man. There was no doubt about it. At that time, he'd already been around forever. And he's still around, God bless 'im.

I lived at Benacre for a year or so, and for most of that time Yoko didn't like me at all. She didn't want John hanging out with me because I was hanging out with those Rolling Stones guys, and some stories were starting to get around about this guy, this loud, wild Texas guy, and she was trying to modify John's . . . well, his *life*, I suppose. From what I understood at the time, she pretty much shut him off from a lot of his rock 'n' roll buddies.

And when I moved out there, I didn't fit her profile of what a good neighbor should be because I was a drinker and a cusser and I'd stay up late at night and take my clothes off and holler—I just did everything that was offensive to her.

When I first moved in over there I went over to John's a couple of times, and I'd take some smoke with me, and we'd have to kind of wait until Yoko was in the other part of the house or had gone shopping or was doing something with her art or whatever and then we'd sneak out. Or John would come over to my house and we'd smoke hash, as much as we could. Or as much as *he* could, and then he'd go home. And he'd call me the next day and I'd ask, "What happened?" and he'd say, "Well, I think she *knows*." Then I wouldn't hear from him for a while.

Then one day I got a call from John saying that Yoko was working on her album and there was a possibility that I might be able to do something on it and get myself into her good graces so that we could hang out together without having to go out behind the barn, so to speak. So I went over there with my horn, and I remember sitting down in their studio listening to this music that Yoko was working on, and it was just . . . Yoko had her own . . . it's hard to describe. If you've never heard her stuff, it's very difficult to put into words. In fact, it seemed to be very difficult for *her* to put into words, too.

Anyway, I was in the studio and I was thinking, My God, what am I gonna do with this? And then I thought, Well, maybe there's a track that has some sort of tempo to it, some recurring chords, a pattern, *something*. In the room were the engineer, Yoko, and John, and there was a door in the studio that opened onto a garden.

Anyway, I got my horn out and put it in the studio and went over and said hi to Yoko and asked her what she wanted me to do. She said, "Come on over here, I'll tell you what I want," and she steered me toward the door so that we were looking outside. Then she proceeded to tell me this long, involved story about this pond in the north of England, and all the creatures of the forest have left the area, and there's just this one bullfrog sitting on a lily pad, the last denizen of the area that's still there, with the cold north wind blowin' up his backside. Winter's comin' on and the summer's gone and there's just this one miserable frog, and he, apparently, was a very integral part of the fabric of her song. And she wanted me to be the bullfrog. To be mournful and sad and have the north wind blowin' up my behind.

So, of course, armed with this information, how could I go wrong? I mean, requests like this came down the pike every day. Frogs, winds, ponds, *hell* yeah.

While she was telling me this, I was looking at John, and John heard what she was telling me and then he kinda looked at me and then kinda looked away. In other words, it was like, You're on your *own,* man. I can't help you, the water's too damn deep. So I was out in the studio, the track was playing in the background, and I got my horn out and put it together. Then, as I normally did, I closed all the keys on the horn and hit a low note—this gets all the pads closed, it gets the air moving through it and warms it up. *Hoooooooooonk.* Low A-flat, man. And Yoko's eyebrows went up about six inches, her eyes lit up, and she said, "That's it! *That's my frog!*"

I don't remember if she called me a genius or told me that I had the sensitivity of a frog or what, but I do remember she was *very* happy. And John was happy, too, because that meant we could hang out and play together some more. What I thought was gonna be the most challenging thing, the most impossible mountain to climb—that there was no way I was ever gonna get through this girl's opinion about me—turns out, all it took was one note and the doors flew open. She treated me completely differently from then on.

Although, I never did spend all that much time with Yoko. Yoko made me nervous. But she'd go off and do things and I'd go over there, and John would play piano and sing and I'd play my horn, and we'd talk about Buddy Holly and I'd talk about Texas, and he'd talk about Germany and he'd talk about Liverpool. And I'd tell him about some of the problems I had being raised in Texas and he'd be like, "Well, you think *you* had it bad . . . " It was funny—anything I'd say, he'd have to one-up me. It was kind of a running joke. I'd say, "Man, I had to get up at six in the morning and cook breakfast for everybody and chop wood before going to school," and he'd say, "You think *that* was bad, I had to get up an hour before I went to bed."

There was this great restaurant we used to go to, too, a place called the Bailiwick, an old stagecoach stopover that had been there forever and ever and ever. They had a really, really good wine selection. An excellent wine selection. And a great restaurant. We'd go down there some afternoons and get something to eat—something besides brown rice and some kinda powder or whatever. None of the things John and I did together ever endeared me to Yoko. The horn thing just bought me more time.

Back then, we had this boys' club kind of a deal. There were nightclubs that we'd go to, like the Speakeasy, places where "the players" would go to hang out. So sometimes we'd be hanging out and somebody'd ask, "Where's so-and-so?" and somebody else'd say, "He's in the studio," so we'd all go to the studio to drop in on him. Hell, I got a lotta sessions that way.

It was a very competitive sort of time, I quickly gathered, between bands like the Stones and the Faces and the Who. The Beatles had pretty much bowed out of the scene, they'd set their mark and were happy to let everybody else go for it. There was Jimmy Page, there was Clapton. The parties in those days—Ringo would have a party and everybody would show up at Ringo's party, then Rod Stewart would have a party and the same people would show up there. It was the same people just moving from venue to venue. And when there wasn't a party, everybody'd show up at the same clubs in London or the same restaurants in Soho. We'd be sittin' at a bar and someone'd say, "Hey, what's Ringo doin'? Let's go see what that penguin-lovin' fart's up to"—because Ringo had a buncha penguins all over his house. Toy penguins, not real ones. But they were everywhere.

Back then it seemed like there were no clocks. It was never too late, it was never too early. When the moment occurred, you went with it. It was never too late to wake anyone up because if they were asleep, well, what the hell were they doin' asleep? They had no business bein' asleep! We're ready to party! This was back when everyone was still in England. You could go to Ringo's house, you could go to Rod's house, you could go to Keith's house, you could go to Mick's house. Ronnie Wood's house, the Wick.

It was a wonderful time. We could just drink and raise hell onstage and people'd just *eat it up*. They *liked* us to be drunk and flamboyant and fucked up. Not only that, they liked to *emulate* us. Rock 'n' roll at that time was a reason to have a party. Yahoo, yippee-ki-yi-yay. It was not goin' to Ticketron and standin' in line. Today, rock stars are isolated. Protected. In the very beginning, it wasn't that way at all. Mick and I would go out together, him driving his own self in his car, there was no security around. It was wonderful.

I met my fair share of interesting people at this time of my life, especially drummers. Crazy drummers I've known and loved. John Bonham was a friend. He was around during the Harry Nilsson London sessions I played on for *Nilsson Schmilsson*. And then there's Keith Moon, one of the wildest and craziest guys I knew. He'd do the most insane things without blinking an eye.

I'd met Keith in passing when the Who first came to the States. The only thing I knew about the Who at the time was that Pete Townshend destroyed his amp and his guitar, and Keith Moon destroyed his drums. That's all I knew. And that wasn't too impressive to me. I thought, Well, OK, the record company's financing this, paying for all their gear, so they're just trashing their shit. And I wasn't really that knocked out with Pete Townshend as a guitar player, either, or as a musician, but really I just knew them through their reputation. I hadn't really heard much of their music at all. When I eventually met Pete I realized that there was more there than just smashing a guitar into an amplifier. The man had substantially more happening. And the same went for Keith. I loved that man.

I first met him at his house. I'd been living in Ascot and I'd heard that Keith Moon lived around the neighborhood. He'd moved in and immediately upset people by building a geodesic dome among all these little Mary Poppins houses. Well, one day I was riding around the peaceful countryside when I heard the sound of an aircraft engine, and I knew there were no landing fields around anywhere. Being an airplane buff, I tried to follow the sound to see where it was coming from, and eventually it led me to this driveway where I saw this geodesic dome, so I knew this was Moonie's house. Then I saw him out in his front yard chasing his chauffeur down in a hovercraft—who he did, in fact, end up running over, by the way, although not at that time—but anyway, he was chasing, I think his name was Dudley, the chauffeur, around his property in a hovercraft. That was our first meeting.

Anyway, we got to be friends, and I'd go over to his house. He loved listening to surf music, which surprised me. I'm not a big surf fan, and surf drummers were always so absolutely *white*. There was no funk involved in 'em at *all*. But anyway, Keith had all these surf records, and I'd say, "Man, don't you have anything else?" and he'd say, "Shut up, Bobby. Let's listen to Dick Dale and the Del-Tones." And so he started to educate me on surf music. And, you know, I didn't wanna piss the guy off, I wanted to be a good friend, a good neighbor, so I'd sit there listening to surf music, thinking this is such a bizarre scene: Keith Moon telling me about the virtues of American West Coast surf music. I mean *early* stuff, stuff like "Wipeout." Stuff that really wasn't very good. We used to get into some heated discussions about his obsession with surf music. I'd ask, "How the fuck can you compare the Beach Boys to Otis Redding—what is wrong with your *brain*?"

Keith's house was a great place to visit. Not only did he have that hovercraft, but he'd also bought an entire pub that he'd had moved onto his property. Which was a good thing for the neighborhood because, unless you were his chauffeur, Keith Moon at home was a lot safer for the general public than Keith Moon on the loose. Here's just one example: One time after a Stones concert, I forget where it was, somewhere north of London, we were staying overnight at a hotel. We were playing smaller towns in England, where they didn't have the big luxury hotels. The best hotel in this town we were playing in was a train station hotel. But it was brand new, and they were real proud of it—it had a big, all-glassed-in front area where you pulled into the driveway.

Anyway, I was at the gig, and afterward Keith showed up and insisted that I get in his new car with him, a Ferrari, to drive back to the hotel. So I got in the car with him, and he was playing me stuff on his new eight-track stereo, blazin' away, and he was drunk and I thought he might've had a little dip into mama's little helpers, too. Well, we kept driving by the hotel because he wouldn't pull in—"C'mon, Bobby, listen to this!"—just circling back around over and over. After the second or third time, I really wanted to get to my room and I really wanted to get outta the car, so I finally started getting real insistent about it, at which point he steamed into the driveway and went *right through* this plate glass window and drove up to the front desk, rolled his window down, and said, "Mr. Keys here can't seem to wait to get into his room, could you assist him, please?"

Obviously he'd pay for it, and people knew who he was. He was legendary for doing stuff like that. But I'd never been with him before when he did it. He just crashed through this ten-foot-tall plate glass front window and drove up to the front desk! "Mr. Keys seems anxious to leave my vehicle." There was a police report to fill out, of course, and they had to kinda pull him out because they couldn't let him drive. He was really drunk. But as far as anything like jail time, anything like that, nothing ever came of it.

7

N THE SPRING of 1971, Mick Jagger married Bianca Pérez-Mora Macias in Saint-Tropez on the French Riviera. May 12, 1971. Mick's wedding was my first trip to the south of France. It was beautiful.

There were two ceremonies. I was a participant in the civil ceremony, not the church service. Bianca, being Catholic, had to have a Catholic wedding, and Mick, being, I don't know, *non*-Catholic, had a civil service. I was Mick's best man.

I did not, however, have to give a speech. I would have, but I don't think anybody was gonna ask me. I would've been *happy* to talk. I had very little to do, actually. All I remember is Ahmet Ertegun was there and I sat next to him. And we all got very fucked-up before the ceremony. Everybody was at the Hotel Byblos in Saint-Tropez, and Marshall Chess and Ronnie Wood and Keith and I were in the bathroom of Marshall's suite. That's the first time I met Ronnie face to face. Or, rather, nose to nose.

The wedding itself was just an excuse to have a giant party, as far as most of us were concerned. Paul McCartney was there and Pete Townshend and Ringo, Eric Clapton, George Harrison. Even the downtime was fun. I remember one of the perks of staying at the Byblos was that, from the window of my room, I could watch the French movie actress Brigitte Bardot sunbathing au naturel outside of the hotel on the beach.

Not long after Mick's wedding, the Rolling Stones moved to the south of France en masse. They were driven abroad by the crazy tax laws they had in England, and since they were gonna be recording their next album there, they brought me and Jim along. Of course, I thought they had millions and millions of dollars. They had all these hit records. I didn't know that they were really dollar-strapped. It's hard to think of someone needing money when everybody, myself included, was living in a big villa in the south of France. It was a beautiful part of the world, it was a beautiful time of life, and if my math serves me well, we were all still in our twenties. God almighty. There we were in paradise—and it *was* a paradise. I mean, it was just beautiful. You'd wake up every morning and you'd go out there and you'd look at this beautiful harbor, and these big, old homes—old, *old* homes, not new McMansions like you see nowadays. Well, look at Villa Nellcôte.

Nellcôte was the house Keith rented that overlooked Villefranche harbor on the Côte d'Azur. It was also where we ended up recording *Exile on Main St.* I stayed at Nellcôte a whole lot. My residence was about five minutes away if you walked and about two minutes away if you drove. Charlie and Bill, now they lived out in the country. They didn't want to live around the Eurotrash. But, see, they didn't just choose their places because an album was being made, they chose 'em because they were gonna set up house-keeping for several years. And it just happened that when the band looked around for studios there just wasn't anything good enough, so it ended up being made in Keith's basement, with their mobile studio parked outside in the driveway.

Mick and Charlie and Bill lived as far away from Keith as they could get and still get to his house in one day. In fact, when Charlie would come he'd have to stay over, he lived so far away. But it was Bill who was really unhappy in France. He couldn't get his English tea and accessories, his Colman's Mustard and Bird's Custard, all that stuff. Bill's just that way. He's the guy, it should also be said, when we went on the road, in his rider—all the Stones had their own riders, Keith would have his specifics, a pool table, whatever, Mick would have his specifics, so many bottles of Dom Pérignon, whatever—all he wanted was a custom-made Ping-Pong table and Ping-Pong paddles and Ping-Pong balls, and nobody would play Ping-Pong with him. I'd play every once in a while, but usually no one was in the mood. Bill just liked what he liked.

We were in France for what seemed like *months* before we were all in the studio at the same time. The way *Exile* was recorded was the way a lot of the Stones' stuff I'd been involved with up to that point—but particularly in this period—was done. Like, there were no words to a lot of the songs. They were mainly just grooves that started out and changed, ideas. That was the whole thing: The main ingredient, the main purpose, was getting the groove down.

And since the studio was in the basement of Keith's house, he was at ground zero all the time. And he had Jimmy Miller, the producer, and Andy Johns, the engineer, living within five or ten minutes from there, so whenever he got the feelin', he'd call 'em up and have 'em come on over. I remember thinking, Man, this is the damnedest way I've ever seen in my life to get a record made, but, hell, I'm in the south of France with the Rolling Stones . . .

Those days started when Keith got up. He'd usually get up with Marlon, his son, in the mornings and take care of Marlon because Anita—Keith's girlfriend and Marlon's mother, Anita Pallenberg—slept quite late. Then he'd put Marlon in his boat, a really nice Riva wooden motorboat, real fast, which he called the good ship *Mandrax*, after a pharmaceutical product very popular in England back then, and come get me. And Marlon loved the boat. He was around four or so at the time.

Another thing, too: Keith Richards did not sleep very much. I mean, a few hours here and there, but that was about it. 'Course, that's about what I was doin', too, because I was pretty much on the same schedule as him, so when he was ready to go, he'd either pull up to the dock and blast away on that air horn that he had on his boat or he'd be standin' there next to my bed goin', "Git yer Texas ass up!" The bay was horseshoe-shaped, and he lived at the tip of the horseshoe, around six o'clock, say, and I lived around eight o'clock. And he'd come by and blast us on his air horn—Jim was staying there, too—and I'd come runnin' down to my dock, jump in his boat, and we'd go down to this little town right near the border with Italy, a place called Menton. This would generally be about seven or eight o'clock in the morning. He'd do this all the time.

So the schedule was, there was no schedule. It was Keith's schedule. There was never really any way of knowing when he'd come by to get us, he'd just announce his presence with that air horn. He'd say "Are you up for breakfast?" and I always would be because, you know, you can't sleep through a fuckin' *air horn*. So we'd go down and get in the boat, and this was when there were a lot of American warships at anchor in Villefranche harbor, and we'd get in there and weave around the warships and sometimes one of the guys on a boat would recognize it was me and Keith— well, they'd recognize Keith, they didn't have any clue who I was—and say stuff like, "Hey, Keith, how're you doin'? Try some of this!"—they'd just come from Southeast Asia and they had tons of Thai weed, and they'd just throw it over to us. Keith and his boat became quite well known toolin' around Villefranche harbor.

Keith also liked to pull into the harbor at Monte Carlo, where this one guy would be, I forget his name, but he was a billionaire-zillionaire shipping guy in the same category as Onassis—you know, he had the biggest private yacht on the south coast of France, had a helicopter on the back of it and all this stuff—and Keith would cruise by and give him the finger. Or make sharp turns and try to splash the people on deck. This was the Keith Richards I really got to know at that time because that fit with my program. I liked to thumb my nose at the elite, the rich—show 'em your ass, give 'em the finger, and tell 'em to fuck off. Splash 'em with water and then move on.

Of course, Keith wasn't always around to help create the entertainment, so on occasion I'd have to resort to doing it on my own. Jim Price and I were living in this beautiful French mansion, a very opulent place with Greek columns overlooking Villefranche harbor. And we'd stay up late at night—well, not Jim so much as me—and although most of my stayin'-up-late time was over at Keith's house, sometimes I'd come back to our house. One time, I remember, we discovered a locked door in our villa that led to a wine cellar with all sorts of stuff, Napoleonic brandy, incredible wine. It was right there if you knew how to break a lock. I mean, lock a door and I wanna *un*lock it.

There was one incident in particular that I'll never forget that took place at our villa. It was around Bastille Day, and I've always had a fascination and love of fireworks. I like things that light up bright and go bang. So I was out there with roman candles and a bunch of other explosives—they didn't have in France what they have here, but what they did have, I got—and I was out there on our veranda shootin' off multiple roman candles all at once. This was just before dawn. You could still see the bright lights across the harbor. And at one point I sorta lost control of the direction of my roman candles and they shot off toward the villa next to ours.

Sure enough, they crashed straight into our neighbor's villa, bangin' into the windows, and bouncin' off of the railings. I remember thinking, Boy, I hope those people aren't home. Meanwhile, Jim was out there hollerin' at me: "Keys, you fuckin' idiot! You're gonna burn the damn neighborhood down!" But it was Bastille Day, I told him. Time to celebrate.

All of a sudden, our neighbor's door flew open and this guy—a diminutive guy, a little guy, wiry—came out in this burgundy silk robe with black lapels over his pajamas. I was gettin' all ready to say, "Ah, fuck off!" or something to that effect, but when I got a better look at him, I did a double take, during which time he said, in this haughty British drawl, "Do you *mind!*" Just as he started to speak, I recognized him: It was David Niven. Well, I liked David Niven, I was a fan, so I felt kinda bad and said something like, "I'm so sorry, sir," and he just turned on his heel and went back inside muttering, "Bloody *Americans.*" 'Course, Jim wasn't happy about that at all. I remember him saying something like, "Bobby, see what you've done? You've got the French against us, and now you've got the English turnin' on us!"

The work hours, meanwhile, were whenever Keith wanted to work, which meant me and Jim and Jimmy Miller and Andy Johns were all on twenty-four-hour call. Although it wasn't always so much work for me—I was there because I wanted to be there and I was damn lucky to be there. Even though I had no involvement at this early stage, Keith wanted me there—"Bobby, you never know," he'd tell me. And actually, one time when I'd just gotten my brand new Selmer baritone saxophone—because most of our instruments had been stolen at one point—I was down in the basement just blowin' on it, and Keith comes down and just starts playing a chord progression. It was "Happy." I wanted to hear what the low note on my baritone was, so when Keith got to the part that goes, "I need a love to keep me happy," man, I got to *nail* that bottom note, and Keith's eyes lit up. It was a *big* sound, it was like all of a sudden a *foghorn* had just come into the room. Made my socks roll up and down and sorta curled his nose hairs. And so he said, "Hey, man, that's a great sound! What else can you do with it?"

I always thought I helped Keith write that song. That's pretty much what he says in print, but you couldn't tell it from the royalty statements, which I never got. But then again, I didn't really do anything. We were just jammin'. He wrote the song, he wrote the lyrics. I just always like to goad him about it: "Hey, man, I was *there*!" To which he says, "Yeah, man, you were there—you shoulda written somethin'! You shoulda said somethin' creative!"

When we first went there—and what was fun about it, too—was there wasn't really a rock 'n' roll crowd around France at that time. Once we were there for a while and people got to know who we were, there'd be some people that'd kinda show up outside Keith's property and listen, but, by and large, we were free to go wherever we wanted to and not get bothered. This little bar called Albert's comes to mind, where we'd head after goin' to Italy. Keith would buy these little fish that they'd serve down there, which I thought were french fries until I noticed that the french fries had eyes in 'em.

Keith liked to go where working people liked to eat. He's not a real fancy restaurant-goer. The restaurants I've been to with him have been, you know, excellent food, but where the locals go. It showed another side of his character: He identified more with the working class. He never hung out in Monte Carlo at the casino, you couldn't drag him there with a team of wild horses. Anyway, we'd eat those fish where the fishermen came in, and I guess they were good. Once I got past the idea of eatin' guts and eyeballs, they *were* kinda like french fries. Not somethin' they served up in Texas very often, though, I can tell you that.

Eventually we'd go back to Keith's house, and by that time we'd have gotten Jimmy Miller and Andy up, and we'd go out to the truck and listen to what got recorded the night before. And then if nobody showed up, Keith would start playing either guitar or bass, and if Charlie didn't show up, Jimmy Miller would play drums. And I was there so I'd play whatever I could play. That's when Jimmy Miller started putting me out in the hallway so the horn wouldn't bleed over into other stuff—we were doing it down in the basement and all we had were mattresses and shit on the walls. It was a homemade job. Jimmy and Andy earned their money.

By the time we were back at Keith's house, it'd be time to roll up a big fat hash joint, then maybe drink a little, and of course when Gram Parsons was there—he was Keith's guest at Nellcôte for a while—he'd play a little piano or whatever. Then Keith would go back to bed. And might not get up again until eleven, twelve, one o'clock in the morning. Might not get up until 8 AM. It was a very loose schedule.

At the time, too, Mick was having to commute between Paris and the south of France because Bianca was pregnant. Mick had to take Bianca to Paris because that's where her doctor was. And Mick also liked to stay in Paris. I remember thinking I'd been down there for a month or more before Keith and Mick and Charlie and Bill and Mick Taylor were all together at the same time with the tape recorder running. It didn't happen that often. And Bill, particularly, would get fed up, and so sometimes he just wouldn't come. If you look at the credits on a lot of albums, Keith played bass on a lot of their stuff. Bill would just get tired of hanging around. And also, Keith was just so into it he'd take Bill's bass part off anyway. He didn't do it all the time, but then again he wasn't shy about it.

Sometimes Jimmy Miller would have to give a little pep talk, like, "OK, guys, we've got umpteen boxes of tape here and so far we only have a couple of songs." Overall, though, Jimmy had a great approach because he knew he couldn't demand that they sit down and record. He knew that. He'd been around the business long enough to have heard all the stories about their behavior. And Glyn Johns, being the engineer in the beginning—Glyn, who was Andy's brother, had worked with the Beatles and did all the early Beatles stuff, actually quite a bit of the Beatles' stuff—also knew sort of what to expect, as did Andy. But still and all, Keith had the setup: He had the tape recorders, the truck was there, the instruments were there, down in the basement. So it was essentially Keith's responsibility, and he'd get up and do it whenever he felt like getting up and doing it. There were times that were frustrating, I know, for other people.

This was the first time I'd been with the Stones from the beginning of a recording experience to the end, and I was amazed at how it worked. I remember asking Jimmy Miller, "Jimmy, is this *normal?*" Because there'd be times when I'd see Keith, who'd probably been up all night, sitting there with a guitar in his hands and a cigarette stickin' out of his mouth, asleep. And it was like, "Are you gonna wake him?" "*I* ain't gonna wake him. Hell, he's liable to *shoot* me." Of course, he wasn't like that all the time. And when he did work, he'd go for several days. He has a constitution unlike anyone else's I've ever come across. I used to think that I had a pretty strong resistance—you know, I could drink as much, stay up, whatever—and I could, but then I couldn't play very well. Keith, he'd just come to and start strumming.

Over time, I could see the direction a given session was taking and pretty well know it wouldn't involve me for hours and hours, so I'd take off for a while. I'd gotten this motorcycle, it was the first year Honda had come out with its 750 model, so when they were in there for a while I'd just hop on that sucker and go. I had this really pretty French movie star who decorated the back of my motorcycle at the time—Nathalie Delon—so if I saw a break in the action as far as I was concerned, I would get out of there. Sometimes I'd have to kind of sneak out because I knew if Keith saw me going, he'd say, "Hey, Bobby, where the fuck are you goin'?" and then I'd have to say something like, "Oh, just to get some cigarettes."

Nathalie was Bianca's best friend. She lived in Paris. But when she came down to the south of France, she'd stay with Mick and Bianca—they had a house just a little bit north of Saint-Tropez, which, on my motorcycle, from Keith's house to Mick's house was about forty-five minutes. If you went by car, it'd take about two hours, but on my motorcycle I could go in between the traffic lanes. It'd be bumper-to-bumper traffic down the Côte d'Azur, and I saw everybody else who had a motorcycle doing it and nobody told me it was illegal, so that's what I'd do. I've never been a real stickler for traffic laws anyway.

We spent *months* in the south of France, and there were just boxes and boxes of tapes. Hours and hours and hours. It got to the point where you weren't quite sure how many songs had been done. It was especially hard because a lot of the things we were doing were just grooves—there weren't any words to some of them. That was something that seemed to come later in their process. From my own personal standpoint, I didn't really *want* the record to be finished. I was having a hell of a lot of fun. Every damn thing was paid for. I don't remember collecting a salary, but

I know I never needed money. Or put it this way: When I needed money I got money.

One of my favorite things to do was when everybody'd be together in the studio and they hit a groove, there were times, because it was so fuckin' hot in there, that I'd go outside, underneath a tree, and listen to the Rolling Stones recording their next album. Sittin' there, man, drinkin' a beer, thinkin', Now, this is some hot shit. And it was.

There were a few songs where I would be in there playing along with them, like "Casino Boogie." I was in there when they were laying that down. And I started to play the solo, but for purposes of song separation, they said, "Hold on till we get it down and then you can do your thing." Which is what Jim and I did. We tried a couple things live. I think we tried some versions of "Happy" live, with Jim and me down the hallway. But as far as playing as a band, we couldn't do that very often because it wasn't very often that everyone was all there at the same time. Mick Taylor was always available, but most of the guys weren't.

Sometimes Jimmy Miller would get instructions from Mick or Keith and tell Jim and me, "OK, you guys go ahead and start workin' on some horn lines for . . . " whatever song, and we'd go down into the studio in the afternoons and do that. And then Keith would come down and listen to it. Jimmy always had a pretty good idea of what he wanted. No doubt about it, he was the absolute best producer for this band.

Mostly, though, Jim and I would work out our own lines. Like on "Bitch"—that was my line. Well, actually, it was Keith's line, I was just copying it, but everybody liked how it sounded, so there

⇓ Robert Keys. Slaton High School, Class of 1961. Courtesy of Slaton High School.

⇓ Top to bottom: J.I. Allison, Buddy Holly, and Joe B. Mauldin. 1958. Courtesy of author.

. . . . . .
KEYS, ROBERT
    Band 57-61; Track 58; Basketball 57-60; Tennis 58-60; DECA 60-61.
    "I have not slept one wink."
. . . . . .

BUDDY HOLLY
&
THE CRICKETS

⇑ The Buddy Knox Band in Seattle, 1961. From Left: Ron Neuberger, Bobby Keys, Buddy Knox, Ray Feldman, Stuart Perry. Courtesy of author.

⇒ Bobby Keys and Jimmy Markham at Tradewinds in Lawton, OK 1964. Courtesy of Jimmy Markham.

⇓ Left to Right: Bobby Keys, Bill Boatman, Jimmy Markham, John Gallie, Geroge Dee at Hobbit Club in North Hollywood, CA 1964. Courtesy of Jimmy Markham.

⇐ J.J. Cale, Bobby Keys, Jimmy Markham at Mirage Club in Santa Monica, CA 1964. Courtesy of Jimmy Markham.

⇒ Left to Right: Bill Boatman, Bobby Keys, Jimmy Markham, unknown, Don White, Bobby Jones in Downtown Tulsa, OK 1967. Courtesy of Jimmy Markham.

⇐ Delaney & Bonnie and Friends in 1968. From left, Bobby Keys, Carl Radle, Jim Gordon, Delany Bramlett. Courtesy of author.

⇑ Bobby Keys recording Exile on Main Street at Villa Nellcôte in France. 1971. © Dominique Tarle

⇓ At Villa Nellcôte. From left: Mick Jagger, Mick Taylor, Keith Richards, Jimmy Miller, Bobby Keys, Jim Price.
© Dominique Tarle

⇑ Stones on the Exile Tour, 1972. From left, Jim Price, Bobby Keys, Bill Wyman, Mick Taylor, Keith Richards, Mick Jagger, Charlie Watts. © Annie Leibovitz

⇓ Stones on the Exile Tour, 1972. From left: Charlie Watts, MIck Jagger, Mick Taylor, Bill Wyman, Nicky Hopkins, Bobby Keys, and Keith Richards, © Annie Leibovitz

⇑ Exile Tour, 1972. From Left: Bobby Keys, Mick Jagger, Keith Richards, and Terry Southern. © Annie Leibovitz

⇑ Jimmy Iovine, John Lennon and Bobby Keys in New York, NY 1974. © 2008 May Pang, from Instamatic Karma

⇐ Bobby Keys and Ronnie Wood
c. 1970s. © Marty Temme.

⇓ The New Barbarians on stage. 1979.
From Left: Bobby Keys, Ronnie Wood,
Stanley Clarke, Keith Richards. Courtesy
of Author.

⇑ New Barbarians, 1979. From Left: Ziggy Modeliste, Bobby Keys, Stanley Clarke, Ian McLagan, Keith Richards and Ron Wood. © Henry Diltz

⇓ J.I. Allison's farm in Tennessee, 1979. From Left: Keith Richards, Bobby Keys and Jane Rose. Courtesy of Jane Rose.

⇑ J.I. Allison's farm in 1979. From Left: Keith Richards, Patti Hansen, and Bobby Keys. Courtesy of Jane Rose.

⇓ From Left: Keith Richards, Bobby Keys and Bill Wyman. Courtesy of Jane Rose.

⇑ Bobby Keys and Keith Richards, 1982. Courtesy of Jane Rose.

⇓ From Left: Chuck Leavell, Bill Wyman, Bobby Keys and Keith Richards, 1989 © Kevin Mazur

⇑ Bobby Keys and Keith Richards, 1990. © Mikio Ariga

⇑ Bobby Keys and Ronnie Wood backstage on the Stones Voodoo Lounge Tour, 1994. Courtesy of author.

⇑ Bobby Keys and his wife Holly on their wedding day, December 18, 1999. Courtesy of author.

⇑ The Horn section at the Licks World Tour, 2003. From left: Bobby Keys, Tim Ries, Kent Smith and Michael Davis. Courtesy of Jane Rose.

⇒ Bobby Keys in 2003. Courtesy of Jane Rose.

⇑ Bobby on the Licks World Tour, 2003. Courtesy of Jane Rose.

⇑ From left: Keith Richards, Charlie Watts, Bobby Keys on the Licks Tour, 2003. Courtesy of Jane Rose.

⇒ Ronnie Wood and Bobby Keys on the Licks Tour, 2003. Courtesy of Jane Rose.

⇑ Keith Richards, Charlie Watts, Bobby Keys, Darryl Jones and Mick Jagger in 2003. Courtesy of Jane Rose.

⇓ Keith Richards and Bobby Keys on the Bigger Bang tour in Australia, 2006. Courtesy of author.

⇒ Bobby with the Stones, 2007. Courtesy of author.

⇓ Keith Richards and Bobby Keys hanging out, 2007. Courtesy of Jane Rose.

was no change to that. Jim Price would voice the chords when we had a block of chords to match when we'd play a horn section part. Keith and Mick had very little to do with the sound of the voice of the horns. The horn lines, Mick would sometimes have suggestions for. Keith never really had any suggestions, but a lot of the horn lines came from his guitar lines.

At some point I realized they must have had enough material, but in the same breath I hoped they'd keep going. And like I said, it was hard to tell sometimes—in fact, I didn't really have any idea—how many completed songs there were. Mick or Keith would start something, but sometimes it was only a verse or whatever, and then Keith, particularly, would keep goin' on and on with it or would put it down and come back to it. But I never really knew how many real, completed songs there were. I know that it was expressly understood by Jimmy and Andy that anytime Keith was down there to record, not to let anything go by because it *might be the one.*

But I don't remember it as one continuous flow. I remember that whole recording process as a series of partial sessions: "Well, Bill and Charlie are here, and Mick's here and Keith's here—OK, turn the machine on." Or even if Keith was just there on his own. Keith was the one who seemed to be the spark who kept it going. But when Mick went to Paris to be with Bianca when she was having their baby, and winter was coming on, people just kind of folded up their tents and left. Everyone just really kind of trailed away, the best I remember it. Jim and I had, I think, something to do with Cocker for a while, and then the next time we got together with the Stones was when they went to the States to mix the album.

I wasn't really involved in the mixing or any of that jazz, but I remember going back to L.A. while the album was being finished, a process that seemed to me to be taking a long time. It was a fun period, though. We were all living in L.A., up in the hills. We weren't staying in hotels, we had houses, some private residences that had been rented for us. It was me and Jim Price and Nicky Hopkins and then the rest of the Stones band, which was Keith and Charlie and Mick and Bill Wyman and Mick Taylor, and they had this record out that we'd recorded, and it was getting a lot of attention. I remember the *Exile* billboard. It was on Sunset Boulevard, right there by Chateau Marmont.

I was staying at George Harrison's house. Actually, the house was rented by George Harrison and I'd taken over the lease because George was going back to England and I was gonna be out there for a while, and he didn't mind me staying there, especially since the Stones' office paid the rent. Although it still ended up costing me a lotta royalty checks.

What happened was Keith and I had a party up there. We had, I don't know, about a zillion people over. There was this girl who was working at the Stones' office who set it up. She'd invited Little Richard, Ricky Nelson, a shit-pot load of people. Eventually, of course, the party kinda got out of hand and, among other bits of minor damage, a bunch of the owner's statuary got tossed into the pool. Which he was not happy about. I don't blame the guy. His property was destroyed. It didn't affect George any, luckily, although I got cut out of many thousands of dollars in royalties.

The last time the Stones had been in the States was in '69, and that ended with the Altamont show, outside of San Francisco, where a fan got killed by the Hells Angels, who were supposed to be running security for the gig. In the late spring of '72, they had a brand new, shiny hit single, "Tumbling Dice," and everything that went along with it, and I was about to embark on my first truly big rock 'n' roll tour with them.

The rehearsals for the tour were held at Universal Studios in Studio C. We'd get there in the late afternoon and stay there until ten or eleven or twelve. Five or six hours, seven hours. Rehearsals were always in the evenings. It's a natural time for playing music, rock 'n' roll particularly. Rock 'n' roll ain't a daytime music, hell, it's a nighttime music. That was the theory.

We devoted two weeks to rehearsals. It wasn't just straight-through rehearsing, though, as I remember it. It was more like rehearse a little bit, take a break, get fitted for clothes, go out for sushi. It was a lot different than any other rehearsals I'd ever done. We were rehearsing in a big soundstage. Rehearsals back then were a lot more casual. It was primarily just going over the stuff. It definitely wasn't overly rehearsed. It's not overly rehearsed now, either, but it sure is *well* rehearsed. But back then, it was just like Keith would start off with Charlie, and then everybody else would jump on in. We'd go through the numbers and they'd decide what songs were gonna be played in what order. I got the impression that once you played it, it was kinda like, "Well, OK, we've done it, now we know it." It wasn't nearly as structured then as it is now.

I remember they had a great costume department there. Right before we left to go on tour, somebody had gotten permission for us to go into the wardrobe warehouse to see if there was anything we wanted to wear. I remember Charlie got this big poofy Cuban shirt.

We were all looking for stuff to wear on the road, and Nudie—this guy who made real flamboyant western wear at the time, he did some stuff for Elvis and Hank Snow and a bunch of country guys—had a shop in fairly close proximity to where we were rehearsing, so I went over there with Keith one afternoon, and Gram Parsons. Keith ordered a T-shirt with the lips logo on it and a big cock with sequins on it. Everybody thought it was a Vienna sausage.

This is also when I noticed Keith was getting a blond streak in his hair. He was squeezing lemon into it. I don't know where he got the idea from, but someone told him that lemon would put streaks in your hair. It was the first time that I noticed it. We had a makeup artist with us, but in addition to that, I noticed that Anita would be putting kohl on Keith's eyelids. I remember lookin' at him and thinkin', *Not me, pal.* I wouldn't tease him about it, but when they'd look at me I'd say, "Uh-uh. I'm good to go." Now, of course, I do use a little Max Factor just to cover up my toothpaste-like complexion, which gets washed out onstage. You get to a certain age and makeup helps—with wrinkles, gives you eyelashes, gives you eyebrows. But in '72, everybody had plenty of eyelashes, and I'd look at Keith, and he'd be dipping a brush into this brown jar, puttin' stuff on, and I'd think, Goddamn, son, what are you, the prince of darkness? I thought it was unusual at the time, but hey, these guys obviously knew shit I didn't know. I'd better not laugh too quick.

I remember Charlie doing it a couple times. He looked ridiculous. Charlie's pretty much his own guy with his own look. He's got his espresso machine set up behind his drums. Occasionally he'll have a little Bombay gin, but very rarely. Charlie's not a drinker.

I'm not sure I ever saw Charlie drunk. I probably don't remember because if I ever saw Charlie drunk, I was probably drunker than Charlie. Yeah, Charlie's always been a pretty steady guy. Whenever Keith and I would get drunk and rowdy, Charlie was always somewhere else. He just really didn't care to be around that shit. He didn't get on us about it ever, but if any action started with any drugs or any chicks and shit, Charlie was *gone*. That's why he's still married to the same woman.

One of the big things about that tour was this new stage-lighting setup. They were always looking for something innovative and different, which was to their credit. Stuff that hadn't been done before. Chip Monck was the stage manager for that tour, the sound man, the guy who put the show on, basically, and his idea was to have the spotlights come from behind the stage and shine up on this big Mylar mirror that hung above us instead of coming from the front of the stage, like they always had before. It was hot, but then everything was hot back then.

What I remember the most from that period, though, was that every day was *exciting*, every day was getting closer to the gigs. This was the first time that I'd be doing a tour with the Stones in the States. There was a lot of positive energy before that spring. Everybody was ready to go out and rock, the record was getting some good exposure. Plus, Stevie Wonder was gonna be opening up the majority of the shows, which was a real kick in the butt because he had a record called *Songs in the Key of Life* that had just come out and it was a monster hit. I guess the powers that be, whoever planned the tour out, thought that it would be a good idea to have Stevie Wonder on the show because it would open up another audience for the Stones, more of a black audience. Which up to that point I don't think anybody'd ever thought about—you know, there were enough white people out there, I guess, that dug the music that it just never occurred to anyone.

Stevie was with us the whole time, pretty much. And he had a great band, man. That band used to really set a high bar for us to follow onstage. But the Stones' band was really good at that time, too. We were getting better and better after all those months in the basement at Nellcôte and then the rehearsals in L.A. We were ready to go on the road and rock. Which is what we did. I'll never forget standing up onstage in the beginning thinking, So *this* is what the big time is, huh?

8

CAN'T SAY exactly what I felt when that airplane lifted off the tarmac and we were actually going out for my first major Rolling
Stones tour. I can remember it was like waiting for Disneyland
to open up, waiting for that tour to start. It was a feeling of . . . I
don't know, of everything that you'd hoped it would be. If you're
looking to get to the top of the rock 'n' roll heap, here all of a sudden I was sittin' on it and getting ready to take off. It's a feeling I'll
never forget, and one I haven't gotten back since. There's nothing
like the first time. Plus, all those *chicks*. And the *money*.

I'd recorded with the Stones and I'd done some gigs with
them in England and Europe prior to the '72 tour, but England
and Europe are different from the States. The venues aren't as
large. Back then, more so than now, it was making it in the States
that counted. If you made it in the States, if you were really
big in the States, you were considered successful—which of

course they were already. I mean, I got there well after the fact was already established that they were the number one rock 'n' roll band in the world. They'd reached that benchmark without any assistance from yours truly here. But by '72 the music sorta shifted another degree, another step, by integrating horns into a lot of the songs they did and by adding saxophone solos—there weren't that many, but hell, one or two was more than I'd ever had before.

It started out good and it just seemed to get better. There was a real camaraderie on the road, particularly between Keith and myself. We got to be very good friends—more so—on that tour. Listened to a lot of music. We used to carry a ton of records, 45s, and a turntable with us, and we'd always listen to what we'd dub the album of the week or the month, which was always something on Chess or some R&B artist. Or country. Keith was getting into country quite a bit at that time, too.

There were no wives along on that tour, either. It was pretty much just boys' night out every night. I mean, it was just a wonderful time: You get up there and you play rock 'n' roll music for the screaming hordes with a shit-hot band with a whole load of hit records, which meant no lack of material, and it just—it was one of those magical periods of time, man, where it just seemed like everything was going along just as good as you could possibly hope it would. And it was. I can't really think of any downside to that at all, other than I got to be pretty handy with a syringe, which later on would prove to be my downfall somewhat.

But by and large it was like entering the gates of rock 'n' roll heaven. I mean, there were just beautiful women everywhere.

The Stones were the darlings of the '70s. There were people like Princess Lee Radziwill traveling with us, and Truman Capote and Terry Southern and all kinds of folks. We'd play places in New York and L.A. and there'd be all these movie stars or stage actors. At the risk of sounding like Forrest Gump, it was just like opening up a box of chocolates and having a big variety of everything—you never knew what you were gonna get from one day to the next. We played forty-eight shows between June 3 and July 26, but it seemed like it lasted all summer. There wasn't a lot of downtime; we were pretty active the whole time. It was like being in a rock 'n' roll fantasy camp.

In fact, the '72 tour was the biggest rock 'n' roll tour of all time in the U.S. at that time. The Stones were big when they did Altamont, which was the first American tour with Mick Taylor, in 1969, but they were bigger when they came back. It seemed like they'd crossed over some cultural or societal border—all of a sudden, instead of it being "Would you let your daughter date a Rolling Stone?" it was like, "Hey, man, Mick might be comin' over to my house—if you're real lucky maybe I'll invite you over." I mean, suddenly they were in demand by people like Dick Cavett. Even he was along for the ride for a while.

There were always people who'd say, "Well, they're still not as big as the Beatles," and maybe they weren't, but it's kinda hard to measure. I mean, the Beatles never did any extensive touring in the States. And the whole business of rock 'n' roll had evolved by then. Bill Graham had a lot to do with that. He took the live concert experience to another level. I thought he did a lot of good stuff. I liked Bill. Some people thought he was stealing from them, and he very well could've been, though I was never in a position to have been concerned about that.

We didn't do nearly as many songs back then. There weren't as many songs in the set on the '72 tour as there are in what it's evolved into now. We only did maybe an hour in '72, sometimes maybe not quite an hour, whereas now it's two, two and a half hours. It's a much longer show. Lot more songs to play.

Then again, we played a lot more places then than we do now, mostly because now it takes so damn long to set everything up. It was just different. It was a lot leaner of an organization back then. Now there are hundreds of people involved. And whereas now there are, I don't know, probably twenty vehicles involved in getting the band from the hotel to the gig—everybody's got their own individual thing, you know, vans and limos, plus all the staff, who have their own vans, plus wardrobe people—in '72 we went to gigs in a camper. We took a fuckin' camper. All of us in the *same fuckin' camper*—me, Keith, Charlie, Bill, both Micks, all of us. Of course, part of that was to be incognito—nobody expected the band to be riding around in a Winnebago. I'm not sure it was a Winnebago specifically, but I distinctly remember it was very Winnebago-like. In fact, it might not have been *good* enough to be a Winnebago.

But then, we did have our own airplane. It wasn't a jet, it was a turboprop. There was nobody but us on it, and it was faster than the Mad Dogs & Englishmen plane. Of course, the Mad Dogs & Englishmen plane was cooler because it was a Super G Constellation, the one that Howard Hughes designed for TWA. The one with the three tails on it. Even so, that was kinda like the sophomore class. For Jim and me, going on tour with the Stones, it was like suddenly we were in the graduating class. For one thing, we had hotel suites at places like the St. Regis and the Beverly Wilshire instead of rooms at the Hyatt. It was definitely ascending another rung on the ladder, which was cool. Very cool.

The atmosphere was pure rock 'n' roll—hedonistic sex, drugs, and rock 'n' roll. We played a gig up in Vancouver first, but our first gig stateside was in Seattle. I remember this because Seattle's where we first met the doctor. Dr. B. was the physician in residence that Mick hired. His specialty was emergency medicine—in case anybody got shot or injured or anything like that, he was there. He was a young guy, single, and really liked the women. *Really* liked 'em. He was basically a sex machine. So he was definitely in the right place because they were all over the place back in '72. It was his *dream* job.

Although it was never officially stated, I was told by people who would've known that the real reason Dr. B. was hired was because Mick had been threatened or the band had been threatened for some kind of reprisal by *somebody* because *somebody* didn't pay *somebody's* lawyer's fee. Hells Angels is what I heard. I mean, it had to be. They'd been threatening Mick and trying to extort money from the Stones ever since Altamont because they were being prosecuted by the state of California for the murder of Meredith Hunter, the guy who got stabbed. Sonny Barger, the head of the biker gang, was in the slam wanting legal representation. This is all hearsay, as in I heard it *said*. But that's what it was, a simple matter of extortion. You know, either you cough up some money or we're gonna blow your little playhouse up.

That's when Mick started moving around on the stage all the time. I mean, *noticeably* more. An interesting coincidence, I always thought. I mean, Mick always moved, but in '72 you'd see him running from one side of the stage to the other. I don't know, maybe it just happened to be a point in time where he thought he ought to bring something else to the stage aside from standin' there singin' and shakin' his maracas. Come to think of it, he stopped doing that, too. And Mick, I thought, was a good maraca shaker. Anyway, it may not have a damn thing to do with anything, but it *did* coincide.

But back to Dr. B. We'd stayed at a place called the Edgewater Hotel in Seattle, and after the show I headed up to my room. This wasn't a fancy-schmancy hotel—it was the kind of place where you had two doubles, and if you wanted to have a suite, you just opened the door between the rooms. Well, when I went into my room I saw Dr. B. in his half of the suite with some girl just *whalin'* away, so I said, "Hey, what the hell's goin' on here?"

I'd been looking for him, actually, because I needed something to take me down after the show, and Dr. B. always had all these high-powered pain-killing drugs in his little black bag: liquid Valium, Talwin, Demerol, all the heavy-hitters. So when he figured out what I was looking for he said, "Just take the bag! Take the whole damn bag and go!" So I thought, Take the bag? Well, all right! "Hey, Keith, I got the bag!" Anyway, that's when we found out that the doc had an Achilles' heel, so when we wanted to, let's say, experiment, we'd found an area that we could bargain in. The doc was a chick freak. And he didn't want anyone to know. But that was OK—our silence could be bought.

I REMEMBER AFTER the very first shows I was really anxious to see the reviews now that the Stones had horns. The album wasn't getting all that well received, which bothered me because it seemed like the horns were brought up as one of the reasons, as if we were trying to be some sort of an imitation Stax soul sorta deal, and that wasn't it at all. So when the tour started, I'd get up real early in the morning and go to the front desk of the hotel and say, "I need a copy of the paper as soon as it comes in," and I'd look at the reviews. Well, it didn't take long to find out that it didn't matter how Jim and I played. I mean, we could've been up there riding checkerboard elephants and they wouldn't have noticed us, man, because it's *Mick*. It was all about Mick. Every now and then a review would say, " . . . and the band was augmented by two horn players."

The fact is, the Stones are a very visual band. Keith would come out there with his shark's tooth in his ear and his leopard skin shit on, and Mick's out there prancin' around. Bill's all clad in suede, standing there not moving a muscle—the guy looked like a wooden Indian. And Charlie, three-drum Charlie. Three drums and a bass drum. But the Glimmer Twins you could always count on for being the focal point. Didn't matter how good Jim and I played.

For that matter, the band all looked primarily to Keith and Mick, too. I mean, Mick was the singer. I remember we had set lists, but they weren't always followed to the letter. And sometimes the tempos would vary a little bit—they'd count 'em off just a little too slow or count 'em off just a little too fast—but none of that really seemed to be a big sticking point with anybody. We got up there and played somewhere around the better part of an hour, but it was *extremely* high energy. I'd come off the stage just *wringing* wet and exhausted.

It was better than anything I'd ever done before. We were playing hit records, hit songs. I mean, in the past, playing with Bobby Vee and playing rock 'n' roll concerts, the kids would appreciate it; they'd clap and they'd holler every now and then, but it was *nothing* like what they did with the Stones. I mean, the fans just *lost* it. In the States, audiences were a lot more fervent than they were in England. It was definitely a different experience. I'd been onstage with Clapton and with George Harrison when I played with Delaney & Bonnie, but it still didn't reach that same level. It just seemed like a whole different crowd of people came to Stones concerts. There was a lot more excitement. You could almost feel it in the morning when you'd wake up before the show, you'd just know that something was gonna happen. I tried to not get too carried away with it—to not get *too* drunk, not get *too* stoned. Which I didn't. Not *too* drunk, anyway, or not *too* stoned.

What it was, was the shows were primarily just the end of a bunch of excitement that had been building over time. We'd pull into these towns and we'd hear these DJs hammerin' away on the radio, "The Stones are in town, the Stones are in town!" They had Stones watches and Stones sightings—it was real teenage drama. And the DJs would really ride that into the ground: They'd dedicate all day long to playing Stones songs, for instance, and at that time there weren't *that* many Stones songs. I mean they had some, but you'd hear the same ones quite a bit—lots of "Satisfaction," lots of "Honky Tonk Women."

And they had all these contests and stuff. I don't know whether they still do that or not, but back then they did. The DJs and, of course, the newspapers. Whenever we checked into hotels, there was always this throng of fans outside, which always made for front page pictures in the local newspapers, whatever they were. I never knew how they knew, but they knew, man. The fans, the real hard-core fans, they knew what time we were getting in, what time the plane would land, and they'd be at the hotels.

That tour in '72 was very eye-opening for me. At places like Madison Square Garden or the Forum, the audience would average maybe twenty thousand a shot, and then we'd play places like RFK Stadium, outdoor places where there'd be fifty, sixty, sometimes seventy thousand people. But still, I wasn't being asked to do something I couldn't do. I wasn't ever afraid to go up on that stage because I knew damn well I could deliver whatever the hell it was they needed to be done with the saxophone. I could do it with my fuckin' eyes closed. Which they usually were. That's the way I play.

It was so damn exciting. We were all in our twenties then, except for Charlie and Bill. At that point, I'd been playing saxophone for about fifteen years. My graduating class was 1961, which I didn't make, but that's what it would've been, and in 1972, eleven years later, I was playing with the greatest rock 'n' roll band in the goddamn solar system. So that was a pretty quick rise.

Everything about those guys, when I first started working with them, was a surprise to me. I mean, it was a surprise to me that I was even involved. But, of course, once I got to know them, it became hard to ever see them again with the same eyes that other people saw them through—just the reverence in which they're held. I still have a great respect for the music that they've written and for their ability to perform onstage. And they're consistent about it. They had their differences, their own personalities, they went their own ways offstage, but when they came together onstage it really was that proverbial magic, that secret ingredient. I mean, Bill Wyman and Keith Richards were as far apart personality-wise as two people could be, at least on the surface. There was very little social interplay anywhere except on the stage.

And it wasn't very social, actually, it was just what they did, those five guys. I've never seen anyone else do it quite like that. Back then, too, bands were living together, bands became family. Look at the Grateful Dead. But here these guys were, five guys who didn't seem to have a whole lot in common offstage, who didn't even seem to really be that friendly offstage, and yet they had this incredible chemistry onstage.

That unique chemistry was definitely part of the magic, though. Because musically, I thought Delaney & Bonnie and Friends were better than the Stones, man for man. Everybody had this great ability. We had Leon Russell, we had Johnny Cale, we had Jim Keltner on drums—I mean, these are *players*. And Delaney and Bonnie singing. Which is not to take anything away from the Stones. The Stones were and are a garage band, the best in the fuckin' world. That's where they started and that's where their roots still are, in my opinion. I mean, they've evolved, as you'd expect anyone to over forty years.

That was part of the Stones' appeal, I guess: Everybody wanted to know what made 'em tick. Which was why there was a film crew along for the ride on that '72 tour. Robert Frank and his crew had been filming sorta behind-the-scenes stuff of a rock 'n' roll band in the middle of a tour: What do they do? How do they unwind? What kind of people are these people when they're not in front of an audience? He'd been on the entire tour but he'd never really been in our faces—although, after seeing the film, I realized he'd captured a lot more stuff than I remember him being around for. Plus one thing I wish I could forget.

We were in Denver, and I guess Robert Frank thought that his film needed more action. Some *rock 'n' roll* action. Usually, as I recall the general sequence of events, after we landed we'd go to the hotel—I'd usually ride with Keith, we were pretty tight back then—go to our separate rooms, and then I'd generally go over to Keith's room to crack a bottle of Jack or a bottle of tequila, whatever. Just to inaugurate our presence in the building.

So we were in Keith's room and Robert and Danny Seymour, his cameraman, came and knocked on the door and said, "Hey, guys, we need some extra rock-guys-at-play footage, some rock 'n' roll stuff." Keith and I looked at each other and said, "Rock 'n' roll stuff?" and he said, "Well, you know . . . "

We did. There'd been all these stories about rock 'n' roll bands tearin' up hotel rooms, restructuring the rooms, throwing the furniture out, and painting the walls, all that jazz. Well, we didn't have any paint or restructuring tools, so I looked at this TV set, and Keith looked at it, too. I forget whether we actually needed to verbally confirm the idea with each other or whether we just up and did it, but we went and picked the son of a bitch up, yanked it out of the wall, took it over to the balcony, and heaved it over. Ha, ha, ha! Wasn't that fun? Wasn't that rock 'n' roll?

And I have regretted that moment ever since. I tell you, if there's one moment I could take back it would be that moment of throwing that damn television set out the window because, of all the music, of all the solos, of all the records I have played on, out of everything I've done in my life that had to do with rock 'n' roll, that plummeting television set seems to be the most ingrained picture in people's mind of what it is I do. The film, *Cocksucker Blues*, only came out recently—I guess there were some legal entanglements—but somehow that incident made its way into the world as soon as it happened. "Oh, you're the guy who threw the TV set out the window with Keith Richards!" Yeah, but, you know, I also did this and this and this—"Yeah, but you're the guy who threw the TV out!"

But I can't really complain. It was the best time of my life as far as playing rock 'n' roll shows. And the *women*! It was just like pickin' cherries off a tree. You'd walk by any number of girls and say, "Hey, come on, let's go have a drink," and they'd go, "*Ahhhhh!*" I mean, that wore thin after a while, but still, it was always available. They were always trying to get up onstage or grab you when you were going into the hotels and all that. Which didn't bother me that much because I wasn't Mick or Keith or Charlie. I was just somebody there along with the rest of the guys.

Charlie never cared for any of that at all. In fact, when we stayed at Hugh Hefner's place in Chicago, Charlie refused to stay there. Actually, I think Shirley, Charlie's wife, refused for Charlie to stay there, but either way, he wouldn't stay there. I don't know if Bill stayed there or not, but I know Keith and me and Mick sure did, and Mick Taylor. That was a highlight in '72, going to Hefner's place in Chicago and staying there. He loaned us his jet even after we'd burned down his bathroom.

You may have heard this one already, but here's my version of what happened. It was toward the beginning of the '72 tour and we'd come to Chicago, we were gonna play a couple of shows there on June 19 and 20, an afternoon show and a couple of night shows. I guess they were somewhere down by the stockyards because I remember there was a *real* strong smell of cow shit the whole time we were down there. Anyway, I don't know who'd lined it up, but someone had made arrangements for us to stay at Hefner's place while we played there, which, I have no idea who that person was, but I'll be giving them my thanks to my dying day. What a wonderful, hedonistic place to be.

I remember we walked in the door and Hef was there, of course—"Hef," he said. "Call me Hef." Well, all right, you betcha, Hughey baby. He was sitting down in his sunken living room playing backgammon with Buddy Rich, the drummer, who *hated* rock 'n' roll. I mean he had *no use* for the likes of our act at *all*. Which didn't bother anybody particularly, except for him. He was all attitude. I've spoken to some friends, horn players that've put in their time in Buddy Rich's band through the years, and they've told stories of him stopping the bus and firing people and kickin' 'em off the bus right then and there.

Anyway, we were met by Hef's secretary and then Hugh himself got up and shook everybody's hand—Buddy Rich didn't, of course; he just sat there and sorta glared at us—and then the staff showed us to our rooms and apprised us of the amenities: We had twenty-four-hour kitchen service, a wine cellar that was unbelievable, and telephones that you could use to call anywhere in the world for free, didn't cost you anything. I thought that was *really* cool. I'm sure we made some calls, I don't remember to who, but there were a lot of other things to do, we found out, other than hang on the telephone. For one thing, there was a whole dormitory full of bunnies living there. I don't know how many were actually there, but it seemed like a couple dozen or a dozen at least. What can I say? It was a young man's paradise. Everything that you could imagine would happen *did* happen. Over and over.

Altogether we spent maybe four or five nights there, I don't recall. One of those nights was particularly memorable. At least in retrospect. Dr. B., the sex freak, was, of course, in heaven at Hef's place. And Keith and I had long since found out that this guy's sexual appetite was enough of a distraction to him that, if we got him lined up with something, then that sorta freed up his little doctor's bag—he took his eyes off of it, sorta lost focus on it. So then I'd sneak in and get the bag and sneak out with it, which is exactly what we did one night at Hefner's joint.

Keith and I had rooms that were joined by a common bathroom at Hef's place, so after I'd gone out, gone over to the doctor's room, and got the goods, we met in the bathroom. I remember it was real bright in there, so I got a towel and put it up over the light fixture above the sink. And then we dove into the bag of goodies, selected whatever it was we wanted, and ministered unto ourselves, just sittin' there on the floor. Well, we'd ministered pretty good to ourselves, and I remember at one point my eyes started tearing up, there were tears running down my face, and when I looked at

Keith, I noticed that the room was full of smoke, and that's why my eyes were waterin' and shit, but I was so damn *stoned* I couldn't get up off of the damn floor. Then, just as I looked up at where I thought the smoke was coming from—well, where it *was* coming from, the light fixture with the damn *towel* over it—the towel just burst into flames.

Well, as soon as that happened the damn sprinkler system went off, along with an alarm. Meanwhile, we were still sittin' on the floor amid all this action goin' on outside the bathroom because by this time, with the fire alarm goin' off and the sprinklers goin' off, quite a few of the staff had assembled outside the bathroom doors and were bangin' on 'em. And neither one of us could get up to open the damn *door*. So all this shit was goin' on, the water was fuckin' comin' outta the ceiling, smoke was comin' out, the thing was blazin' up, pieces of the towel were fallin' into the sink and onto the floor, and it was just—all *hell* was breakin' loose all over the place, man. Finally, somebody broke down the door or found the key, somebody got the door open somehow, and there's Keith and me down on the floor lookin' like a couple of drowned rats. We couldn't move. We were what you'd call *slack-jawed*.

I remember this one guy came in with Hugh's right-hand woman, and they just looked at us—they saw the medication surrounding us and the floor was all fuckin' wet, and they just kinda looked at us. I really don't remember what came out of their mouths, if anything. I'm sure something *must* have, but if I said what it was I'd be makin' it up. Whatever it was, it just sorta boiled down to a look of disgust and something like, "You guys oughta be more careful." And then they just sorta cleared out, and left us sitting in the debris and the water and the smoke and the ashes.

Hefner, to his credit, never brought it up. I thought he was going to be very, very upset. At the *least*. We didn't exactly fit the profile of his normal houseguests to begin with. He always had these jazzers, these cool types, but not an entire rock 'n' roll band, a bunch of dangerous sons of bitches that were pretty . . . energetic, shall we say. Not bridled by convention. He even loaned us his bunny jet, the black 747 with the rabbit on the tail, which we flew down to Kansas City for a gig and then back to Chicago.

The doctor, meanwhile, was busy in his room the whole time. He didn't give a damn. He had other things on his agenda. He did kinda keep an eye on his bag a little closer after that, but I could still figure out some way to distract him and get to the honey pot. I mean, he was professionally bound not to just *give* us stuff, but he was also young, and he was a chick freak, and here we were in the fuckin' Playboy mansion. So most of the time he saw that there was more merit in letting us get by with it as long as we didn't kill ourselves. He knew our sort of *wants*, and he'd say, "Hey, look, if you're gonna do this shit at least let me give it to you since I *am* a *doctor*." Which, of course, we were happy to agree to.

Ian Stewart was our road manager, although he was also more than that. Stew was the guy who'd come back to the dressing rooms and tell us when to go onstage. No one would go toward the stage until Stew said so. All the promoters would come back there and tell us we had to go on, but Stew was the guy who brought the Stones onstage and made sure that the stage was ready. And he always had such a charming way of telling everyone it was time to go: "All right, my little lovely showers of shit, my little three-chord wonders, time to go!"

The funny thing is, in his boogie-woogie piano realm, boy, he was a motherfucker. He could play. He was really special. But he was always very self-effacing about his piano-playing, he never gave himself the credit. I remember at some point asking someone what Stew's deal was, which was when I found out that he was in fact the original piano player for the Stones. I had no idea because when I came on Nicky Hopkins was playing piano with 'em and I thought, Well, that's Nicky Hopkins, he's the best, that explains that. It's very unusual that you find somebody who was one of the actual founding members of a band take what would seem to be a secondary seat in the organization as opposed to being onstage—I mean, he's driving the guys to the gig. He'd play on some stuff, but not a lot. Even so, I know how well loved he was by Keith and Charlie and Mick and Bill. Of all the bitching they'd do about each other, I never heard anybody bitch about Stew. Ever.

I loved him, too. The first car that I bought in England I bought from Stew. It was a Riley Elf. I hadn't even *heard* of a Riley before. Stew was also instrumental in getting me into the band, or bringing Jim Price and me to Mick's attention as a horn section. I'd met Mick and Keith as a saxophone player, but as a horn section it was Ian Stewart who brought us to Mick's and Keith's and Charlie's and Bill's attention because of the Delaney & Bonnie Southern gospel-rock thing. He was a big fan of Leon Russell's and Dr. John's. The fact that Jim Price and I got to play with the Rolling Stones had a lot to do with Ian Stewart.

Although he wasn't officially a Rolling Stone, Stew still managed to create some perks for himself here and there. When we were doing our first tour in Europe we started to notice, during the Scotland leg, that every damn place we stayed at was a golf resort. Stew was a big golfer. I guess he just assumed no one would notice—"These guys live in another world, drink themselves to sleep, doesn't matter where they wake up, whether it's a golf course or not." There ensued a complaint or two, but he still did it. Didn't change his modus operandi.

Toward the end of June we did a couple shows in Fort Worth, Texas. Stew came backstage to find me and said, "There's some mates of yours waiting for you out front." I said, "What do you mean?" He said, "There are some girls out there who went to school with you." I said, "Really?" I was hoping it was my high school sweetheart eating her heart out. I didn't know who it was gonna be, but I remember thinking, Well, all right, you guys didn't believe in me in ol' Slaton, did you? Look at me *now*. Who's laughing *now?* I even remember what I had on: some black leather-stitched, highly decorative pants and a black satin shirt with birds of paradise all over it. I wanted to say, "Tell 'em all back home what I'm doin'—playing with a *big* rock 'n' roll band. Y'all came and you *paid*." I didn't say that, but that's what I was thinking.

Turned out not to be my high school sweetheart. It was her best friend. Which was OK, too. I liked high school for the most part, even though I never graduated. When I came out they just couldn't *believe* it. "What are you doin', Robert? What are you *doin'* with these guys? Well, now, how did you get mixed up with them? You're not *English*!" They had all sorts of concerns and questions. "What about all this *devil* worship, and all this *sex* and *drugs* and stuff? Well, Robert, what have you *done*? Is it *exciting*?" I don't recall what I said. I just had a few minutes with 'em because I had to go and get ready for the show.

That was really about the only time I ran into old acquaintances because when I left Texas, I *left* Texas. And didn't go back for a long, long time. I'll never forget that afternoon, though: "Well, Robert, your hair's so *long*!" "Yeah, well, that's the way Mick likes it"—yeah, I kinda played that one up, too: "Mick and I, me and Keith and Mick and, you know, Truman." And then I threw in a few movie stars that weren't actually around, but what the hell— "Yeah, I was over at Marlon's the other night, drinkin' beer, you know . . . " "Marlon *Brando*?" "Yeah, yeah, Marlon's a big fan. Keith named his kid after Marlon." Yeah, I used to get some mileage outta that. Hey, why not?

That was the fun part of those Fort Worth shows, the unexpected part. The other thing that stands out in my memory about those shows was something that had been on my mind ever since I saw the tour itinerary over a month earlier. Fort Worth, Texas, was the last place that I'd known my grandfather to have moved to, who I hadn't seen since, I guess, 1960. He'd retired from the Santa Fe Railroad. After my grandmother died, I left and went on the road. Last time I'd even spoken to my grandfather was when I'd called him and he told me the FBI was lookin' for me for draft evasion.

Anyway, a lotta time had passed, and here I was back in the United States with the Rolling Stones, a big-name group, successful.

I was trying to locate my grandfather to kinda say, "Hey, you know all those times you said I wasn't gonna amount to a hill a' beans? Well, OK."

When we got to Texas I called my brother to see if he had any idea where my grandfather was, and he told me to call Debbie, our sister, and she gave me the last known telephone number and address of Harrison Keys. I called the number and it had been disconnected, but there was a referral. So I called the number and this lady answered the phone, and I said, "I'm looking for Harrison Keys," and she asked, "Who wants to speak to him?" I said, "Well, this is his grandson, Robert." And there was a *gasp* on the other end of the line, and she didn't say anything for a while. I said, "Hello?" and she said, "Um . . . well . . . your grandfather is taking a nap right now. Can you call back in an hour?" I thought maybe she was just puttin' me off.

Anyway, I called back in an hour and he answered the phone. I said, "Hey, Granddad, it's Robert." He said, "Well, how are you?" I said, "I'm doin' fine. I'd like to see you." He said, "OK. But you'll have to come right away because I've got something to do," or something like that. But we agreed that I would come over, so I got a cab, gave the driver the address my grandfather had given me, and headed out.

I was really undecided as to how I should be feeling, to tell you the truth. I mean, I *wanted* to see him, but there was always this shadow in the back of my mind. Did he pull the trigger?

OK, let me go back for a minute to the fall of 1960. I was sixteen years old. I was at school one morning when Doc Babb called me down to his office. I thought I was gettin' thrown outta school again for some reason, but he said, "Son, I've got some bad news for you. Robert, your grandmother's dead."

I had just left her less than an hour earlier to come to school. I said, "How?" I thought she'd had a heart attack or something. That's what you attribute to grandmothers. But Doc Babb didn't answer me right away, he just took me back to my house and there was a police car there and an ambulance. They'd already taken my grandmother away. Then, as he pulled up to the house, Doc said, "Now, Robert, I didn't wanna tell you this earlier, but your grandmother died of a gunshot wound."

So I went into the house, and my grandfather was there, and he looked real ashen and shaken. My grandparents' room was right off to the right as you went through the front door, and I looked in there and I saw a big ol' pool of blood on the bed. I said, "What *happened* here?" and the police officer said, "Well, she died of a self-inflicted gunshot wound."

Now, I had just seen my grandmother less than an hour or two earlier, and everything was fine. There was no indication that there was any deep depression or anything like that, so this really shocked me. I said, "*Self-inflicted?*"

Because this is the problem: My grandmother had arthritis so bad she could barely sign a check, and my grandfather had a gun that it took me both hands to pull the trigger on, and I was a lot stronger than my grandmother. So I had all of that in my mind—how the hell did she pull the trigger?—and I couldn't imagine what could've caused such a dramatic mood swing in the short period of time between when I'd left her after eatin' breakfast and goin' to school and when Doc came and got me outta class. I was in shock. She was the only person who I really answered to. And I knew that she really cared about me.

All of this was hitting me at one time—first I find out she's dead, then I find out that it was from a gunshot wound . . . Well, I didn't say anything to the police, I didn't tell them she couldn't have done it because she didn't have the strength in her hands, but it's always been in my mind. But I couldn't see my grandfather doing it either because he just didn't get that emotional about anything.

Everybody was so incredulous at the thought of my grandmother killing herself. There was never any indication that she could possibly be heading in that direction whatsoever. But there was never any indication of foul play, either. I don't know how in-depth the Slaton Police Department's investigation went. I don't think they fingerprinted my grandfather, but I don't know. Anyway, they clearly didn't find enough evidence to conclude that it *wasn't* a self-inflicted gunshot wound. Still, it was just something I couldn't accept.

I hung around for a little while after that, but my grandfather and I were just at the opposite ends of the spectrum, so I left as soon as I could and went out on the road. And aside from talking to him on the phone once or twice, I hadn't been in contact with my grandfather since.

Well, by the end of June 1972, I was 29, and I'd made up my mind to go and see my grandfather. So I did. I saw him for about an hour. We didn't say anything about my grandmother. It was more like me askin' him, "Well, how've you been, how's your new wife . . . ?" I don't recall. Small talk. And I guess, even though my grandfather and I weren't real close, even though we didn't have a typical grandfather-grandson relationship, still, he was my grandfather. I wanted to see him, and I saw him. Then I went to do my gig. I remember thinking, I wish he was here just to see that it *wasn't* the biggest mistake in the world for me to drop outta school and become a musician. But he wasn't there.

OTHER THAN THAT little side trip, the tour was almost like a vacation. Nobody had their old ladies on the road with them, so after the show we'd go back to Keith's room, where there would be much drinking and much smoking and talking about music and listening to music. Keith carried a lot of music with him and I started carrying it with me, too. Back then, we had record players and cassette players. I remember I'd bought this monstrosity that I had to buy a steamer trunk to carry in. It was a record player with jacks to plug in an eight-track player or a cassette player. Hell, you could plug a microphone into it and sing along if you wanted to.

And then I had all these albums. The Chi-Lites were big on our playlist back then. A lot of times Keith would come to my room and Mick would come to my room to listen to music, and my room would be party central. Which was fine with them because it kept people out of their rooms. And it was fine with me 'cause I was feeling real sociable back then. So we'd play a gig and get back to the hotel, and there were always *options*. They would know who we were at the hotels, so if you were lookin' for anything, you could pretty much get it.

Also, too, Keith and I started recording all the shows. We had these little Sony TC-120 cassette players that came in a little briefcase-type thing—that thing I had to pay for outta my paycheck back on the Mad Dogs tour. And Mick was in the mix back then, too. But I remember most of the time things ended up in Keith's room. I'd go to Mick's room, but things always ended up in Keith's room. Still do.

As for everyone else, depending upon the city, there were literally hundreds of people hanging around. Getting into the hotel lobby was a challenge. Not for *me*, particularly—in fact, I welcomed that challenge if it ever came my way. "You wanna take a picture of me? Sure!" Those nights lasted until the next day, and then the next day turned into another night. It was nonstop until the batteries ran completely out of juice and you just finally crashed. Then you got up and took a pill and had a couple of shots and did it all again. Back then, the only real requirement was to *make the fucking gig*. Get your ass onstage in some sort of condition to play, and the rest of the time do whatever you want to. Just *make the gig*.

When you're in your twenties and you go out there in front of tens of thousands of people who're all jacked up beyond their eyebrows—they'd be bouncin' up and down to see you and you'd get out there and they'd bounce even *higher*—it gives you a whole bunch of adrenaline. So by the time you leave the building and get back to the hotel, you'd need to come down somehow. Glug, glug, glug. Plus a little of this, a little of that. And when you'd had enough of this and that, then things finally slowed down.

Around the middle of that tour we had a break, and Keith and me and Stan Moore, this big black security guy, drove through the South, stopping at pool halls and bars all along the way. By 1972, even in the rural South, we didn't look totally alien despite the long hair and the way we dressed, but the minute Keith opened his mouth we were immediately found out. Not necessarily as being the Rolling Stones, but certainly as foreigners. "Are they Freedom Riders?"

I sort of assigned myself the job of Southern ambassador. "You want some barbecue? Follow me. You want some beer? Follow me." With Stan driving us around, chauffeuring this Englishman—Keith—and this Texan, it was a rather eclectic little caravan we had there going through Dixieland.

Other than our short excursion down South, if we were in any given town for a few days, the day didn't start until nighttime. The days were for sleeping. Our waking time was spent listening to music, listening to records. We'd start out by cracking open a fresh bottle of Jack Daniel's and a fresh bottle of tequila, smoking some cigarettes, rolling up some dope, smoking some dope. Wasn't a lotta cocaine at the time, it was mostly just booze and pills. It just seemed to kinda go on and on and on, sorta the same thing over and over. Then you'd play the odd gig every so often. Time was elastic.

That was another thing. We weren't what you'd call sticklers for sticking to a schedule or starting on time. I remember being in the hotel room in New York at, like, nine o'clock in the evening, and we were supposed to have already started at eight o'clock at Madison Square Garden, and Keith and me'd still be trying to get it together. Everybody else would be pretty much ready to go. Keith and I were probably primarily the ones who would still be rousing ourselves for departure—gettin' dressed, havin' another drink, havin' a cigarette, callin' downstairs, sayin', "Where's that fuckin' club sandwich, man?"

And then we'd go to the gigs, finally. Peter Rudge, who was the tour manager, used to come up and plead with us and threaten us and yell at us—he used everything at his disposal to get us off our asses and into the car or the camper and get us onstage. It was like that *all* the time. It wasn't exactly a military operation. Which was OK because nobody ever left. I mean the kids would sit there for *hours*, man.

The most extreme case on the '72 tour was when we played the Boston Garden after we'd been delayed in Warwick, Rhode Island, coming in from Canada. We couldn't land in Boston because of the weather or something, so we had to be diverted to Warwick, a little town that was not set up for international customs and things of that nature. So we land there, and we're sitting around bored and drunk, and at some point there was some sort of confrontation. I don't remember exactly what happened—I don't know who said what or how it all came about, but all of a sudden it was *them* against *us*. They had Keith and they had Mick and I don't know who else, and they were totin' 'em away, man, and *I could not get myself arrested.* Bill Graham was yellin' at me, "Shut up, Bobby, be quiet, we got enough problems as it is," and I was sort of at the door sayin', "Hey, you can't take my friends, blah blah blah blah!" Anyway, they did. And they didn't take me. I really wanted to get arrested, too. I wanted to go where the guys were goin'.

Well, finally they figured out that they had this bunch of very *excitable* young men in their midst and that, meanwhile, there was a riot goin' on in Boston. The mayor of Boston at the time was a guy named Kevin White, and he called the governor of Massachusetts, who called the governor of Rhode Island and said, "Look, man, I've got a riot goin' on down here—I've got the Boston Garden packed with kids and they're gonna tear the joint apart if the Stones don't show up, so *let those fuckers go!*" And through the magic of telephonic negotiations, all of a sudden they were out.

Next thing we knew, we were in these cars and we had a police escort from the Warwick police station to the border of Massachusetts, where we were picked up by Massachusetts state troopers and taken to the Boston Garden. And we had all this shit. Keith carried this bag he called "Doc" with him, and there was always at least twenty years of hard time in that bag, man. So we're whizzing down the highway, having been passed off from the Rhode Island cops to the Massachusetts cops, when it suddenly dawned on us: "Shit, we can do anything we want to and these fuckers can't arrest us!" We had a *free zone* goin' there.

That's not the end of that story, though. Apparently an electrical storm took place in Rhode Island that night, and at the time, according to the newspaper report, that we went onstage, all the electricity went out in Warwick. Lightning had stricken the town's electrical generators, causing all the electricity to go out the minute we went onstage in Massachusetts, and it didn't come back on until we left. Now, I don't know if that's really true or not. I think I remember reading something about it in the paper. But even if it isn't true, just the *thought* of it—"OK, you fuck with us and we'll bring the wrath of Mother Nature down on you and shut you down until we finish playin'"—I always thought was kinda cool.

The ultimate show on that tour, of course, was Mick's birthday at Madison Square Garden. That was a great event. We played there for three days, and the last gig, which was on the day of Jagger's birthday, July 26, was just one big party. We had this great pie fight onstage at the end of the gig. It was somebody's bright idea to bake up several hundred meringue pies—they were just pie shells with meringue, there was no flavoring in them or anything—so that we could have this massive pie fight onstage. Stevie Wonder just got *completely* hammered. That poor bastard couldn't do a damn thing about it 'cause of course he couldn't see it comin'. He just looked like a *mountain* of meringue. And there were cops down at the front of the stage, or security, New York security, and I just had an uncontrollable urge to grab a couple of pies and *let 'em have it*. And I did. And then other folks got the idea, and all of a sudden, man, all the cops were gettin' it. Which they didn't care for that *at all*.

Anyway, that was an afternoon show, and we went from there back to the hotel. I think we were staying at the St. Regis Hotel. And that night they had a party for Mick's birthday, and I'll never forget the bands they had lined up: One of 'em was Count Basie—this was on the rooftop gardens of the hotel, the ballroom there—and the other was Muddy Waters. It was just a wonderful night. All these people were there, Bob Dylan was there, all of New York's rock 'n' roll hierarchy, along with fashion models and writers—all the lip-synchers and finger-poppers that you could imagine. That was one helluva day. One helluva *week*, actually.

The whole tour was probably a little over two months including rehearsal time. Touring is fun when you're on the stage. When

the band's together and you're playing music, it's fun. The rest
of the time it can be very tedious and it can be very disruptive.
Or it can be relaxing. You have those options. You have lots of
options open to you. No one's locked in their rooms, everyone has
the means to go out and go see a movie or rent a car, go out to eat,
whatever. It's gotten a hell of a lot easier. But the times when it's
the easiest are when you're onstage playing. That's when it's easiest for me, and I think it's the same with everybody else. Those
couple of hours onstage make all the pain-in-the-ass time spent
sittin' around suckin' ice cubes worthwhile.

I was a lucky motherfucker. That's the simple truth of it. I've
said it before and I'll always say it: My life was not the result of
any design or master plan. I mean, I always wanted to play rock
'n' roll and make a lotta money and get a lotta chicks—what the
hell else was there to aspire to?—but I never planned it to happen
the way it did. And in 1972, man, I thought, This is it. This is just
it. And in 1972, that *was* it. I don't remember how much money
I was making—I wasn't making millions, I wasn't even making
hundreds of thousands—but it was 1972, and I had a yard a' hard,
a bucket o' balls, and a billfold full of hundred dollar bills. And I
knew Keith Richards and Mick Jagger and could call 'em up. Not
to mention John Lennon and George Harrison and Ringo Starr. I
was shittin' in tall cotton, pal. It was just a wonderful time to be
on this planet for Bobby Keys.

It really hit me that the tour was coming to a close when I was
watching TV and Truman Capote came on *The Tonight Show*. Keith
loves this story, although there's not much to it. For some reason,
while Truman was on tour with us, he took a special interest in

me, which I had no idea was happening, or had happened. So when he shows up on *The Tonight Show* and Johnny Carson asked him how his tour with the Stones went, he just started goin' on and on about *me*. After all the teasing subsided, I remember thinking, OK, that brings *that* to a close.

When the tour ended in New York, everybody went their different ways. Keith and I went on the *QE2* back to England. Keith likes to take a little time to decompress, as he says, after a tour. What better opportunity than to get on a boat? Plus, we had *bags* of shit that we knew we could get onboard a boat—especially since we were VIPs—a whole lot easier than we could a plane.

Five days. A very drunk five days. Very drunk, very stoned. A lotta pills, lotsa booze. We won't talk about all that except to say we got back to England in essentially a semi-comatose state. One night out at sea we were invited to have dinner at the captain's table, where Keith nose-dived into his roast beef and mashed potatoes. *Splat!* I laughed and said something like, "Mr. Richards seems to have retired early." None of the other people at the table laughed at *all*. I thought it was hysterical, but nobody else thought it was funny. Dinner at the captain's table is apparently a big deal on the *QE2*. They frown on people passing out in the middle of it.

Getting back to England brought the tour officially to a close. When it's over and everybody goes home, it's hard. You're used to this routine, day after day after day, where you have a purpose, you have something to do. Even if you have nothing to do, you've got somebody to do nothing *with*. But after the tour, when everybody's gone, there's nothing to do and no one to do it with, so then you go out and try to keep the momentum going. And therein lies the rub. You can't manufacture those twenty or thirty thousand people a day that give you the fuckin' juice to look forward to the next day. All of a sudden, man, it's all quiet. So you go out at night, to bars and clubs and restaurants, so all the people who saw you being wonderful can tell you how wonderful you were when they saw you and ask you when you're gonna do it again, and ask you what it was like. Even when the tour's over, you can keep it goin' for a little while just by being out in public, basking in the fallout, the residual whiffle dust. But it's not the same.

9

T THIS POINT in time, I wasn't making long-range plans. I just figured, I'm here, I'm in the mix, and when there's a move to be made, somebody from the office will call me and they'll send me a ticket and I'll go wherever I'm supposed to be. That's pretty much how I planned my life at that time—somebody from the Stones' office will call me and tell me what I'm supposed to do. And that's what they *did* do. But sometimes there was more time in between Stones gigs than I had the money for, so I had to get advances.

The next Stones album was gonna be made in Jamaica, and I didn't really want to commit myself to anything else. I mean, hey, I was still young, I'd just finished doing the biggest, most successful tour with the highest-profile rock 'n' roll band going, so I wasn't about to go play with Wingding and the Zippos down at the local union hall. I wasn't really looking for another gig. I mean, I *got* the gig, the dream gig. I was just waiting for the next Stones album to come along. After driving a Rolls-Royce, why would I wanna go look for a fuckin' Volkswagen?

That was my attitude back then. Unfortunately, it was a very *poor* attitude. I could've really used my time and position to a lot greater advantage had I not thought that I was mister fucking wonderful and that this shit was just gonna be available to me anytime I wanted it. But this was what I seemed to be thinking at the time. Sure enough, down the road it proved that that was not the case at *all.* I look back and I think, Why didn't I do this? Why didn't I do that? *Because I thought it would never end.*

When you're not on the payroll and you want to continue the Beverly Wilshire lifestyle but you're only geared for a Holiday Inn existence, things are gonna catch up to you. I was on a different page than the rest of the world. I just didn't *consider* the fact that this fuckin' sleigh ride was ever gonna end. And then the snow melted. Nothin' left but mud.

I wasn't totally stupid, though. Richard Perry still called me in for a lotta sessions back then, and generally I'd do 'em. One session that turned out to make something of a splash came about in September of '72, shortly before the guys took off for Jamaica. It was for Carly Simon.

I like Carly. I introduced Mick to Carly. They ended up spending the night together. In *my* hotel room. In fact, it was me who got him down to the session to sing on "You're So Vain." That's him singin' with her on it. I'd already done some sessions with her, and Richard asked me if I could get Mick down to the studio, and I did—this was back when Mick used to listen to me occasionally.

So he came down and he sang with her on that track, and then they ended up going out to dinner.

That song's about Jagger. That's from Carly to me. That's what she said. Well, she said it *could* be about him, that's definitely one way to read it, but that it's really about a lotta people. As a matter of fact, she and Mick sang really well together. I'd be sitting in the control room watching 'em sing "You're So Vain" thinking, Man, there's two serious sets of chops in there.

As it happens, Jim and I didn't end up going out to Jamaica for the recording of *Goats Head Soup*. We did all of our overdubbing in England, at Stargroves—Jagger's house. They took the mobile recording studio out there.

IN JANUARY OF '73 we went to Australia for a month-long tour. Another album had been recorded, but in a lot of ways it was just an extension of the '72 U.S. tour—plenty of rock 'n' roll excess.

We played one memorable—or not so memorable, depending on how you look at it—show at the Oolong Tennis Courts in Melbourne. This was at the height of me and Keith's bottle of Jack a day, bottle of tequila a day, and just whatever else we could get our little hands on to amp up the situation. Well, in Melbourne, I forget where we'd gotten them, but somebody had given us some psychedelics. LSD. So, hey, down the ol' gullet they go, man. This was, like, an hour and a half, two hours before the show.

A couple hours later, things were just *poppin'*—Wow, look at the colors! Reality had taken on a lighthearted, funny-ha-ha sorta slant. Everything was making us laugh. And the way things worked in the Rolling Stones' world was weird enough already: I remember they had this carriage, purportedly used by the queen, hooked up to these horses to take us out to the center of this field— they say it's a tennis court, but it's a field in a big stadium, like a soccer stadium.

We're on our way to the stage in this carriage with coachmen and footmen and everything, along with the rest of the band, and Keith and I were just beside ourselves. And we're not getting a lot of support from our bandmates. Mick just sorta glared at us, silently fuming. We'd tested ourselves before in various states of awareness and pulled it off pretty good, but this was a little more than I'd bargained for.

By the time we were onstage, I thought I'd gotten myself together somewhat—I mean, I *knew* the songs. But of course every-thing looked and sounded different. So we were onstage playing, and suddenly I was overcome by the feeling that I was following my saxophone, that my saxophone was *leading* me around the stage. And it was like a cartoon saxophone, like a wet noodle. I was just tryin' to keep the damn thing in my mouth. This was mid-show. And I'd look at Keith and we'd just wanna laugh. I'd sorta forgotten that there were fifty or sixty thousand people out there.

Eventually, it got to the point I had to focus everything I could on remembering what song we were playing and where we were. I was trying to go into automatic pilot, trying to look halfway nor-mal, even though I didn't *feel* normal at all. The funny thing is, I was in a really good mood. I could hardly keep from laughing. The people out in the audience must've thought I was an *extremely* happy guy.

Well, we made it through, we made it back to the hotel, and then Keith and I were on our own again. This was back when we taped all the shows. So we went back to Keith's room and listened to the tape of the show and it sounded *great*. We were *fantastic*. A couple of days later we went back and revisited that tape, though, and while it was OK, it wasn't as fantastic as we thought it was. Not by a long shot. Maybe the reason nobody ever told us not to take LSD before a show again was because nobody really had to. We figured that out on our own.

Looking back on it, there seemed to be a lotta psychedelics in Australia at that time, and a lotta people givin' 'em to us, because there was another incident on that tour. I honestly don't know whose Ferrari it was or how it all came about, but at one point three different elements—LSD, a Ferrari, and the thought, the *vision* of thousands of bounding, jumping herds of kangaroos—combined to lead Keith and me on a lone mission into the Australian outback.

Everything started at night and carried on over into the day back then. I don't know where we started—I want to say Adelaide, but I'm not sure—but I remember it was a long ways from wherever it was we'd begun to where we imagined we'd find these herds of kangaroos, this vision we felt compelled to chase. In the end, we drove through miles and miles, *hundreds* of miles of back roads, and the only kangaroo we saw was in a pen behind a gas station. That was our big kangaroo sighting.

We ended up sometime the next day at the next tour stop, wherever we were supposed to be. It was one of those things that in theory, at three o'clock in the morning, lit up on a thousand micrograms of LSD, seemed like a great thing to do. Of course, some of the things you thought were gonna be cool didn't really pan out that way. This was one of 'em. One poor, sickly little kangaroo tied up behind a gas station didn't really warrant all that effort.

Keith and I got away with a lot back then. Which is not to say I haven't endured my fair share of talkings-to, though. I have. I've been spoken to in harsh tones several times in the past by tour managers, guys like Peter Rudge. I guess it's because they know they can't go to Keith and say anything because he'll just tell 'em to fuck off. So they'd try to appeal to me because they'd look at me as being the instigator, or at least the enabler. But because of everyone's respect and regard for Keith, and because I was under Keith's umbrella of protection, I got away with a lotta shit that I know would otherwise have gotten me either fired, shot, or thrown in jail a long time ago. Or all of the above.

After the Australian tour, I went back to England. That would've been when I moved from Ascot to Boveney, a little village between Slough and Maidenhead, west of London. I don't remember exactly what precipitated the move. I think we got asked to leave, to tell you the truth. The word "eviction" comes to mind. I'd had some pretty good parties out there in Ascot.

My severance with the Stones came about six months later, on the tour that Billy Preston was on with us toward the end of 1973. What happened was, I had a very bad heroin problem, and I just finally realized it one night. It dawned on me after I dumped my car into a canal in Holland and nearly drowned my wife at the time as well as myself. After we made it back to the hotel, I remember looking at my son Huck in his crib and it made me feel really bad. I thought he deserved a hell of a lot more than a junkie for an old man. After that, the wife and kid went back to England and I tried to stick it out on tour. But I just couldn't make it. So I decided at that point that the only way I could get away from that shit was to literally get away from it, to geographically get away from it, and that meant leaving the Stones. So that's the first thing I did.

It didn't take a genius to figure out that a couple guys in the band were really fucked up. Especially when the other people in the band were not, as Messrs. Watts, Jagger, and Wyman could tell you. That wore on them a lot. It was the least musically involved of any period I've ever spent with the Stones 'cause there was the distraction of heavy drugs. And it was a really big distraction.

My leaving the tour surprised Keith, I think. He was the only one I could call. I felt so, so bad about leavin' the band, but I just couldn't stay and do anything. I was just . . . it was past the point of me being useful. I had no musical validity at that time at all. I was just wrung out. I wasn't a musician, I was a junkie.

Even so, it was not a popular decision. When I called Keith after I got back to England, he said, "Keys, *nobody* quits the Rolling Stones. *Nobody.*" I don't remember if he said "the Rolling Stones" or "my band" or both, but I just said, "Man, I couldn't handle it." I tried to relate to him what my reasons were, although I don't think I was that coherent. Then he said something like, "Well, you better make it count"—meaning, "You better really get off the shit."

I just kind of left in the middle of the night, so to speak, without telling anyone what was happening. There were several attempts made to schedule me a flight to get back for the rest of the tour, but at the time I was just lyin' in bed, still tryin' to score dope, and just feelin' sick, and I didn't feel like goin' on the road. I was so down, man. I didn't feel like seeing anybody. I just wanted to go to sleep. So I didn't go back on the road.

At that time, I was just tryin' to get back to square one. I wasn't really thinking about anything else. I wasn't thinking about my future with the Stones, or even my future as a saxophone player. I wasn't thinking about much of anything at all.

Not surprisingly, given the circumstances, I don't remember exactly what happened from there. I know I talked to Keith several more times on the phone, and that he arranged for me to go to this clinic called Harrow House, outside of London, which he paid for out of his own pocket. I don't remember how long I was in there, but I know it doesn't take as many days to get heroin out of your system physically as it does to get the *want*, the *addiction*, out. The psychological aspect of it is a hell of a lot worse than the physical aspect. The physical aspect I don't remember because the clinic kept me sedated to the point where there was nothing *to* remember. I don't remember any of the physical withdrawal process. I just remember that when I went home I didn't feel real good, and I was still goin' around the house checking for where I might have possibly stashed something.

When you're screwed up on that shit you do all kinds of things you wouldn't normally do. At the time you don't realize how pathetic and how fucked up it is. I'd find old syringes and, even though there was nothing in 'em, I'd think, Well, maybe there's a *trace* of something. I ended up trying to inject myself with water. It's really pitiful when you get to that state.

Ultimately, I had to leave England to completely get away because I still knew where I could get it there, even though I didn't have the means at the time—I couldn't get out and drive anywhere, but I still knew I could get it. It seemed like there was a period of time when heroin was very prominent on the scene in England. Not so much in the States, but in England there was a lot of it in play. So the final step to getting away from it was to come back to the States.

We left England and ended up in Massachusetts, where my wife's parents lived. I stayed there for a couple days, but that was just not working out well at all. I was still cold turkey, and on top of that I was stuck in suburbia. It was not a good mix. So I got in touch with this guy Freddie Sessler. I knew Freddie would help me out.

Freddie was the type of guy who, when he first came to New York, he looked up and saw how many lightbulbs were used on the city streets and in the buildings and thought, Well, I wonder who sells them their lightbulbs, then found out and figured out how to sell 'em cheaper. He was a pretty amazing character. Keith and I met him at the same time in '72. There was a guy named Brad Klein, a friend of ours who used to have really good smoke. He was a nice guy, although he was not too well liked by the other half of the Stones camp, Mick's guys. This was when I started to perceive that the Keith-and-Mick divide was starting to widen some. Mick had married Bianca and was going more for the upper end of the social element, people like Princess Lee Radziwill and others. And of course Keith's inclination was to go more toward the

Terry Southern end of the spectrum, which was also my inclination. Anyway, Freddie was a friend of Brad's.

Back then, anybody who wanted to make an impression or get past the outer guard, so to speak, could work their way in either by being very hip or by having some very hip drugs. And Freddie, who was a short guy with a potbelly, bald on top, and with a big, bulbous nose, fit into the latter camp. He was a survivor of the Nazis from Poland. His family was wiped out. He remembers escaping to Russia. And this, I know, fascinated Keith because Keith always had a big interest in anything to do with World War II. Can't blame him—as he looked at it, when he was a kid, Hitler was tryin' to drop bombs on him every day he could. And Freddie had some fascinating stories about dodging the Nazis.

Freddie was also a real immigrant success story—he came to the States, made several fortunes, lost several fortunes, married women and divorced 'em (which I could relate to that). At first, though, I never believed him. He'd say stuff like, "Oh, yeah, man, when I was a kid I'd hang out at such and such a place and Sinatra would come in, and I got to know Sinatra." I used to think it was bullshit, but I came to find out as time went along that it was all true. I used to wonder why Keith was so fascinated with him—I mean, yeah, the guy had some good blow, but so what, there was a lotta people in this world that had good blow. But it turned out he *was* a very fascinating guy.

He and Keith were very, very good friends. I know Keith really loved the guy because he got really pissed off at him at times, and it takes somebody that Keith really likes for him to get mad at. If he doesn't really like you and you're bothering him he'll just tell you to fuck off and go away, but if he really likes you and gets mad at you he gets very passionate about expressing that. I know he's expressed it to me when I've gotten my hand caught in cookie jars it shouldn't have been in.

Anyway, Freddie Sessler helped me resolve some litigation having to do with a divorce I'd gone through a year or so earlier. He was friends with this guy who was the former attorney general for the state of New York. He got him on my case and it was taken care of. Freddie was a friend. He was tryin' to do some good for me. He was also friends with some other musicians, the guys in the band Mountain, so he made a call and I ended up doin' a gig with them. One show. Got a couple grand for it. I didn't have any money at the time, so a couple grand was a welcome addition. I was also staying with Freddie during that time in his apartment in New York.

Once my legal difficulties in New York were over, I left Massachusetts with my wife at the time and my son and went to L.A. We ended up in Harry Nilsson's apartment. I didn't get there in very good financial condition, so Harry let me have an apartment that he had leased but was no longer staying in. I'd met Harry in London in 1971. Richard Perry had enlisted Jim Price and me to do the horns on *Nilsson Schmilsson*.

Harry and I got along great. He was a bit of a boozer and a really smart guy, very witty. But he was a Yankee. There was always kind of a cats-and-dogs-type situation between me and Yankees. Even so, it didn't take long for me to realize Harry was a bird of the same feather as me.

At first, though, I was suspicious. He'd had the record "Everybody's Talkin'," but prior to that I'd heard he was just some working stiff bank teller or something, and therefore not a worthy rock 'n' roll person, just someone who'd gotten lucky. And here he was in London now—this was back in 1971—and I was gonna work with him. But I'd also heard that John Lennon thought he was real quality talent, and that spoke a lot to me. Still, when I met him I thought he looked like a pasty-faced, pansy-ass bank teller. Turned out he *had* worked in a bank once and hated it, but he'd done a lot of other things in his life, too. And he was writing some good songs.

There was more to Harry than met the eye. When I first met him, I'd already kinda pigeonholed him—he was a non-rocker, got lucky once, OK, I'll make some money off of this session and move on. But Harry was a unique person. He liked rock 'n' roll, he had a really good voice, and his songs were clever. His play on words and his lyrics were clever. He once gave me a book he wrote for his son called *The Point*, which was kind of an *Animal Farm*–type story. There were a lot of levels to that story, a lot of depth. And that was exactly what Harry himself was like.

Anyway, after listening to what he was doing and then hangin' with him after the sessions, we got to be real good friends—to the point where we spent a lotta time together and didn't spend much time goin' home, so his wife was always looking for him and my wife was always looking for me. We kinda got to this stage where anytime we got together we were liable to not show up back home for a couple of days. I can't really explain it, just sometimes you have a connection with someone. Harry had a lotta mischief in him. He kinda took the place of Keith in my life as far as a boozin' partner, a raisin'-hell partner.

We weren't out chasing women or anything like that, though. It was just a lotta drinking. I never remember seeing Harry out womanizing, but, boy, he had lots of opinions on everything else. He was such a smart guy, and he wasn't wishy-washy on any subject. He was an expert in *every* one of 'em. And of course I thought I was, too, so we'd have two experts at the bar, one from New York and one from Texas. And we became even more expert the more we drank. And we did a lotta drinkin' together. We used to describe ourselves as "uncommonly smart, extremely good-looking, and capable of making career decisions." That was our motto.

I really liked being with Harry. I even liked arguing with him, which we did a lot because I'm a rock 'n' roll guy and Harry was not what you'd call mainstream rock 'n' roll as such. But he knew about it. He was a very musical guy. In the beginning, I looked at him as a silky-voiced folk-singer kinda guy like Gilbert O'Sullivan, the guy who sang "Alone Again (Naturally)." That sort of singer. I didn't think Harry had that much spunk in him. But I underestimated Harry's spunk level *enormously*. That boy was *full* of spunk.

And his powers of observation were fantastic. When we used to go out to the pubs after sessions, he'd sit there and make up little songs or little stories about whoever walked in. He'd tell you where they'd come from, what kinda day they were having, and all that stuff. He could translate anything into a story; he could make up some guy's whole life story just by watchin' him drink a beer at the pub. It was complete fiction, obviously, but he'd go on and tell you about this guy's kids, his wife, everything. Harry told great stories.

And not just in the pubs, but in his music, too. Musically, Harry knew what he wanted. He had some very definite ideas. He would go over and over and over his songs until he got what he wanted. He was very passionate about his thoughts.

He got particularly passionate after John Lennon, who he was very close to, got shot in 1980. He got involved in banning handguns, which, despite all of his efforts, never really got banned. Which is too bad. When John got shot, it seemed to me that Harry put everything else in his life on hold and just devoted all of his efforts and time into talking to people and getting people to sign petitions.

Harry died in his sleep on January 15, 1994. He had a lotta complications in his system. Kissed his wife, told her he loved her, and he never woke up again.

BUT THAT'S A ways away from where we were when he gave me a place to stay in L.A.—twenty years away. Back in late '73, he gave me the use of his apartment on La Cienega Boulevard and Fountain Avenue. My next-door neighbor there was the guy from the TV show *Highway Patrol*. I stayed there for several months just trying to figure out what was goin' on. I don't know how the hell I was living. I guess I was doing some work. I had to be. That whole period is difficult to recall. It's like trying to pick up Jell-O—I can see it and it's there but I can't quite hold it.

I've never believed that one drug leads to another. I know the reason I got hooked on heroin is because I took heroin. I thought I *couldn't* get hooked. I thought I could take this shit but it couldn't take me. But I was wrong. That shit took me and whacked me around. I've never known anyone to get out of it without bearing some scars.

I'd gotten off of it by the time I was back in L.A.—I'd kicked it, I'd assumed, for good—until one afternoon when I went up to Marshall Chess's house. Somebody up there had some smack, and I didn't know what it was. I thought I was taking a shot of cocaine, but I wasn't. It was pure smack. So pretty much one of the first things I did when I got myself back to L.A. was I OD'd.

Just a couple years ago I talked to a guy who was there. Apparently, he was the one who called the paramedics. I was very happy to be able to thank him in person. He said everyone else in the house was so fucked-up that day that they weren't doing anything. There's no worse people to be in charge of a situation that requires some clear thinking than a bunch of junkies all smacked-out.

The paramedics ended up taking me to the L.A. County hospital. When I woke up, my only memory for the first couple of days was my Social Security number and Jim Keltner's name and phone number. I didn't know I was married, didn't know my wife's name. I'd call Keltner up, and I guess it would just be a few minutes later and I'd call back, not remembering I'd already talked to him.

One thing I *do* remember is Jim saying to me, "Bobby, I love you, you're my friend, you're my brother, but I can't afford to have you as a friend anymore if you're gonna do this shit." Jim had already had a really good friend who'd overdosed and died, and he just said, "Look, I don't want to have to go through that again." He told me he could never be my friend as long as I was involved with heroin. And that really impressed me. Here's one of my best buds in life—outside of Keith, he's who I'd consider my *best* friend— telling me this.

After that, I never really wanted to take any more heroin. I didn't want to be around people who did, either. Jim really put it in stark, black-and-white reality for me by saying he couldn't be my friend if I kept doing it. So the two people who got me off heroin were Keith Richards, initially, and then Jim for the final push.

When I was recovering from that overdose, I felt jittery, kinda weak, like I just wanted to withdraw within myself and go to sleep. I didn't want to see anybody, I didn't want to be around anybody. I ended up going to this doctor in Beverly Hills, a psychologist, because of my amnesia, which lasted quite a while. Prior to that, my memory was very good. Afterward, especially for certain periods, I really struggled. It brought a lot of vagueness into my life. I don't know if that's a common problem or not. I haven't talked to anyone else who's OD'd and lived. Most of my friends who OD'd were never around afterward to carry on a conversation, unless you believe in the séance method.

The most intense period of amnesia lasted for about six months. I would leave to go to the studio and not remember how to get back home. I'd remember that I *had* a home, but not how to get there. I was going down to a studio called the Record Plant a lot at the time, and I was living up on 4321 Parva Avenue, near Griffith Park, and the Record Plant was just off of La Cienega on Third Street. I was doing a bunch of different sessions. Al Kooper got me to play on a Lynyrd Skynyrd album, *Second Helping*. I'm sure there were others.

After a session was over, I'd go out and get into my car and just sit there and try to remember where the hell it was I had to go. It was very scary, very disorienting, although it didn't make me panic so much as it pissed me off. I didn't panic because I knew what I could do was call a cab and follow him home. I had my address written down, but I didn't know where the hell that address was in the city. So I'd give the address to the cab and follow it, taking notes.

My whole ability to recall things was shot. I'd be introduced to people and by the time we'd finish shaking hands I'd have forgotten their names. That happened literally all the time. Unless I knew someone from before, I had real trouble. Eventually I learned how to deal with it, what I had to do to compensate, which was to relate people to song titles that I remembered. To this day I have a terrible time remembering names.

All of this was happening in the spring of 1974, and it was during that time that I started to work with John Lennon and Harry Nilsson again. Of course, that didn't help my memory regrowth any. A lotta drinkin' and blow. John was hangin' with May Pang, who had been John and Yoko's secretary. Yoko, it was my understanding, had assigned May to be Yoko-in-absentia, to kinda keep an eye on John, keep an eye on the guys who were hangin' around John. And I remember she did put up a valiant effort to stem a lot of the activity that was going on. But, of course, if John wanted to do something, it would've taken a lot more than one little Asian lady to stop him.

There was an inside circle of loonies in L.A. at that time: Keith Moon, Ringo Starr, Jim Keltner—although Jim was never really a loony—Jesse Ed Davis (the guitar player from Oklahoma), and Harry and John and myself. Jesse Ed Davis was known as "Indian Ed" because he was a full-blown Indian. He was also a hell of a slide guitar player, blues guitar player. I first met him before he came to L.A., when he was playin' with Conway Twitty.

Back then in L.A., it seemed like when one guy would finish his project, another guy from the team would take up another project, which sorta kept everyone working. Ringo would do his album, Keith Moon would do his album, John would do his album, Harry would do his album, and throughout that process other things would come up occasionally. Like, I was in the studio with John and there was a producer from San Francisco in there who produced Country Joe and the Fish who thought I'd be perfect for a Country Joe track, which I did. But most of my time was spent with the boys at the Record Plant, or with Harry at RCA. We also spent a lot of time at Martoni's, an Italian restaurant near RCA where we'd while away a lot of our extended breaks, bringing our love and joy and humor to the outside public, who didn't always appreciate it as much as we thought they should.

By now I'd known John for several years, but in L.A. it was different. In England, it was John the neighbor who lived next door. In L.A., it was always John and Ringo and Keith Moon and Harry—somebody. Jesse Ed Davis. Not everybody all the time but it was *somebody* all the time. In Ascot, when we were neighbors, I'd go over to his house on those beautiful English mornings, with all the flowers around, and sit out there in the backyard and smoke some hash. He liked talking about Texas and he liked talking about Buddy Holly and Roy Orbison. In L.A., it was kinda wild. John would later refer to this period as his "Lost Weekend," even though it was closer to a year long. I always thought that was a pretty accurate description.

In fact, John still had a lotta music in him and it wasn't getting done in L.A., and because of that, I guess, he moved back to New York. Which seemed to do the trick 'cause by the early summer of '74 he was ready to record his *Walls and Bridges* album. That's when I got a call from May Pang. John wanted me to be on the album.

I remember the first thing May asked me was if I could leave California behind in California and not bring anything with me, which I knew what that meant: Bring your saxophone but leave all the other shit behind. Because when John moved back to New York, he'd straightened up. He'd gotten away from the West Coast debauchery. Don't be California Bob, be Saxophone Bob. Which was a good idea.

And I did leave all that behind when I came to New York because she told me that John had had enough, and I believed her—I'd seen all of us get way over the top there for a while. She was saying John needed this, that it was time for John to put out a good record.

When I got to New York—I remember being really impressed because John put me up in a suite in the Waldorf Astoria—there was a message waiting for me with a number to call, and it was John's house. He'd just moved into the Dakota. He said, "Well, when are we gonna see you, when can you come over?" I said, "Right now." So I went over there, and that's when I asked John about the album.

Walls and Bridges was gonna be the first solo album he'd put out in a while, the first stuff that he'd written in a while. Anyway, he took his little Sony cassette player and played me the stuff that

I was gonna be working on. He told me that he had all these really good guys lined up for the horn section—Howard Johnson, the Brecker Brothers, basically New York's A team—and he also told me he'd already had the charts done. I said, "Charts? I don't know how to read any charts." And so we went into the stairwell and he took his acoustic guitar and he showed me what to play. He just sat a couple stairs above me with his guitar and I sat a couple stairs below him with my horn and he'd tell me, "OK, come in here." We did that for all the songs I needed to know.

I remember one of the first songs he played for me was "Whatever Gets You Through the Night," which didn't have any horn section stuff on it, but it was something he wanted me to play on. He said, "Well, this is how it starts . . . " and he played me the track that he'd done with Elton John in Caribou Studios in Colorado, which was where that track was done. Elton John was singing harmony on that and playing piano. John said, "So, you're gonna start the song out," and I thought, Uh-oh, shades of Elvis. So I just started playin' around with things and at one point I hit that high note and he said, "*That's* what we gotta come in on. Come in on that." So, OK: I got the first note. Now I only have about three hundred to follow.

But we went on and played it through several times until I got the parts, and he'd say stuff here and there, like, "You know, you don't need to play so many notes, you can simplify it a little bit," things like that. And so, really, although I played the solo on the song—which went on to become the only number one single he ever had as a solo artist during his lifetime—it was John's idea structurally what to do and when to do it.

And then we went on to other stuff, the stuff that had the horn section on it. It wasn't real complicated stuff, but stuff that, if all I'd known about it was how it was written out on staff paper, I would've been at a loss. But since John had coached me in the stairwell of his apartment on where to do what, I was able to go to the studio the next day and, when they passed out the sheet music, I knew what was there. I was really so thankful because it saved me from certain death by embarrassment. 'Cause I couldn't read any music at all.

Only one of a million reasons to love that man. He was just that way. I really miss him.

10

DURING THE MID- to late '70s, I stuck mostly to session work, although early on I did a couple of monumental—as in, monumentally *long*—tours with Joe Cocker.

A few years earlier, I would've just stayed put and waited for the next Stones tour to come along, but at that point in time I was on very shaky ground with pretty much everyone in that band. In '76, it was just more than could be accomplished, I guess, allowing me back into the fold 'cause there were still some very strong feelings about me and my untimely exit. It took a while for the right opportunity to present itself and also for Keith, I think, to get back into more of a leadership role before he could really ever do anything for me. Not to mention that Keith and Mick were at particularly opposite ends of the spectrum at that point.

So with nothing on the horizon any time soon as far as the Stones were concerned, I was left to my own devices, so to speak.

And, too, by 1976, I was single again and living in a house in the Valley with Joe and Nicky Hopkins, who'd left the Stones' touring band in '73 to work on his own stuff. Nicky started playing with Joe on Joe's '74 album *I Can Stand a Little Rain*, and both of us had recorded *Jamaica Say You Will* with Joe in '75. With Joe, it seemed like when the money got short, we'd go out and play. 'Course, the money was always short.

Michael Lang, who was one of the guys who'd put Woodstock together, had become Joe's manager by this point, and he'd gotten a band together for a tour of New Zealand, Australia, and South America, and Nicky and I were available. I needed the work, and I loved working with Joe, so it worked out well for me. We made a deal with Michael for the money and the time and everything, and they flew us to Boston and picked us up and we went to Provincetown on Cape Cod. That's where we went to rehearse.

The rest of the band was a bunch of guys from Worcester called the American Standard Band, and they'd already worked up a lotta Joe's stuff—"Feelin' Alright," "Delta Lady," the usual ones. And they were a good band, I guess, for a bunch of Yankees. Actually, they were really good. But they were very young. It was the first time I'd ever been called "Mr." by any band I'd ever played in before. The drummer's name was John Riley, and he'd say, "Well, Mr. Keys—" and I'd say, "Man, if you call me 'Mr. Keys' again, I'm gonna take your goddamn pants off and throw 'em up in a tree.'" He was a little guy. Then he'd say, "Sorry, Mr. Keys!" and I'd say, "There you go. That's it. Grab 'im, boys." Anyway, I got to be good friends with them. But, God, that kid never could stop calling me

"Mr."—he'd say, "OK, I'll never call you 'Mr. Keys' again. Is that OK, Mr. Bobby?"

I still run into ol' John Riley every now and then. The last time I was in Boston playing with the Stones, he brought his family up. He doesn't play drums anymore. But they were a good band. I liked those guys. They took care of all the musical details. Walking in, I was real skeptical—"How could you *dare* get a bunch of kids out of a nightclub to go play a gig of such importance with such *giants* of the industry such as us?" But those kids did a real good job.

Still, they traveled separately. I don't know if it was a matter of money or if their manager just didn't want to expose them to the potential hazards that three buzzards like us posed. I mean, they were the all-American types, the Pat Boone types, and me and Nicky and Joe were the unholy trinity.

For instance, because we were going thousands of miles unescorted, Michael Lang, had entrusted me to be the responsible person among Joe and Nicky and me while we traveled from L.A. to New Zealand. Well, that was fine with me. It seemed like it would be fairly uncomplicated: We had people who put us on the plane in California, and people who were waiting to take us off the plane in New Zealand. But back then, nothing was uncomplicated.

This was in the age of boom boxes hitting the market. Big ol' boom boxes. And Joe and Nicky were really into Derek and Clive, two characters performed by Peter Cook and Dudley Moore. It was a British comedy thing—they'd get really drunk and just talk about anything that came into their minds. And they had some pretty disgusting topics of conversation. Lots of vulgarity. Really *rank* stuff.

Anyway, we got on the plane and everything was OK until we took off and got going a little bit. We were up in first class, the very front seats, and there were quite a few people behind us. But we didn't pay much attention to 'em. Then Joe got a little tipsy. As did Nicky and as did I. And they started listening to this Derek and Clive stuff on the plane. Well, it offended everybody else on that airplane. It didn't take too long for a few of those choice words to come out, and all these purple-haired New Zealanders returning from their trip to the States were really offended by the language.

So then the stewardess came up and said, "Would you mind keeping the offensive language down?" Well, that was the wrong thing to say because they were gonna do exactly the opposite of whatever was asked of them. Up went the volume, full tilt. Then the stewardess came back with the copilot or somebody, and he said, "You're gonna have to turn that down." Well, there was some resistance to that suggestion, until finally it ended with the boom box being removed and put away.

The problem was, Nicky and Joe had that tape memorized. Verbatim. Every disgusting skit on the tape. And in character. So they just started reelin' 'em off, man. At that point, there was no more boom box to take away, just Joe and Nicky. The stewardess was warning me, "You're gonna have to do something about your friends." I said, "Lady, I'm sorry, but I have no control over 'em." And anyway, I didn't care. They weren't bothering me.

By this time, though, everybody on that airplane was dead set against anything to do with us. So, finally, they landed the plane

in Pago Pago, American Samoa. They said, "OK, everybody, fas-
ten your seat belts, we're making an unscheduled stop." So they
landed the plane and had these cops from Pago Pago come onboard
and escort us off of the airplane.

I had a wad of money with me, so bribery was my first thought
on taking care of the situation—appealing to their weaker side—
and, sure enough, one of the cops and I negotiated a deal. He had
a brother-in-law who had a hotel by the airport, and he was gonna
take us there and rent us a room. The room was something like a
thousand dollars. And to keep from goin' to the slam, I had to hire
this cop and a buddy of his as our security force. Meanwhile, Joe
and Nicky were still in la-la land, they didn't care—"Look, coconut
trees!"

JOE COCKER: *As I remember it, the stewardess or somebody
came up and said something like, "We've got a bit of a
layover, would you like to get some fresh air? There's a nice
lounge outside you might enjoy." So of course we said, "Oh
yeah, sure, why not?" And the next thing we know, we're
on the tarmac and the plane's takin' off on us.*

The next morning I get this phone call from Michael Lang saying, "Stay put, stay where you are!" I said, "No problem. We don't
have any money left." After taking care of the local constabulary,
we were tapped.

A couple of days later—there wasn't exactly a full schedule
of planes coming into Pago Pago from the States at that time—
Michael Lang made it over with a sack of money to pay for the
damages. We had to pay for a landing fee, all kinds of stuff. And

it was *expensive*. It was really expensive. Needless to say, I was never trusted as the scout leader of our little pack again.

JOE COCKER: *Looking at it today, I mean, I was an alcoholic. Every now and then we'd have a pretty good show, but Nicky and I were incorrigible. And he had stomach ulcers, so they gave him all these heavy downers to cope with it, and then he'd drink triple White Russians, which were like, you know, heavy things. Before a show he could put a dozen of those guys away. So sometimes we were a liability, I mean, my God.*

Nicky would always carry around this big case—one of the first guys I knew to do that without looking too effeminate. We'd be in an elevator going down to the lobby or wherever, and he'd pull a screwdriver out of his pocket and he'd go, "Joe—keep a lookout!" He'd take these signs that said, I don't know, DO NOT TAKE YOUR TROUSERS OFF IN PUBLIC *or whatever. Anything. He'd say, "I gotta have that, I gotta have that."*

We should've called him just plain Nick Hopkins, he liked to nick things so much. His house was full of stuff from the tours. I mean, he brought back huge things— lamps. He'd say, "Joe, cover for me!" and I'd say, "Whaddya mean, 'cover for me'?"

NICKY HOPKINS WAS a fucking *genius*. Pure, pure music, man. Ian Stewart, the guy who first played keyboards with the Stones, described Nicky's playing once as "diamond tiaras." Just little gems of music. Nicky was on all of the good Stones records plus the '72 tour and the '73 tour, and then he moved to the States and started to pursue his own interests, his own solo career. Everybody *loved* his playing.

He had some problems with alcohol for a while, but never drugs. I had a sorta self-appointed position of looking after him when we were on tours together. When he was straight, he wouldn't say a word to a butterfly, but when he got drunk—he was highly allergic to alcohol, he'd black out after two drinks—he didn't care what he said to anybody. And loudly.

My mother got him out of a deal in Mexico one time when we were playing in Juarez, at a gymnasium in the afternoon. This was with Joe Cocker. Nicky didn't have his passport or something and he was drunk and he was really, really pissing off the officials. Luckily my mother happened to be there—she was involved in state politics in New Mexico, which made her a diplomat of sorts, and she also spoke fluent Spanish, so she got him out of that scrape. She came in real handy for border incidents.

I knew that Nicky had had a whole lotta surgery done over the years. That boy had health problems from the day that I met him. Very, very frail. Looked liked Linus. I always remember him as Linus from the *Peanuts* comic strip. If you saw him without his shirt on, you could see that his whole lower abdomen and stomach were just a patchwork of scars from past surgeries.

Nicky passed away on September 6, 1994. I remember exactly where I was when I found out: in Boston, on tour with the Stones. I got the call from my wife, after which I called whoever it was that was acting as the responsible party at the time—I don't recall who it was—but I still couldn't find out what had happened, so I called a doctor friend of mine who I'd recommended to Nicky to see. Well, what had happened was that before a recent surgery, things were not prepared properly and he had a bowel or something constrict and turn under. It was a horribly painful way to die.

There's a high mortality rate in this business. It's got its share of drug abuse and the consequences that come from that, but that wasn't the case with Nicky.

Anyway, back on the Cocker tour, we'd made it to South America by the time Elvis died—*"El Rey es muerto!"*—in 1977. In South America, things started to get really weird. In one country, and I can't recall which one, we were met, once we landed, by CIA operatives. And I mean, on the *plane*.

Apparently there was this guy who owned a bunch of radio stations in whatever country we were in who was sympathetic to American oil interests, and he wanted to have his picture taken with us so that younger people could identify with him. So when we landed, they held us on the plane until these guys came on and said, "You go with us." We asked, "Who are you?" and they said, "Government." Blue shirts and sneakers. CIA.

Then they said, "Look, if you need anything, ask us. Don't go out on the street to get it." My ears perked up: *need anything*? So I asked, "What do you mean?" One of them said, "Just don't go out and try to buy anything." I said, "Look—I'm a pot-smoker, and I really do need some pot." He started to say something, but before he could finish I said, "And I've also heard there's great cocaine here." He said, "Please, please just don't even *mention* that to anyone else—leave it to me."

So we got off the plane and were taken to a van—we didn't go through customs, we didn't go through immigration—and they took us to the hotel. I see that there's a guard at the hotel, and I'm thinking maybe I shot my mouth off at the wrong time because I don't see anything materializing in front of me that I'd asked for, and I just told a U.S. government agent I wanted drugs. That might not have been the brightest move. But he did come up with it. He came up with the goods.

That whole leg was sorta surreal. For one gig, we were playing a soccer field there—Luna Park—and I remember walking out onto that pitch, man, and all of a sudden these guys came running at me from three different directions, wavin' their arms and hollerin' and stuff, and I thought, Are they fans? But they didn't look like fans. Anyway, it was because I had walked out onto their soccer pitch. Hallowed ground. Here's this American out there stompin' around in cowboy boots. I loved playing with Joe, but some of those tours were a little *under-planned.*

JOE COCKER: *One of the things I remember the most about Bobby is that he was always really nice, almost fatherly with me. After shows we'd get stoned and we'd always wanna find a bar 'cause we'd always get so wound up at performances, and we'd be somewhere in South America and we'd ask, "Where can we get a drink?" and they'd say, "Nah, you can't get a drink," and we'd be fuming. And I'd always end up with Bobby in a room—either he'd come to mine or I'd go to his—and he'd call up, "Hello, room service? Mr. Cocker would love a sandwich. Is it possible to get a sandwich?" Or he would always try to get me a king-sized bed: "Mr. Cocker requires a king-sized bed."*

Whether there was ever a proper tour booked is a good question. I think we just went out and made a start and thought, I hope this gets better as we go along. Michael Lang wasn't the perfect manager. It wasn't that the tours didn't make any money, it was that Michael would cover his own ass first, and I would just be like, "What happened?" It was really corrupt then. We knew there wasn't gonna be any money at the end of it, so it was sheer adventure.

IN 1978 WE recorded Joe's *Luxury You Can Afford* album. I remember those sessions well because Joe let me contract the horn section, and I got Ray Charles's horn section to play with me. We did it in New Orleans because that's where Allen Toussaint lived. I got to bring in Fathead Newman, Hank Crawford, and Harold Battiste.

This, for me, was big. Very big. I mean, this was Ray Charles's "A" band, which meant they were the "A" players in one of the best bands in the business. I didn't want that session to end, so I kept it going for as long as I could. I'd go down there and smoke some pot with Fathead, and he'd tell me about his times—David Newman, a.k.a. Fathead Newman. Man, he played with some interesting people. He played with Lionel Hampton to get outta Texas, where he was from. He knew King Curtis. But he played most of the time with Ray Charles, on all his significant stuff. And he had his own album out on Atlantic.

I remember asking him where he got the name "Fathead," and he said it was a hipster term for somebody who was high on pot. There was a time when all tenor men had nicknames: "King" Curtis, "Fathead" Newman, "Ping Pong" Austin, "Big Al" Sears, Eddie "Lockjaw" Davis. I never got a nickname. By the time I figured out a good nickname for myself, they were passé. It's probably for the best, though. I was belittled and berated so loudly for even trying—"What, you think you're a 'King' or a 'Count'? 'Count Bobby'?" Plus, if you have to think up your own nickname, it's probably not gonna work. "Baron" Bob? Don't think so.

Playing with Fathead and Hank and Harold was . . . it was religious. It really was. It was like going to church and *liking* it. I mean, here were these guys who I'd listened to and admired for all this time—Ray Charles's horn section was the *ultimate* horn section, and they had been since before the Memphis Horns. They even surpassed the James Brown horn section. They were the benchmark, the quintessential guys. The *men.* In fact, for years and years I kept a copy of the union contract from those sessions with all the guys' names on it along with mine. That was my prize possession until it got lost in a move.

Getting Fathead and the boys to play on the album was also a little bit of a personal thing between Joe and me—or for me, at least—because years before, when we were first playing together, Fathead Newman came up in conversation and Joe knew all about him. He knew horn players. I knew he knew his music and he knew Ray Charles, but a lotta those guys, the singers, they don't know who's playin' the saxophone on that shit, but Joe did. I remember thinking, Well, all right, he's not your typical LV (lead vocalist). He actually knows who's playin' in the band with the guys.

We did a North American tour following the *Luxury You Can Afford* album that I remember being a whole lotta fun. Maybe too much fun sometimes. Because like on certain other occasions where too much fun was had—filling a bathtub with champagne in the Alps, filling a pool with statuary in L.A.—there was usually some sorta bill to pay when the smoke cleared. In one case on tour with Cocker, *literally* after the smoke cleared.

WE WERE PLAYING a leg throughout the South. We were in Alabama somewhere. I remember it must have been sometime in June, sometime preceding the Fourth of July, because there were fireworks stands all over the place, and I bought this big ol' sack of fireworks. I spent a lotta money on fireworks back then. I loved 'em. I love things that blow up. Anyway, I put the sack in my room. We were staying at a Holiday Inn in, I think, Sheffield, Alabama.

Meanwhile, we'd been to Mexico sometime earlier on that tour where I'd bought myself a serape. I'd begun to wear a serape as a part of my stage wear. It had its advantages. For one thing, you didn't have to iron it. This was still with the American Standard Band as the backing band, and they had a couple of horn players as well as guitar, bass, and drums, and then there was Joe, Nicky, and myself.

So we went to the gig. Well, some friends of mine from California showed up before the show, a guy named Ronnie Godwin and some of his friends, and we started drinking tequila. You know, a serape, tequila—hey, what else are you gonna do?

Later, we were onstage playing, having a good time, and I don't know what possessed me, but I decided it would be cool to go out in a blaze of glory, so to speak, so I ran back and forth across the stage, layin' down a line of lighter fluid. I thought it'd light up in one big poof and go away. Obviously, I wasn't thinking too clearly.

Joe wasn't paying attention, he was wailin' away, so he didn't see me going back and forth with the lighter fluid. This was toward the end of the show. I thought I was gonna really light the joint up, really get people's attention. So I pulled out my cigarette lighter and lit it, and—*whooosh!*—it went up. All of a sudden I got smoke in my eyes, and by the time I could see anything I saw that *I* was on fire. The strings on the bottom of my serape had caught on fire. So I was smoldering, and I had my horn strapped on and I couldn't get my horn off and my serape off at the same time, and it was starting to become something of a distraction—this was mid-song, remember, and I was getting flambéed. Finally, Michael Lang just walked over and sprayed beer all over me and put it out.

Well, that wasn't enough, apparently. At some point, I got the microphone and extended an open invitation for everybody to come back to my room at the Holiday Inn for a party. And people took me up on it. So all these people showed up to my room. Meanwhile, don't forget, I had bought a big garbage bag full of fucking explosives. So we were all in my Holiday Inn hotel room and somebody flipped a lit cigarette into my bag of fireworks. This was, like, two o'clock in the morning; people could barely stand up. All of a sudden there was this *Whizz! Bang! Wham! Bam! Blooey!* and everybody hit the door at once and scrambled outside.

By the time I got out there, all the other patrons of the hotel were out there, too, either leaning over the balcony or in the court-yard. Because this wasn't something you could cover up. We had a pyrotechnic fucking *extravaganza* going on inside Room 231. So we were all out there in the courtyard and the room was blazin' up, and by this time the fire department had arrived, and the people who owned the joint were standin' out there and they were lookin' real grim. People were saying to them, "What happened?" and I heard 'em say, "It was that damn *rock 'n' roll* band, you know how they are!" Plus, it seemed like every three or four minutes, even after it had died down, there'd be a stray pop or whistle. Seemed like it took an eternity. Just as soon as I'd think the last one had gone off there'd be a *zzzzZZZZ-POW!*

I knew this was gonna be another problem for me. I felt like I was watching the tour profit literally go up in smoke. So Michael Lang came over and said, "Bobby, this is not cool. The police want to arrest you. They want to arrest everybody who was there. I've talked them out of that, but you're gonna have to buy that hotel room." I said, "What do you mean, '*buy* it'?" He said, "Well, I've spoken to the owners, and they won't press charges, but you have to pay for all damages."

Well, I thought, that's reasonable. I'll do that. How much could it cost to redecorate a Holiday Inn hotel room? I found out. And it ain't cheap. Not only was it the cost of redecorating the room, it was the money charged for every damn day that room wasn't rented. And it seemed to take 'em a *long* time to renovate that son of a bitch. When I finally got presented with the bill from Michael Lang, which was five figures, I told him I damn well better get a plaque on the door saying THE BOBBY KEYS MEMORIAL SUITE. I don't know whether or not they ever put the plaque up. I'd like to think they did.

The '78 North American tour was the last tour I ever did with Joe, but we've always kept in touch over the years. Not long after that tour, I stayed with him for a while when he was living in a house on Jane Fonda's property in Santa Barbara. That's when I talked him into buying a satellite dish so I could watch the Dallas Cowboys play football. He didn't care about football at all—he liked soccer and cricket—but he got it anyway. So we got a guy up there on a Sunday to install it and point it toward the satellite, and finally found the football game, but we could only get it in Spanish.

It was also at that house where, one morning, we were sitting in the kitchen next to an open window doin' a little blow, and Jane walked by—she was outside watering the morning glories or whatever—peered in, and said, "Are you still doing *that*? I thought that went out of style."

She was probably right. I saw Joe not long ago and he's doing great—healthier than ever, still doing worldwide tours, happy, successful. But looking back, I sometimes can't help but wonder how the hell people like Joe and I are still sittin' upright, perpendicular to the horizon, forming complete sentences. Because at one time, it didn't seem like we would be.

Even so, I always think of those days as happy days. Maybe that's because I've always liked Joe so much as a person. I mean, the music's always been good—sometimes it was better than others—but the music was only part of it. Playing with guys like Nicky and Joe, that's what made those times special.

DURING THE COUPLE of years I was off getting clean and touring with Joe, Keith Richards was battling his own demons. That whole time, I'd think of Keith and I'd wonder, but I had no idea how to even go about the first stage of getting in touch with him, or what I would say even if I did. Because I knew from the word that I'd had that he was going through his own period of rehabilitation or whatever. I knew I'd hear from him again, I just didn't know when.

Sure enough, later on that year, Keith gave me a call. He was down in Jamaica with Freddie Sessler. Freddie had gone to Jamaica to start a clinic that did research on using rattlesnake venom to develop a cure for cancer or something like that. And Keith was living there at the time, so he flew me down to join him. I used to end up at Keith's house in Jamaica every once in a while during that period. He'd call up and say, "Hey, get your horn, Jane'll get you a ticket, come on down." And that's what I'd do.

At that time, Keith was absorbing a lot of the Jamaican style of music—not the commercial stuff, but the really backwoods stuff. A very basic style. In fact, he recorded an album of it years later: *Wingless Angels*. Anyway, back then, he'd have these guys come and we'd sit around the pool at night and play this stuff *forever*. Those nights involved lots of pot.

Keith was always playing Buddy Holly songs, always singin' 'em, and somewhere in one of those conversations I remember saying to him, after the subject of J.I. and Joe B. came up, "Well, hell, let's go visit 'em." So we did. Patty Hansen, Jane Rose (Keith's personal manager), Freddie Sessler, Keith, and myself. We took a Learjet from Jamaica to Nashville. J.I. Allison, Joe B. Mauldin, and Sonny Curtis and their respective wives all met us at the airport, and we went out to J.I.'s place in Lyles, Tennessee, for a while, four or five days or so. During which time there was a lotta singin', a lotta talkin', a lotta drinkin'. Keith and J.I. loved just sittin' around and singin' and playin' the guitar. J.I. had one of the original guitars that the Everly Brothers used. In fact, there's a picture of Keith asleep with it in his arms.

Keith Richards in rural Tennessee was about as interesting a sight to see as you'd think it would be. One night, we all went out to this local restaurant and the locals couldn't get over the fact that here he was sittin' in there. And of course, J.I.'s wife, Joanie, was real nervous 'cause we're smokin' pot out in the open, had a big sack of cocaine, goin' in and out of the bathroom, I mean just wide open about it all—and their friends were the local cops. Very liberal cops, it turned out.

Another thing I remember about that trip was Elvis the pig. J.I. had a pink-and-black pig named Elvis, and Patty and Jane became attached to Elvis, this cute little pig. Well, the next time we saw J.I. and Joe B. and those guys was in Houston, and I don't remember if it was Jane or Patty, but one of 'em asked, "How's Elvis?" and J.I. just patted his stomach and said, "He tasted real good." They were horrified. But, you know, J.I. lives on a farm, and that's what you do on farms, you raise critters and you eat 'em.

J.I. ALLISON: *Bobby called one night and said, "Hey, man, we were gonna come out to see you, we just got through doin' this album." This was in '78, something they did out in Jamaica or somethin'. They were gonna just come through and hang out a day or two. I loved it. Keith liked*

shootin' guns, and I had what we call a "snake charmer"—
this fourteen-inch shotgun with a pistol grip. He liked that.

That was just a whole new lifestyle to me. I mean, when
we were at the peak of our success with Buddy, we didn't
have a roadie. Didn't know what they were. Didn't have a
monitor system, either; we'd just play like we played in the
garage. So all that stuff was beyond me.

But they did leave some nice notes layin' around.
When Keith came, he brought me a bottle of Château
Latour, 1934. I still have it. I wouldn't open it for a million
dollars. It's the wine that Hitler hoarded when he was in
France. When I was outside at one point talking to Bobby, I
said, "Man, that must've cost over a hundred dollars," and
he said, "Fourteen hundred dollars."

That's just outta my way of thinking, you know? I mean,
when we did a four-month tour in 1957, we were with Fats
Domino, Eddie Cochran, Buddy Knox—everybody who
had a rock 'n' roll record out. The Drifters, the Platters.
And we'd do, like, two songs, and then they'd say, "And
now we have . . . " Everybody did these package shows:
"The Greatest Rock 'n' Roll Stars of '57" or somethin' like
that. We made a thousand dollars a week and there were
four of us. And then they'd take the commissions outta
that, and that made $800 a week, so it was $200 a week to
buy your own hotel room and all that. 'Course, hotel rooms
were cheaper back then.

IN 1979, THE New Barbarians were formed. The New Barbarians consisted of Stanley Clarke on bass; Joseph "Zigaboo" Modeliste from New Orleans, from the Meters, on drums; Ian McClagan on keyboards; Keith and Ronnie on guitars; and me on sax. We were introduced onstage by Dan Aykroyd, a guy who's always got good pot. He's a big, big pothead. I've always liked him even more for that. He's a good guy. Very knowledgeable, music-wise.

The Barbarians were Ronnie's band. Keith joined at Ronnie's request. When those two are clickin', they're great together onstage. They have a kind of older brother–younger brother relationship: Keith's the older brother, Ronnie's the younger brother, and sometimes it's kinda like, "Get away, kid, you bother me," although Keith has a great respect, I know, for Woody as a guitar player and as a person. Woody's a great person. And a really talented fella. He's a hell of an artist.

The first gig the Barbarians did was Keith's "Get Out of Canadian Jail Free" gig. We had to play this gig in Windsor, Ontario, as a part of Keith's deal with the Canadian government to get him off the hook for a drug thing. The Stones played, too. This girl in Canada, Rita, who still keeps in touch with Keith, and he with her, thought of a simple solution that all the high-powered attorneys missed, that went right over their heads, and that was to do a benefit for a charity. And being blind herself, her charity was for the blind. That was the first gig the New Barbarians did.

That band, from the get-go, was put together to be a one-shot deal. One tour only. But we had some good shows. The New Barbarians were the only band to have ever sold out Madison Square Garden having never had a record or a record deal. There was never an album under the name the New Barbarians. There was a live album, a bootleg, but never an official album. We were on the road, really, to promote Ronnie's new solo album, which was *Gimme Some Neck*, and also to put a little money in everybody's pockets. We did a tour of the States and we did one gig outside of London, in Knebworth. And that was the last gig that the New Barbarians played. We played that one without Stanley Clarke. They got another guy to play, Phil Chen, a bass player who'd played with Rod Stewart.

The Barbarians was a fun gig. It started out kind of under a cloud, though, because at first the promoter was selling the show by advertising that Bob Dylan was gonna be there, that Rod Stewart was gonna be there. He was an idiot. Ticket sales weren't up to where he thought they ought to be, I guess, and he was afraid he was gonna lose his ass, so he decided to just start sayin' shit. It was crazy.

I forget where exactly this happened, what city we were in—maybe Detroit because I think we were staying overnight in Wisconsin—but it was sometime toward the beginning of the tour. Anyway, we got to the gig, and usually you could kinda take it for granted at this point in time that people were gonna like you, but the audience was clearly not as receptive as they normally were. Plus, they kept hollering out, "Where's Bob? Where's Bob?" I remember thinking, Well, *right here.*

We had no idea what was going on. It was really, really confusing. The whole thing was a drag, and the papers really slammed everybody, and it pissed Keith off to the point of distraction. Woody's manager was a guy named Jason Cooper, a big ol' beefy guy, and when Keith found out what had happened and how come the papers were saying all these bad things, he grabbed Jason Cooper and put a knife to his throat and told him to get the fuck out and if he saw him again he was gonna put a bullet between his eyes. And you know what? There was a helicopter out there to Wisconsin within thirty minutes. He was on that helicopter and he was gone and we never saw him again.

There are some things you just don't do. There are some things that just really piss people off, especially people like Keith. Imagine how it made him feel when someone said, "You know, we weren't getting enough ticket sales from just you guys, so . . . " Well, Woody's manager didn't say that outright, but by doing what he did, he essentially said, "Well, the tickets aren't moving and the promoter's starting to get a little edgy, so maybe it would help if we said mystery guests might be coming in, Bob Dylan might show up, Rod Stewart might show up, etc." Which people would've believed because of the Faces connection between Woody and Rod Stewart and because Bob Dylan wrote "Seven Days," a song that Woody had recorded, and they'd been in the studio together. But no matter what the connection, if you wanna know how to piss Keith off, and me, too—hell, any musician I can think of, really— that's one of the ways to do it.

Never did play a live gig with Bob Dylan. Or Rod Stewart. I've played in the studio with Rod, though, and I've been to a live gig of his in Paris. He had a great band. But he is really a Scotsman. Whereas with the Stones, you'd have all these trimmings and whistles and bells, wine tables and wine captains and all this shit, Rod's got the big ol' economy thirty-two-piece Kentucky Fried

Chicken tub of wings and legs and Mexican orange soda pop. Really good band, though.

While the rest of that tour was mostly a whole lotta fun, one other unfortunate incident did come to pass. On a stop in L.A., we recorded a track at RCA that turned out to be the last track that Lowell George, who'd just left his longtime band Little Feat, played on before he died. It was for Zigaboo Modeliste's solo album. We did a song called "Fingerprint File," which was done by the Meters originally, but Ziggy wanted to cut it for himself, so we went into the studio and recut it with Stanley Clarke and the rest of the guys in the New Barbarians and Lowell George. Just a couple of nights later, he was dead. I don't even know if that record was ever released.

Aside from that, though, it got me pointed in the right direction. Everything I did back in those days that involved Keith I hoped was a step back into the fold. It was like, All right, if I can get through this New Barbarians tour without shittin' and fallin' back in it, then that'll make the next step, whatever it's gonna be, easier. That was the thought process, anyway.

11

THE '80S, BY and large, were not my best years, to tell you the truth. But there were some bright spots. I met my wife Holly in Albuquerque in June of '84, while I was visiting my family—I'd run outta money and needed a place to stay, so I went back home and sponged off of my mom for a while—and then we moved to Texas, where I hooked up with Joe Ely. Joe's one of my Lubbock buddies. Actually, I wasn't familiar with Joe from home because I was a couple years older than him and had left town before he got started, but I remember him doing a gig with the Stones in Arizona. Ian Stewart came backstage and said, "Hey, Bobby, there's some of your lot here, some band from Lubbock. The Joe Ely Band."

Didn't ring a bell. But I'd heard of some of the guys who were in the band. Lloyd Maines was the steel player. So Ian Stewart took me down to their dressing room, and here's all these guys, real friendly. 'Course, I was with the Rolling Stones at the time—this was when I was taggin' along on the '81 tour, playin' shows when I could—so I was like, Here I am, Wonderful Bob. Which I wasn't really all that wonderful back then, come to think of it. I was still a ways away from workin' my way back into the fold, although I didn't know that at the time.

Anyway. I didn't really know what to expect when I listened to 'em open for the Stones, but man, they were great. They had so much energy, Joe had so much energy onstage. It was Texas rock 'n' roll full tilt. West Texas rock 'n' roll with a steel guitar. I didn't have time before the show to hang out with them for long, but I listened to 'em onstage and I was really impressed. Then by the time I went onstage with the Rolling Stones and we were done, they were long gone.

The next time I saw Joe was back in Lubbock. There was a fella called Jay Boy Adams who invited me to come to Lubbock and play at this event that Joe had taken a major part in organizing. It was called the Tornado Jam, in response, if I remember right, to a tornado that had done some damage to Lubbock some years earlier. This was the third and final year of the event, May 11, 1982. And that's where Joe and I sort of rekindled our friendship.

Right about that time the Stones went on hiatus for a few years. Time off from the Stones always kinda put me in a popcorn machine—there was no telling where I'd end up. Anyway, this time I ended up in Texas, back in Lubbock, stayin' with this fella Davis McLarty, a drummer who played with Joe. We had a little band there called the Ace Liquidators, which included some members of Joe's band—Joe had sort of a floating cast of musicians, I guess depending upon availability or whatever.

After several months in Lubbock with that band, I headed out of town for a bit, I don't remember exactly why—it might've been to visit Keith in England; I know I spent some time with him there that year—and while I'd been gone, the band up and moved to Austin. So when I got back, that's where I moved, too.

It was in Austin that I got back together with Joe and did some recording out at his house and then went on the road. One of the results of that tour was the CD *Live From Fitzgerald's*. He'd bought a brand new van for us to ride around in. We went all the way from the South up to Chicago and then points east, to the coast, and then on back to the West Coast. During that time, the band got very good. It was a hell of a band. It's called the Reunion Band now. I still play with 'em every once in a while.

I'd spent a lotta time workin' my way back down the ladder over the previous couple of years. Hell, I ended up goin' all the way back to where I'd come from—*literally* all the way back to Lubbock—to see if I could get outta there again. And Joe, for me back then, was a rung or three back up the ladder. With Joe, I was playing places like New York and Chicago again, and not in the balcony of a Chili's restaurant in El Paso, Texas, which I had had the misfortune of playing in the recent past.

The thing I really admire about Joe is his work ethic. He gets up onstage and no matter how many people or how few people are there, he gives it his all. For the first time in a long time, it rekindled the spark again for me and it was really fun to just play. Plus, it's comfortable to be around him 'cause he's Lubbock. Even though I didn't know him at home I could smell it all over him, just like I can smell it on myself. Lubbock leaves its mark.

Joe had an interesting life I found out as I got to know him. He ran away and joined the circus when he was a kid. That, on top of him being from Lubbock and being a really good singer and songwriter and the way he presents himself onstage—I've got a lot of respect for the guy. I don't think we've ever had a cross word, which is very unusual, to know someone for as many years as I've known Joe and never have a misunderstanding or anything like that.

We were different in a lot of ways, though, Joe and I—it wasn't like I'd call him up and we'd go hang out at a bar. But we were close on the road. I remember one morning in Texas after an all-night drink-a-thon, he was trying to demonstrate to me how you could write a song about anything. I told him I'd love to be able to write songs, but all my lyrics end up being endless verses of tragedy and triumph, not really songs.

He said, "OK, look around the room and pick something out." I pointed to my saxophone, and he immediately started writing a song about it. Its name, of course, was Elmer, and in no time he came up with some really good lyrics. He was writing from the point of view of the saxophone: it getting up out of its case, stretching, getting ready to go to a gig. I don't recall exactly what he wrote—as I said, it was the morning after a long night—but he proved his point, at least when it came to his own songwriting abilities.

I played with Joe at a time when it was really important for me to have a gig. I was *way* between gigs with the Stones—Keith and Mick were really not getting along well, which meant the future looked kinda grim when it came to any Stones stuff—so I was very happy to be playing with Joe. The music was really good and the band was really good. The traveling got to be a little tedious—seven guys in a van, and I was in my forties. Probably had a minimum of a hundred dates that year. But I was lucky to be along for the ride.

I remember we had one little adventure somewhere in Arizona. For some reason the club owner at one gig didn't come up with the deposit or the rest of the money we were owed before we were supposed to play. We'd set up there, did the sound check and everything. This was on a long road trip, and I remember this gig was at a little joint, sorta substandard, and David Palse, our road manager, went to get the rest of the money and the guy didn't have it.

Well, we started sayin' the hell with this, let's pack up our shit and go. But the guy wouldn't let us pack our shit up. And he was a big ol' guy: "Oh, no, that equipment's not goin' anywhere. You guys are gonna play here tonight." It was our equipment, but when you've got some four-hundred-pound Bubba there with a double-barreled shotgun settin' just off of his elbow, you don't have much of an argument to come back with.

Now, I'm not quite clear on the exact details of what followed. Some say it was me, but I don't remember doing it, and it seems to me I would remember. Either way, somebody called the fire department and reported a fire at the club, so when they came out there, we had a reason to get our instruments outta there. By the time the dust settled, we were gone.

I really liked playing with Joe a lot. 'Course, it was a different situation—it wasn't the Stones, it wasn't Joe Cocker. Smaller audiences, everything was scaled back. We had six guys and a roadie traveling in a van together, which was certainly a different slant on things. No more private jets and limos. But, hey, man, it was a good band, it was good music, and everybody was really cool, so I didn't really miss all that. I missed the *money*, but otherwise it was really good for me. It got me into playing again on a really regular basis, which I hadn't done for a while. It was very therapeutic for me.

Plus, Joe's just a good guy, a responsible guy, and that's always a good type of person for me to be around. I don't know, it seems like, for some reason—and I missed out on this—but most of the musicians I know from Lubbock who're still alive and still playing are very stable, solid citizens in their lives, and I'm still blowin' around in the wind up there somewhere.

TOWARD THE END of 1987, I got a phone call from Ronnie Wood's manager. Ronnie and I have always been friends and have always had a mutual respect for each other. I'd known him for years before he became a Stone. Ronnie's one of the most likeable, easiest-goin' guys you'll ever meet in your life. Plus he is a musician's *musician's* musician and he's a hanger-outer's *hanger-outer's* hanger-outer. There's no reserve about him. What you see is exactly what you get. It's always balls-to-the-wall fun and rock 'n' roll—if you wanted that on your menu, you'd see him.

Also, too, he's one of the sweetest, most understanding guys. Talkin' with Woody, it always impressed me how much he loved his family, his brothers, his sisters, his father, his mother. He spoke about 'em with so much love and credited them with where he got his direction, his love of music, and also where he got his sense of humor. So he's always had this quality about him, this love of family, but also this wild, abandoned, toss-the-dice-and-see-where-they-land thing, too.

Anyway, I was living outside of Nashville at the time, at J.I.'s place. Ronnie's manager said Ronnie wanted me to come to Miami Beach because he was opening up a club, and the grand opening was slated for New Year's Eve. This was just a few days prior to that. So we made arrangements and got the funding for me to make the move, and I put my family in the car and we drove down to Miami Beach.

They were refurbishing all the old Art Deco buildings and hotels at that time, and they put us up in this hotel that was half-finished and half-not-finished. It was kind of an uncomfortable situation, but it was OK. We were there to play at the grand opening of Woody's new club, which itself wasn't quite finished yet. This was gonna be great fun. I hadn't had a gig in a while. I'd been living in Nashville, Death Valley for sax players.

I didn't see Ronnie until a couple of days after I got there. The only person I knew there, the only person I recognized, was this guy Big Joe, who'd done security for Keith and had been on some Stones tours. I'd spoken to Woody on the phone, but I couldn't seem to connect with him in person. He seemed to be otherwise occupied. There were some very nefarious characters involved in this shindig as I came to find out, and as Woody came to find out.

Well, rehearsing for the gig kept being put off and put off and put off because nothing was getting finished. But while we were waiting to rehearse—or, more accurately, while we were waiting for the place to get finished because they didn't finish it until the day of the gig—I finally saw Ronnie. It was great to see him, and he was glad to see me. We finally got it together and we played the show, New Year's Eve 1987, and it went great. The next day, Ronnie had a proposal for me.

I said, "You got a nice club here, Ronnie, what're you gonna do with it?" He said, "Well, I wanna feature live music." He had a point—there was no place in Miami Beach at the time that had much in the way of live music. Then he told me he couldn't stay in the U.S., that he had to leave for tax purposes every so often, and that he wanted me to keep an eye on the place for him and be in charge of the live music. Suddenly I had a gig.

When Woody left because of his tax situation, I stayed on to be talent coordinator of Woody's on the Beach. Director of bullshit. And I directed a *lotta* bullshit. Johnny Starbuck, who'd been a longtime roadie and guitar tech for the Stones, was hired to be my sidekick, my assistant talent coordinator. And the first thing we set out to do was put together a house band.

The problem was, we didn't know any musicians in Miami. So Starbuck and I would go out on these talent hunts. We'd get the paper and see what places had live music and go out and make a few contacts. And one contact would always lead to another—you can't meet a musician without him telling you about two more. And that's how we got the band together. Woody's Orphans, as we were called.

It was a pretty good little band. Two Cuban drummers, a guitar player, a blond-headed biker type on bass—good players, good guys. Once that was done, Starbuck and I had to figure out something for the band to do.

That's when it hit me: I'd played a gig somewhere with Jimmy Markham where it was talent show night. We'd play a set, and then for the second set people from the audience would sit in. They'd come in before the show and sign up on a list—"Joe Blow, I play guitar and I wanna sing my own personal song" or whatever, and if it was something the band knew, we'd play along with him, or if it was something we didn't know or that he'd written, he'd play it himself. We took the worst night of the week, which traditionally was Monday night, and we promoted that kind of a theme with it. And it got to be pretty successful. Monday nights turned out to be lined-up-down-the-street time.

But even as things got going music-wise, there was still something kinda off about the place. Keith never did like Woody's involvement in that thing. Woody kind of invested his presence— he was the face of the club, Woody's on the Beach. There were various rumors going around as to where the actual funding was coming from—somewhere *south* was the rumor. I don't know. But I have very strong suspicions. I was always paid in cash, in hundred-dollar bills. I never had to sign a receipt. And I'd get paid sometimes at two or three o'clock in the morning. Or if I ran out of money, I'd just ask for more and they'd give it to me.

I could never get it straight how much I was being paid. Not only could I never get straight how much I was being paid, nobody could ever tell me what I was supposed to *do*. So what I did, aside from the weekly band gig, was sit in my hotel room with my wife and kid and order room service and go down to the bar. And since I didn't always have cash on me, I'd just put it on the bill. I ended up puttin' a *lotta* shit on that bill.

Personally, I think it was a place where they brought drug money in and laundered it. That's exactly what I think it was. I'd be an idiot to think it was anything else. I mean, I never got paid with anything like a payroll check, never had any taxes taken out, always got paid in cash. Not to mention there was an extraordinary amount of cocaine around at the time. There was a section of the club, a private part of Woody's, where you had to have a membership to get in—pretty pricey—and it was one of those things, right in the middle of the *Miami Vice* period, everybody was wearing bright linen jackets with the sleeves rolled up and lots of chains, and just coke everywhere. I never did that. Wear the bright jackets with lots of chains, that is.

Not long after Woody left the country, the money began to slow down. I'd have to call people several days in advance to try to track the sons of bitches down to get some money. It finally got to the point where I said, "Fuck it, this is just not any fun anymore." I was getting into some very bad habits, stayin' out forever and ever and ever, hangin' out in some really seedy places for all the wrong reasons. Everything was readily available anytime, day or night. Whatever you wanted, life or death, it was there.

Fortunately, that's when Keith called. He was going into the studio to do some recording for the first X-Pensive Winos album, *Talk Is Cheap*, his first solo work. He brought me to New York to play on that, which I was very happy to do. The session consisted of me playing on a couple of tracks, and then Keith and the Winos—they were already the Winos, they'd already recorded the record except for the last couple of things, which I was involved with—headed to South America. They had a gig in Argentina, and

I couldn't go for some reason. I think by the time they asked me it was too late to get the permits and shit. When they got back, Keith called and said, "OK, we're gonna start the States tour, and we're gonna be rehearsing in Atlanta and we want you to be there." So I resigned my position at Woody's on the Beach and headed to Georgia.

But before I left Miami behind, Starbuck had a surprise for me. When I did the session in New York, Keith had wanted me to play baritone, and I didn't have a baritone sax. I had to rent one. So before I headed out on the road, in a grandiose gesture, Starbuck said, "Aw, hell, man, let's go buy one. Where do you buy a baritone sax?" I said, "New York." He said, "Let's go." So, out of his own pocket, Starbuck got us two first-class tickets from Miami to New York and bought me a brand new baritone sax.

The X-Pensive Winos were a great band. They were multitalented cats. Charley Drayton was the bass player, but he was also the drummer on some stuff and a keyboard player. Steve Jordan was a drummer and a keyboard player. But when everybody was at their assigned positions, it was Ivan Neville (son of Aaron Neville of the Neville Brothers) on keyboards, Charlie Drayton on bass, Keith on guitar, Waddy Wachtel on guitar, Steve Jordan on drums, and myself on the saxophonic device.

Waddy Wachtel had done a lotta stuff with Stevie Nicks and Linda Ronstadt, and he played with Jackson Browne and a lot of other people. He was part of the sort of early guard of the California/West Coast/Texas-transplant (although he's from Brooklyn) scene. I love him. He's a funny guy. Steve played in the very first *Saturday Night Live* band, when *Saturday Night Live* was really in its heyday. Since then, he's done some producing and he's played on a shit-pot load of records in New York. He's at the top of the A-list of drummers.

By the time I hooked up with the guys in Atlanta toward the end of November 1988, I didn't have much rehearsal time with 'em because I didn't play any of their first gigs in Argentina. But then, I only played on two tracks on the album, so a lotta their songs didn't have any sax on 'em. Which means being up onstage with nothing to do for certain segments of the show.

I remember addressing the issue with Keith—"Well, what do you want me to do?"—and he said something like, "I don't care. Dance? Or, I don't know, play some rhythm stuff." Well, I wasn't gonna dance. So he gave me this little egg, this shaker, and said, "Take this." So I did, man. I took that egg and I thought, OK, I don't think he's doin' this just to piss me off 'cause on the record you can hear a very definite *chukka-chukka* sound, so I guess he really wants that sound in there.

So, OK: When you're playin' an egg onstage, and you got Keith and all these other high-powered cats just blazin' away, and all you got is this one damned egg with some sand in it, you're kinda *under-gunned*. But I'm a team player, and this was my first show with the Winos, so I thought, OK, man, if I am destined to be an egg-shaker on this tour, I'm gonna be the *best damned egg-shaker that has ever shook anybody's eggs*. I got into it. There's actually a video of it out there—several seconds, up close, of me and my egg. And I was right in time, man.

I got fond of my egg on that tour. But let's face it, there's not a lotta demand for the egg-shakers of the world. It has definitely been an overlooked corner of the market, exceptional egg-shakers. And that just isn't right. What people don't realize is it's *hard* to shake an egg onstage with Keith Richards.

Our next gig was in Memphis. A guy named Cowboy drove the bus. Cowboy and I got to be good friends. Johnny Starbuck and Chuch Magee were our road managers. These are guys who'd done the Stones, worked with Rod Stewart, big-time shit, and all of a sudden here we were in a bus. I mean, we were big-time guys, but we were playing little places to promote the *Talk Is Cheap* album. And Keith was right in there, man.

See, that's one difference between Keith and Mick: Mick would never even consider setting foot on a tour bus to go across town, much less across the country. Although I should mention, out of fairness to Mick, we didn't stay on that tour bus *all* that long. I think we had it for the first leg, and then it became obvious it wasn't gettin' us to where we wanted to be as fast as we could get there if we were in a jet airplane, so we moved up to a jet airplane.

One of the best things about the Winos was that nothing was set in stone—we didn't have to hit a certain beat or arrive at the bridge at a particular time in order to coordinate with a video display or a set of flash pots or any of that shit. In a way it was like the Rolling Stones from years ago, when there was no set limit to the guitar solo, or to any solo, or even to any particular part of the song.

Keith loved it. It was the last bastion of freedom for him, getting away from the corporate rock, the timed show, everything at a specific tempo. We'd walk out and hunker down on the stage in a circle and say, "Well, let's have some fun, let's play some rock 'n' roll." We'd just talk, ask each other what everybody wanted to play, and then turn around, the lights would come up, and we'd sorta walk over to our instruments, pick the shit up, and start playing. What a concept, huh?

After that first Winos tour, I came back briefly to Woody's on the Beach. The tour took about a month to six weeks, something like that, and I went back to Miami because I needed a gig. But then when bodies started showing up around the neighborhood, figuratively and, so I was told, literally, I went to the bank and took out every last penny from my bank account, pulled out of Miami, and we drove to Nashville. I guess I was just tryin' to get back home without really knowin' it. Tennessee isn't Texas, but two of my oldest friends in the world lived outside of Nashville, so that's where I decided to go. I came to Tennessee and stayed out at J.I.'s house and spent time talkin' with Joe B., who didn't live too far away, and it was kinda like goin' home again. And it felt good.

By the spring of 1989, I was leading a much quieter life. Coming from Miami out to J.I.'s guesthouse out in the country, fishin' at the little pond he has out there, it was a period of regrouping, of regathering myself. And it felt good getting out of that environment of goin' out all night and sleeping most of the day, which was just goin' around in circles, not gettin' anything accomplished. Going to J.I.'s house helped to break that cycle. Besides that, he's responsible for me—he signed off on me.

That period of regrouping got me ready to go back out on the road with the Stones, which the Stones were getting ready to do. I remember I was watching MTV when they made their announcement about their upcoming American tour, and they did a little

publicity stunt—they drove through downtown Manhattan on the
back of a truck, playing. And Patty, Keith's wife, told me later that
people in the crowd were yelling, "Where's Bobby? Where's Bobby
Keys?" She said Mick didn't pay any attention to it, but Keith said
something like, *"He's comin'!"*

12

IT'S BEEN SAID that I'm the only guy who's ever split with the Stones and been allowed back into the fold, so to speak. Well, that may be true, but the fact is, in my mind, I never really considered myself out of the fold. I mean, I knew I screwed up. I knew people were angry. But whenever it would be time for another Stones tour, I just knew that that was where I was supposed to be. I knew I was the best man for the job, even if it wasn't particularly obvious to everyone in the organization.

My only link to staying in that band at all was Keith. He kept saying, "Just hang in there, Bobby, I'll handle it." And he'd compensate me. The money came outta his pocket. He'd send me a ticket and say, "Come on, bring your horn, we'll find you something to do." So I'd go. I'd be in and around the fringes, but I was still skatin' on thin ice.

After I left the European tour in '73, there were a couple more tours in the '70s, but I was only able to play a handful of shows. By the '80s, Keith and Mick were not getting along at all, and the Stones didn't tour again until the end of the decade—the Steel Wheels tour. Preparations for that tour began in the summer of '89, and I remember talking to Keith off and on, campaigning real hard to get the gig and looking for his help.

He and Mick still weren't at a very warm and fuzzy part of their relationship at this time. The last time the Stones toured, in 1981 in the U.S. and '82 in Europe, the only songs I played on were "Honky Tonk Women" and "Brown Sugar," and there was another guy named Ernie Watts who played all the other solos. And then after him, there was a guy named Daddy G., a.k.a. Gene Barge, but after a while I started takin' over my own solos because I played 'em better than he did.

All of this was irritating the hell out of Mick, so Mick had gotten a guy to play keyboards for this upcoming tour, Matt Clifford, who also sidelined as a saxophone player and who'd played with Mick on his solo stuff. Keith said when he saw this friend of Mick's get out a saxophone and start playing the solo on "Brown Sugar," that's when he told his personal manager, Jane Rose, to give me a call.

Jane Rose made the arrangements. They were rehearsing in New York, at Nassau Coliseum on Long Island, so I flew in and was met at the airport by a car that took me to the hotel. I didn't even have my own room. I was met there by Tony Russell, who said I could stay in his room for the time being, which sounded a little strange, so I asked him what was going on. "Well, Mick doesn't know anything about you being here," Tony told me. "Keith's gonna have to slide you through the back door."

Which is exactly what he did. Tony said, "Look, I'm gonna leave you here and go to the rehearsal, and sometime when the time is right, I'll come and get you and bring you back over there." So I sat in the hotel room for several hours, feelin' like I was in some sort of FBI protection program, until Tony came back to take me over there. When we got there, I was told to sit in the car outside in the parking lot. Then Tony appeared at the back door of the place and waved me in. So I got my horn and I was walking to the back door, and the instant I opened it I was nose to nose with Mick Jagger.

Mick looked at me and asked, "What're *you* doin' here?" I said, "I don't know, Keith called." I don't remember what Mick said after that. I think he just turned around on his heel and walked away. He never spoke to me once for that entire tour. Apparently, he was still upset with me for having quit the tour years ago, but also because I was now in Keith's camp and not Mick's. His attitude to this day has only slightly mellowed.

Anyway, once he saw me in the doorway, that blew the covert part of the mission, so Keith just said, "Fuck it, come on in. If he wants to hire Matt Clifford, then I'll hire you." And that's kinda what it came down to. I played on Keith's songs and I played on "Brown Sugar." For those first couple tours there was always another sax player.

JIM KELTNER: *I could explain what Bobby does with the saxophone technically, but I think a better way to describe it is this, which I always found interesting and a very lovely story. Now, I can't speak for the Stones, exactly, or what they might've been seeking to do at any particular point in time, but I know that probably the temptation was, since they were such a huge, such an iconic band, and had already gained the nickname "World's Greatest Rock Band," I think at some point the temptation to get an amazing tenor sax player was too strong.*

And so they tried a bunch of different people. They had Sonny Rollins. They had Ernie Watts. They had different jazz guys who were really accomplished players. And I believe that what happened each time those guys would play with the Stones is that eventually they would realize that the Stones sounded like the Stones were supposed to sound when Bobby Keys played with them, and not when these great virtuoso players played with them. It was kind of a mismatch, in a way. Bobby plays with the spirit of rock 'n' roll to the bone. That's what he knows, that's what he came up with in Lubbock, Texas. And so when he plays, that's what you hear—you hear Lubbock, Texas, you hear all those experiences he'd gone through playing with people like Buddy Knox, all of that.

THAT FIRST TOUR back full time, I was traveling with everybody and staying with everybody but only appearing onstage twice. The rest of the time I was offstage. After a while I started playing on "Satisfaction," too, making it three appearances onstage. At some point Mick sent the accountant around to my room to make a deal:

"Well, Bobby, it's apparent that you're here, so we're gonna have to do something about you. We're gonna have to pay you. And this is what we've come up with . . . " This was strictly Jagger. He knew I was only playing on a few songs, and the offer was to pay me $100 per song that I played on. Three hundred dollars a gig. So I went to Keith, and he said, "Bobby, just take it and don't worry. I'll compensate you." Which he did.

It was great hangin' out with Keith again on the road, and seein' Charlie, and even Bill Wyman. Bill actually told me after the tour was over, "Well, Bobby, I was one of 'em who was dead set against you ever gettin' back into the gig because, you know, *nobody* quits the Stones and gets back in. That's just the way it is." But I'd straightened up, I was being a very good boy, and he noticed that, and by the end of the tour he was convinced, and he told me so. Charlie was, too.

In some ways, though, I'm still convincing them. With Jagger, it'll take an eternity. In reality, it took several tours for me to truly get back. 'Cause it's real easy to put up a front for a while and get by with it, but it's only over the course of time that you can see if there's any reality to my saying I'm never gonna touch heroin again. Which I haven't. But it takes time for somebody to believe it.

I trashed an awful lot of trust. Well, I don't know if I ever had an *awful* lot of trust, but whatever trust there was, I trashed it, man. And I'm totally responsible for that. But it's been maybe six tours now and still goin'. And even if Mick still doesn't exactly trust me completely, he knows I'll be there and I'll do my job. And he knows, too, that when the introductions are bein' passed around the stage, aside from Charlie and Mick and Ronnie and Keith, I'm recognized by the general public more than anyone else up on that stage. Because I've *been* there longer than anyone else, and I've played on a lotta the records that people actually remember. That's also why now I'm referred to as the "section leader." Which is really just lip service, but I'll take it.

OF COURSE, THE road is not what it used to be. On the recent tours, people tend to stick to themselves more. I'll hook up with Keith occasionally to play dominoes or listen to music—pretty much, for Keith and me on tour, it's all just rock 'n' roll and dominoes anymore—but for a couple of tours there I was tryin' to learn how to play golf. Which really disgusted my pal Keith.

This was in '94 or '95, on the Voodoo Lounge tour, which was a yearlong tour. We had the world famous Voodoo Lounge golf team in full swing that year—we all had these little jackets with the tongue logo and a golf pin sticking up at the end of the tongue with a little flag on it, which kinda piqued certain members of the tour group.

The Voodoo Lounge golf team was comprised of Michael Cole, who was the ramrod of the outfit since he was the promoter and had all the hookups to all the cool golf courses; his right-hand man; three members of the horn section, including myself, Kent Smith, and Mike Davis; and then sometimes we'd bring alternates along like the publicity girl because sometimes we'd need a little comic relief aside from myself. We played all kinds of amazing courses—we played Spyglass, we played all over the world.

Anyway, we were in Hawaii this one time, and we were staying in this resort that had a golf course. And I'd been over to Keith's room listening to music and carousing the night before. Our tee times would always be, like, seven o'clock in the morning, sometimes earlier, which only made Keith try to keep me up as late as he could and fill me with as much alcohol as he could the night before. But I'd struggle onto the course the next day anyway, and so this one time I was feelin' pretty raggedy, and I don't recall which fairway it was, which hole we were on, but I got out my driver, the extra-big Big Bertha, which I didn't have any control over whatsoever, and I whacked the hell out of the ball.

Now, Michael Cole had our balls made up with the tongue logo right on the ball, so they were impossible not to recognize. Anyway, I *whammed* that thing, man, and it hooked left around the corner of the fairway, and I couldn't see where it went 'cause it went straight off the course and behind the trees. A few seconds later I heard a gunshot. I thought, What the hell is that? I mean, I know what a gunshot sounds like, and that was a *gunshot.*

So I got into the golf cart and steamed off lookin' for my ball. Now, at this hotel, the better rooms are lined, like apartments, along the fairways of the golf course, and when I came around the corner I saw Lisa Fischer, one of the backup singers, out on a balcony and I thought, Oh, this must be our wing. And then I saw Keith—he's got his shirt off and his Arab shawl around his head, and he's standing there on his patio with a pistol in his hand and smoke coming out of the muzzle.

When I hit my ball it had hooked into the trees, ricocheted, and landed smack dab in the middle of his breakfast. So he shot it. He's always got a gun with him, and he *shot* my golf ball. I don't know if he's ever shot anyone else's golf ball, but he shot mine. So by the time I got around the corner and he saw me, he was yelling, "*Keys!*"—and he was holding this smoking shell that used to be my golf ball—"*That's a ten-stroke fucking penalty, and if you ever do it again, I'll do the same to you! You ruined my fucking breakfast!*"

He wasn't really mad at me, but it shocked the hell out of him. I knew what condition he was in, and here he was, gettin' ready to eat his eggs Benedict, and all of a sudden *splat!* Ten-stroke penalty.

Reentering the Rolling Stones fold was, if nothing else, a process. It took a long, long time. Even after I got back on tour, I didn't have Mick's endorsement until the Bridges to Babylon tour. On the previous tour, the Voodoo Lounge tour, the band was backed by a group called the Uptown Horns, but Mick didn't want the Uptown Horns back on the Bridges tour because he was told by some of his advisors that they didn't really "fit the look," whatever the hell that means.

So Mick had found these guys, the New West Horns, and he came to me and said, "Bobby, I'm gonna trust your judgment. We've got these guys comin' up to audition." Well, it turned out that Keith had found a set of guys *he* wanted to use, too, so we were gonna audition Keith's guys one night and Mick's guys the next night. And Mick said, "Bobby, it's your decision."

Well, no problem—it was gonna be Keith's guys. They're *in.* So we went to the rehearsal and Keith's guys played, and they played fine, they were rock 'n' roll–type guys, got along with everyone. They were fine. The next night was Mick's guys' night, the New West Horns. They looked like college-type, clean-cut young guys. Didn't really have the rock 'n' roll attitude that Keith and I are typically drawn to. But when they played, they sounded good. *Really* good.

Well, I'd already told the other guys, Keith's guys, "Hey, I gotta go through this other perfunctory thing first, just listen to 'em out of respect, but you guys are in." But when I listened to Mick's guys I knew they were the real deal. So I called up Keith and said, "Hey, man, these guys are *better*, they really are. I've gotta make a decision but I kinda wanted to talk to you about it first." He said, "Bobby, it's your call. If you think they're better, hire 'em." And that's how we got the guys who're with us today.

When I told Mick that I chose his guys, I thought that was gonna bring about some sorta revelation with regard to his attitude toward me—or at least I thought he might start sayin' hello—but it didn't, really. Either way, it was the thing to do because these guys were better. The other guys were good, but they weren't really a section unto themselves. They were just three or four guys playin' together. The New West guys, they're a section. And that makes a difference.

To tell the truth, the horn parts aren't that demanding. I mean, some of the solos might be, but I've been playin' 'em for so long that I don't even have to think about 'em. Besides that, the audience doesn't pay too much attention to what the horn section's playing—it's all Mick and Keith. I could've hired some chimpanzees with horns up there riding around on tricycles and no one in the audience would've noticed. Still, it was a pleasant surprise to be asked by Mick to make that decision—at least he was acknowledging my presence.

And after all these years, I still love being in the presence of everybody in that band. When we all first get together for a new tour, for instance, seeing Charlie's like seeing somebody you just saw yesterday. I mean, that's the way it is with Keith, too, but Keith and I see each other in between tours and talk. Charlie and I pretty much have no contact from the last gig until the next rehearsal.

Charlie is a unique individual: He collects horses but he doesn't ride; he collects cars but doesn't drive. He has full suits made of the type that would've been worn in his cars' heyday. He's also a great collector of jazz music as well as Civil War maps and books and all sorts of stuff. He's really very well read about that part of American history.

Charlie's a guy who folds his socks. He's a very fastidious guy. If you look at him up onstage, he's got this little stand with his espresso and a towel neatly folded on a rack. He dresses immaculately. Silk socks—not cotton socks, silk socks—and shoes like Edward G. Robinson would wear, black-and-white or brown-and-white spectator-style shoes. Here he is, so far out of anything that has to do with conventional rock star living, and he's one of the greatest drummers in rock 'n' roll.

He plays his drums like an instrument. With Charlie and with Keith, Charlie's the engine and Keith's the driver, the conductor. Charlie holds it all together. I've been onstage before with the Stones where everything else has broken down except for Charlie. Like, if the electricity goes off, or when the electricity goes off in people's minds—sometimes it goes dark onstage but the lights are still burning—either way, Charlie knows where the light is.

I have a great affection for him and a lot of respect. I've seen all the pitfalls that offer themselves in an environment like playing with the Rolling Stones for that many years and, not that he's impervious or bulletproof or anything, but I mean, as far as being distracted by the trappings of that kinda lifestyle, he's the least affected. I guess that's why he's got such a special place in my heart—just looking at the environment that he's had to put up with without compromising too much of himself, that's pretty damn hard to do.

He's just different than any other drummer I've ever met in my life. And he's the drummer who, anytime I mention him to other drummers, they'll be fascinated. And Charlie plays the simplest stuff in the world. He's only got three drums up there on the stage with him, four including the bass drum. Bass, snare, shell tom, floor tom, and two cymbals. And that's it. That's all he's ever had. While people were going drum-crazy back in the '60s and '70s, Charlie kept the same setup. Things like that just endeared him to me. That and the fact that his favorite instrument's the saxophone.

It's hard to tell somebody what the difference between good and great is, but I can tell you that Charlie is great. He's great in his understanding of the music he's playing and how he plays it with the people he's playing with. He's an accompanist, he's not a banger. He really enhances the music, and in really subtle ways. And I love his tempo. That's the number one prerequisite as far as a drummer goes, and Charlie's a timekeeper. It doesn't mean you have to have perfect tempo—he and Keith together really make up something special.

Another guy who's become an integral part of the band since the '80s is Chuck Leavell. Chuck's a great Southern-style piano player, which is the kinda keyboards I really like. He's a Georgia boy. ("Boy Georgia," that's what Keith calls him, much to Chuck's chagrin.) He comes from the same sorta musical background that Delaney & Bonnie came from, that Southern rock, Southern gospel music. He's a gifted keyboard player. And he's a very nice guy, very congenial.

Chuck's also taken on the responsibility of being the onstage musical director for the Stones. And he knows the music. He's done his research. When he first took on the job, I thought, Oh, he's just a glorified song counter-offer. But he knows what he's doing up there.

When Chuck came onboard, after Ian McLagan, that first time on tour he just played piano, but then at some point Mick and Keith asked him to take over the duties of musical director. This was when they'd decided to tighten up the band's stage presentation and music. So Chuck broke down a lotta the songs into the actual arrangements that were played on the records. There needed to be a consistency with the tempos and everything else. Now what happens is Chuck has his set list and he goes in before the show and discusses the lineup—what the running order's gonna be—with Keith and Mick. All the songs are broken down to number of beats per minute, etc., and so then he sets the number of beats on his little machine and he counts us off—and to get us all in it together he has to count *loud*—so that we've got the same tempo every time we play a given song. And that coordinates with the flash pots and the JumboTron and whatever other effects they're gonna have for that particular song.

Someone else who's been with the Stones for the last few tours is Darryl Jones. On bass Darryl's a gentle soul. I thought he was gonna be a real jazz guy when he came onboard. He played with Miles Davis when he was a teenager, and I thought he might have a Miles Davis attitude along with it, but he is nothing at all like that. Darryl's been great. He never screws up. And he's so nice. He's into various Eastern philosophies and martial arts. Kinda brings the band into balance, so to speak.

It's just a pleasure to work with the whole cast of characters, man. You know, the horn guys we've got—Kent Smith, Mike Davis, and Tim Ries—we're really lucky to have. For one thing, they've adapted to a lifestyle that's not easy to adapt to. And the fact that they're the cleanest-living sons of bitches I've ever been associated with helps me, too. Plus, working with quality musicians like these guys keeps me on my toes. They can all read, for instance. They read like New Yorkers. I read like a Texas guitar player. And they've helped me so much with that.

It's a pleasure, too, to work with singers like Blondie Chaplin, Bernard Fowler, and Lisa Fischer. Blondie's got his own credentials. He's worked with the Beach Boys. He also plays a little rhythm guitar. And then Bernard and Lisa carry the bulk of the backup singing— in fact, it's Lisa who does the big duet with Mick on "Gimmie Shelter," and Bernard, I guess you'd call him the leader of the vocal section. He put 'em all together and he rehearses 'em. They're really important to the band, and the best I've ever worked with.

There's a real team effort to get this band onstage. It takes hairdressers, dog walkers, fire eaters—it takes a whole cast of citizens to get this little show on the road. Caroline and Isabel, for example. We call 'em Fluff and Puff. They handle the makeup and wardrobe. They're the ones who'd call me up all the time when I'd get back to my hotel room and say, "Bobby, where are your clothes? We need to clean your clothes!" They're the only women I've ever taken orders from outside of my mother. These are the people who make the whole thing work.

So that's what the Stones are like these days, at least on tour. Pretty calm, for the most part. Professional. Now, *off* tour, a couple of us can still scare up some excitement if the mood takes us. And, at least when I'm with Keith, the mood still seems to get around to taking us every once in a while.

A few years ago, in the early spring of 2009, I got a call from Keith to come down to his place in the Turks and Caicos Islands to hang out, throwing in, "Bring your horn, we might have a gig." I had no idea what he was talking about, but I took my horn anyway. When I got down there, Steve Jordan from the X-Pensive Winos was there and Bruce Willis, the actor, was there. Bruce had a house nearby, and he and Keith had become friends because Bruce was also a pot-smoker. Anyway, they were all in Keith's living room having a drink, hangin' out. About five or ten minutes into the conversation, it came up that Bruce was getting married the next day and that Keith and Steve and I were gonna play for the ceremony. Everybody'd been drinking, so I didn't really think much of it at the time.

Well, it turned out to be true. Bruce wanted "Harlem Nocturne" and "Sleepwalk," luckily both songs I knew, to be played at the ceremony. And also his daughter Rumer was gonna sing "You Are My Sunshine." So we had three songs to learn. The ceremony was gonna take place on the beach. I knew my parts, Keith sorta learned his, and Steve just had a cardboard box to bang on.

The next day we stumbled over the sand dunes to the wedding. I remember sloggin' through the sand tryin' to play "Harlem Nocturne," this really pretty song, and I was panting and sweating and wheezing and sand flies were bitin' me. It was not a setting that was really all that conducive to playing music. Then, after the ceremony, we went back to Bruce's house and continued the drinking, and then back to Keith's house and continued the drinking, and basically got really, really drunk.

Donna Karan, as it happened, had a house in the same neighborhood and she was having a party that night, too, and Keith suggested—because we were all liquored up and had nobody to play for and nobody to mess with, and he was definitely in the mood to mess with somebody—that we go over to Donna Karan's house and play the Ritchie Valens song "Oh Donna." So we got in the golf cart and went to this big mansion, this big stack-a-rocks down the road. This had to be about one or two o'clock, maybe even three o'clock in the morning.

Well, we pulled up to this place and knocked on the door but nobody answered. After about half a minute, Keith just kicked the door open and said, "Come on, boys, let's start playin'!" So we struck up "Oh Donna." We were in this giant entry hall with a stairway goin' around and up to the second floor, and this guy showed up on the landing up above us, turned the lights on, looked, and rubbed his eyes. And that was when we noticed this was not a party. So Keith said, "Donna Karan's house?" and the guy just stuck his arm out and pointed his finger to the left, too angry for words. He never said a thing. At that, we all just kinda shuffled backward, went into reverse back out the door, and quietly shut it.

OF COURSE, LIFE goes on outside of the Stones. My wife Holly and I ended up in Nashville over twenty years ago by process of elimination, more than anything else. Couldn't go to L.A., had to get out of Miami. And we had a lotta old friends in the Nashville area: J.I., Joe B., Jimmy Markham, and others.

When we first got to town there were a fair amount of opportunities to play. I played with Markham quite a bit back then, those dives he used to play. Markham always had a joint stashed away, somewhere we could go play. We never made *any* money. Markham's got a real knack for finding joints like that. If only they paid.

Nicky Hopkins was living in Nashville when we first moved there, too, so we'd do gigs together every once in a while. We did a couple at the Hard Rock Cafe when it first opened up, me and Nicky and Markham. But Nicky was sickly by that point, he wasn't doin' so well, his health was failing him. We tried to do more gigs, but Nicky just didn't have his health. He was very frail.

Eventually, the local gigs between Stones tours kinda petered out. I mean, you couldn't sustain a living playing with Markham making $35, $45, $50 a night, one night a week or two nights a month.

It wasn't until I concentrated on the music itself—not foolin' around with music as a part of the experience, but on actually playing music—that things started to pick up. It wasn't happening while I was using music for recreational purposes. When I started to clean my act up, I noticed I got a lot more done, so I thought, Well, hell, man, this is better than doin' nothin', so I cleaned up pretty much everything. The really nasty habits I did away with completely. I don't even really drink all that much anymore.

That's when I started to play again with some regularity. I've got a bunch of guys that I've been doin' shows with recently, some really good, experienced players: Dan Baird, a producer, singer, and guitar player probably best known as the leader of the

Georgia Satellites, on lead vocals and guitar; Steve Gorman, from the Black Crowes, on drums; Mike Webb, who also plays with the band Poco, on keyboards; Robert Kearns, currently with Lynyrd Skynyrd, on bass; and Chark Von Kinsolving, a longtime fixture in the Nashville rock 'n' roll music scene, on lead guitar. And, of course, myself, on the saxophonic device.

The reason I got that band together was out of the frustration of not being able to play in Nashville. I was just sitting in with people. Then I met Chark in the summer of 2010 at the Eleventh Annual Americana Music Festival, where he'd put together a kind of all-star band to play *Exile on Main St.* the whole way through as one of the festival's showcases. Well, I really liked the way Chark played, so I mentioned to him that I'd like to get a band together and do some work around town, and he said he could help me do that. And he has. He's the one who brought everyone together. And it's been fun so far. It's still in the early developmental stages, but it's been a lot of fun.

And I still do sessions as they come along. Recently I've done a couple of shows in New York with Chuck Leavell, and the guitarist on those gigs was a guy named Tom Vukovich, and he's from Nashville. I mentioned to him to call me if he heard of anyone looking for a sax player, and a couple of days later he did: Dave Stewart, formerly of the Eurythmics but also a big-time player, writer, and producer who works with Mick in the band SuperHeavy, happened to be in Nashville working on an album at the time. I went in and did a session, and Dave called back and had me play on a couple more. Just another instance of being in the right place at the right time, I guess.

MY LIFE HAS been as unrehearsed as a hiccup. I've said it before and I'll say it again. It really has come down to being at the right place at the right time, and having enough ability to do the gig.

I started playing the saxophone through a series of accidental circumstances—mostly, it was available—but it's turned out to be the longest relationship, by far, I've ever had in my life. And it's still a work in progress. I think a little bit more now about my playing—before, I used to just stick it in my mouth and blow and whatever came out, came out. I'd sorta just toss the dice and see what would come up. And I've been very lucky. But now that I'm where I am, at this stage of the game I recognize that it's an ongoing learning process. For one thing, I've learned that I don't know as much as I thought I knew thirty years ago. I listen more than I used to. I trust myself more. It's more of a conscious thing than an unconscious thing now. It's like fine-tuning something that I've been doing for a long time.

After a while, if you live long enough, you do learn a few licks. I enjoy playing. I love it just as much now as I did when I was a teenager. I especially like to play shit I've never played before. Wherever I've been around the world, I've always tried to find some locals to jam with. Because they couldn't speak any English, so it was all just feel, you know? It wasn't like, "Well, we're gonna go to the bridge here, and then we're gonna change the E and A"—there was *none* of that. It was just like, "Well, if you feel froggy, hop on." And that's more fun to me, man. Do somethin' you've never done before.

And sometimes you might hit a wrong note. Make a misstep or two. But, hell, if I'm gonna play a wrong note, I'm gonna play it with as *much* conviction as I have. Because that's rock 'n' roll.

DISCOGRAPHY

A SELECTIVE DISCOGRAPHY OF STUDIO RECORDINGS

Ace, *No Strings*, horn

American Flyer, *Spirit of a Woman*, horn

Andrew Gold, *Andrew Gold*, horn

Audience, *Lunch*, saxophone, sax (tenor)

B.B. King, *In London*, horn, saxophone, sax (tenor)

Barbra Streisand, *Barbra Joan Streisand*, horn

Billy Preston, *Late at Night*, saxophone

Bonnie Bramlett, *I'm Still the Same*, saxophone

Carl Carlton, *Love and Respect*, saxophone

Carly Simon, *No Secrets*, saxophone, sax (tenor)

Carly Simon, *Hotcakes*, saxophone, sax (baritone), sax (tenor), trombone

Chris Jagger, *Chris Jagger*, saxophone

Chuck Berry, *Hail! Hail! Rock 'N' Roll*, saxophone

Chuck Leavell, *What's in That Bag?*, saxophone

Country Joe & the Fish, *Reunion*, saxophone

Country Joe McDonald, *Paradise with an Ocean View*, saxophone

Dana Gillespie, *Weren't Born a Man*, saxophone

Delaney & Bonnie, *Accept No Substitute*, saxophone

Delaney & Bonnie, *On Tour with Eric Clapton*, saxophone

Delaney & Bonnie, *Motel Shot*, saxophone

Delaney & Bonnie, *D & B Together* (Bonus Tracks), vocals, musician

Dr. John, *The Sun, Moon & Herbs*, saxophone, sax

Eric Carmen, *Boats Against the Current*, horn, saxophone

Eric Clapton, *Eric Clapton*, saxophone

Eric Mercury, *Eric Mercury*, horn

Etta James, *Come a Little Closer*, horn
Faces, *Long Player*, saxophone, sax
Fanny, *Fanny Hill*, saxophone
Gary Wright, *Footprint*, saxophone
Genya Ravan, *Goldie Zelkowitz*, saxophone
Geoff Muldaur, *Motion*, horn
George Harrison, *All Things Must Pass*, saxophone
George Harrison, *All Things Must Pass* (30th Anniversary Edition), sax
Graham Nash, *Songs for Beginners*, saxophone
Harry Nilsson, *Nilsson Schmilsson*, saxophone
Harry Nilsson, *Nilsson Schmilsson* (Bonus Tracks), saxophone
Harry Nilsson, *Nilsson Schmilsson* (Import with Bonus Tracks), saxophone
Harry Nilsson, *Son of Schmilsson*, horn, saxophone, sax (tenor), soloist
Harry Nilsson, *Pussy Cats*, saxophone
Harry Nilsson, *Son of Dracula*, saxophone
Harry Nilsson, *Duit on Mon Dei*, saxophone
Harry Nilsson, . . . *That's the Way It Is*, saxophone
Harry Nilsson, . . . *That's the Way It Is* (Expanded), saxophone
Humble Pie, *Rock On*, saxophone
Ian McLagan, *Troublemaker*, horn
Ian McLagan, *Bump in the Night*, horn
Jim Carroll, *Catholic Boy*, saxophone
Jim Price, *Kids Nowadays Ain't Got No Shame*, saxophone, sax (tenor)
Jim Price, *Sundego's Travelling Orchestra*, saxophone
Joe Cocker, *Mad Dogs & Englishmen*, saxophone
Joe Cocker, *Live in L.A.*, saxophone
Joe Cocker, *Jamaica Say You Will*, sax (tenor)
Joe Cocker, *Luxury You Can Afford*, saxophone
Joe Ely, *Lord of the Highway*, saxophone
Joey Stec, *Joey Stec*, sax (baritone), sax (tenor)
John Hiatt, *Beneath This Gruff Exterior*, sax (baritone)
John Lennon, *Sometime in New York City/Live Jam*, saxophone
John Lennon, *Walls and Bridges*, horn, saxophone, tenor (vocal)
John Lennon, *Rock 'n' Roll*, saxophone
John Martyn, *Inside Out*, saxophone

John Simon, *Don't Forget What I Told You*, vocals

John Simon, *John Simon's Album*, sax (tenor)

Keith Moon, *Two Sides of the Moon*, saxophone

Keith Richards, *Talk Is Cheap*, sax (baritone), sax (tenor)

Keith Richards, *Live at the Hollywood Palladium* (December 15, 1988), saxophone

Keith Richards, *Live at the Hollywood Palladium* (Box Set & CD Limited Edition), saxophone

Kracker, *Kracker Brand*, saxophone

Leo Sayer, *Endless Flight* (Expanded), horn

Lesley Duncan, *Maybe It's Lost*, saxophone

Lynyrd Skynyrd, *Second Helping*, horn, saxophone

Marc Benno, *Ambush*, saxophone

Martha Reeves, *Martha Reeves*, horn

Marvin Gaye, *Let's Get It On* (Deluxe Edition), saxophone

Michael Pinder, *The Promise*, saxophone

Nicky Hopkins, *The Tin Man Was a Dreamer*, saxophone

Ringo Starr, *Ringo*, saxophone, sax (tenor)

Ringo Starr, *Goodnight Vienna*, horn, saxophone

Ron Wood, *Mahoney's Last Stand* (Japan Bonus Tracks), sax (tenor), brass

Ron Wood, *Mahoney's Last Stand* (U.S.), horn, sax (tenor), brass

Ron Wood, *Gimme Some Neck*, saxophone

Ron Wood, *1234*, saxophone

Ronnie Lane, *Mahoney's Last Stand* (U.K.), sax (tenor), brass

Rossetta Hightower, *Hightower*, saxophone

Shawn Phillips, *Bright White*, saxophone

Sheryl Crow, *The Globe Sessions*, sax (alto), sax (baritone), sax (tenor), soloist

Sheryl Crow, *The Globe Sessions* (DVD), sax (alto), sax (baritone), sax (tenor)

Sheryl Crow, *The Globe Sessions* (Australia Bonus CD), sax (alto), sax (baritone), sax (tenor)

Sky, *Sailor's Delight*, horn

Sky, *Don't Hold Back*, saxophone

The Cate Brothers, *In One Eye and Out the Other*, horn

The Crickets, *Double Exposure*, saxophone

The Rolling Stones, *Let It Bleed*, horn, saxophone, sax (tenor)

The Rolling Stones, *Sticky Fingers*, horn, saxophone
The Rolling Stones, *Get Yer Ya-Yas Out—Revisited*, saxophone
The Rolling Stones, *Exile on Main St.*, horn, saxophone
The Rolling Stones, *Goats Head Soup*, sax (baritone), sax (tenor)
The Rolling Stones, *Headin' for an Overload*, saxophone
The Rolling Stones, *Emotional Rescue*, horn, saxophone
The Rolling Stones, *Rome, 1990*, saxophone
The Rolling Stones, *Flashpoint*, saxophone, synthesizer
The Rolling Stones, *Stripped*, saxophone
The Rolling Stones, *No Security*, saxophone
The Rolling Stones, *No Security* (Japan Bonus Track), saxophone
The Rolling Stones, *Poland, 1998*, saxophone
Third World War, *Third World War*, saxophone
Van Dyke Parks, *Clang of the Yankee Reaper*, saxophone
Various Artists, *Dick Tracy* (Original Soundtrack), guitar
Various Artists, *For Our Children Too*, sax (baritone)
Various Artists, *From East Memphis to Kingston*, performer
Various Artists, *The Shag*, bass, guitar
Various Artists, *Weird Nightmare: Meditations on Mingus*, sax (tenor)
Warren Zevon, *Warren Zevon*, saxophone
Yoko Ono, *Fly*, saxophone, claves

FILMS

1971 *Mad Dogs & Englishmen*
1972 *Cocksucker Blues*
1973 *Ladies and Gentlemen: The Rolling Stones*
1982 *Let's Spend the Night Together*
1991 *Rolling Stones Live at the Max*
1993 *Weird Nightmare*

LIST OF NOTABLE TOURS AND PERFORMANCES

The Dick Clark Caravan of Stars Tour 1964

Delaney & Bonnie and Friends Tour (opening for Blind Faith) 1969

Delaney & Bonnie and Friends on Tour with Eric Clapton 1969

Joe Cocker Mad Dogs & Englishmen Tour 1969–70

The Rolling Stones U.K. Tour 1971

The Rolling Stones American Tour 1972

The Rolling Stones Pacific Tour 1973

Joe Cocker on Tour 1976–77

The New Barbarians U.S. Tour 1979

The Rolling Stones Tattoo You Tour 1981

The Rolling Stones European Tour 1982

Joe Ely on Tour 1984–85

The Rolling Stones Steel Wheels/Urban Jungle Tour 1989

Keith Richards and the X-Pensive Winos Tour 1989

The Rolling Stones Voodoo Lounge Tour 1994–95

The Rolling Stones Bridges to Babylon Tour 1997–98

The Rolling Stones No Security Tour 1999

The Rolling Stones Licks Tour 2002–03

The Rolling Stones A Bigger Bang Tour 2005–07

ACKNOWLEDGMENTS

WE'D LIKE TO thank Charlie Winton for his personal guidance, expertise, and friendship throughout the entire undertaking; Keith Richards for his generous and kind words and for his inspiration; J.I. Allison, Joe B. Mauldin, Joe Cocker, Jim Keltner, Jane Rose, May Pang, and Jimmy Markham for sharing their time, memories, and photographs; as well as Loni Efron, Annie Leibovitz, Dominique Tarle, David Tillier, David Salemi, Henry Diltz, Kevin Mazur, and Mikio Ariga for providing photographic support. Howell O'Rear, whose passion for this project brought us together and whose expertise sealed the deal; Phil Ollila, whose magnanimous help and experience were priceless; and the team at Counterpoint—Kelly Winton, Mathew Grace, Megan Jones, Julie Pinkerton, and Lorna Garano—for their assistance in all aspects of the publishing process. And last but not least, a special thanks to our families, Holly and Jesse Keys and Stephanie, Otis, and Lulu Ditenhafer, for their love and support.

INDEX